Mommy jitters can be compared to wedding jitters a bride and groom feel just before their marriage—except they're worse. When you have a baby you're making a drastic change in your life that can't be undone. And if you haven't had experience with babies, you're stepping into unknown territory. The best thing that can be said about mommy jitters is that they're usually very brief in duration, vanishing as soon as you get your little one home and discover that motherhood isn't so hard after all.

The M🌑MMY BOOK

BY KAREN H. HULL

**Advice for New Mothers
From Women Who've Been There**

HarperPaperbacks
A Division of HarperCollinsPublishers

HarperPaperbacks *A Division of* HarperCollins*Publishers*
10 East 53rd Street, New York, N.Y. 10022

This book is published by arrangement
with Zondervan Publishing House.

Cover illustration by The Imagebank/Whitney Lane

First HarperPaperbacks printing: May 1991

Printed in the United States of America

HarperPaperbacks and colophon are trademarks of
HarperCollins*Publishers*

10 9 8 7 6 5 4 3 2 1

To Jon, Megan, and Anna

... Contents

...
Acknowledgments

Special thanks to Chris Thomas for giving me the idea for this project (and to her sister, Debby Clack, for giving *her* the idea) as well as for her encouragement and organizational help. Also to Jan Strader for allowing me to use her handwritten book of friends' advice as a starting point.

Special thanks also to Dr. Daniel Leviten for donating his time and knowledge, and to the many parents who read and gave their approval of the finished manuscript.

Most of all, very special thanks to the more than sixty-five mothers who ultimately became involved in *The Mommy Book*. May the advice they've shared in its pages help others to become as good at parenting as they are.

Introduction: Advice About Advice

No one is more inexperienced than a new mother. On finding out you're pregnant, you tell yourself that after carrying a child inside you for nine months you'll be prepared to be a perfect mommy. But as your abdomen swells (and your feet, your hands, and your hips), you approach your due date with the sinking feeling that you're no more ready to be a mother than you were nine months—or nine years—ago. The little person inside your womb seems somehow unreal, no matter how hard he kicks and squirms. You want to be a good mother, but you begin to wonder whether you will be.

As if the self-doubts aren't enough, you're assaulted on all sides by unasked-for advice. The reason for this is that, as insecure and anxious to learn as the new mother is, there is no one more eager to dispense advice than the experienced one. And she really does have a lot to give. The problem is that the experienced mom usually isn't around when she's needed. She casts her pearls at the most inopportune moments: in the church hallway when you're already late for Sunday school; at the social gathering when you really wanted to forget about diapers and feedings for a change; or in a phone call just as you were about to take a nap. Too, the manner and frequency with which she gives counsel often puts the sensitive new mother on her defense. The question is how to get adviser and advisee together in such a way that the new mother can really use the advice.

We hope this book will help. The idea was conceived when my neighbor Jan had her baby three months after my own little girl, Megan, was born. A group of mothers from our church put together a small book of advice for Jan, each writing several pages of practical tips that had helped with her own children.

When the book was complete and we all took a look inside, we were amazed at the creativity, common sense, and wisdom that had come from our group effort. Tips that seemed obvious to the mother who had written them often astounded the rest of us with their practical simplicity.

The Mommy Book takes the best advice from that project and widens the contributing circle of mothers to include other creative Christian women who are committed to raising secure, happy, healthy children. Many of them don't have college degrees, and they don't claim to be experts—but they are. You don't do something twenty-four hours a day for years, and do it well, without gaining a certain amount of expertise. In the back of this book you'll find a "Meet the Mommies" section, giving a bit of background on each of our moms. You may want to go ahead and read through it to acquaint yourself with them before reading and taking their advice. Or you may want to just look up each mother as you come across her.

Perhaps the most important advice in this book comes here, before the first chapter. It's from "Aunt Connie," who, with her husband, "Uncle Shelby," pastors five hundred children at a large church in central Florida: "Listen to everyone's advice. Smile and be gracious. Then, when they're gone, do what you believe is right. Some of their ideas you'll be able to use and some you won't. After all, you and your husband are the ones who have to decide what's best for your child."

1
...
Surviving Mommyhood
(Or, Things They Never Told You in Childbirth Class)

Now, don't let the title of this chapter give you the wrong idea. We, the mommies in this book, love our children and happen to believe that being a mother is the single most fulfilling profession around when it's handled the right way. It's just that life with a newborn baby, especially when it's your first, takes a little adjustment.

Well, no, not really. It takes a *lot* of adjustment.

In this chapter we'll try to give you an idea of the changes you can expect and ways we dealt with them in our own lives. Think of it as a briefing session being given just before you leave the carefree land of Independence, where you've spent your life up till now, to live in Parenthood, a country shrouded in weird super-

1

stitions and where the inhabitants practice all sorts of odd customs.

The analogy is more accurate than you might think. You really can fall victim to culture shock during your first weeks in Parenthood, especially if you're unaware of the ways people must conduct themselves there in order to succeed. And the most fascinating thing about Parenthood is that the little person who ushers you into it and takes up residence with you is constantly changing and demanding that you change too.

But once you adapt to the necessary changes, you'll find that Parenthood is a great place to be and you wouldn't go back to Independence for the world.

And it's a good thing.

Great Expectations

There are two basic types of expectant mothers: the Nervous Expectant Mother and the Smug Expectant Mother. The N.E.M. has no idea what motherhood will be like, and she fears the worst. The S.E.M., on the other hand, tells everyone how long she plans to be in labor and insists to all who will listen, "There's no need for the baby to disrupt our lifestyle. He'll just have to fit into our schedule."

Although the S.E.M. is undoubtedly more at ease during her pregnancy, on the whole the N.E.M. is the better off of the two. When her baby is born she usually discovers that things aren't as hard as she expected them to be, and she relaxes as she gets to know her baby. On the other hand, there's nothing like the devastation experienced by the S.E.M. who has just had the rug pulled out from under her, with all her grand expectations of an accommodating baby crumbled to dust.

Believe me, I know.

If you've already made it through your baby's first few months you probably won't find too much new material in this chapter. You'll want to read it anyway, though, for the nod-and-giggle value—that is, you'll find yourself nodding involuntarily when you come across something that happened to you and giggling when you think of the unsuspecting expectant mothers who are about to go through it.

If you're pregnant with your first child, you're about to have some of your fondest fantasies of motherhood blown to smithereens. That isn't meant to scare you— it's meant to give you the comfort of knowing, during the first weeks and months after your baby arrives, that yours isn't the only one who turned out to be a real-life squalling human infant instead of a china doll.

You're not alone if you expect your baby to be a model child. Our moms did too. "I thought it was going to be easy, like all the commercials and TV programs showed," says Adrienne. "I just knew I'd have a rosy-cheeked baby who went to bed when I wanted him to and was always good and sweet, and who ate without spitting everything out."

Chris adds, "I thought I might have to get up maybe once or twice a night, and I thought there'd be a few dirty diapers, and that's about the extent of the badness I expected. I expected the baby to sleep maybe eight hours a day, and I'd be working around the house all the time and would hardly even know it was there except when it was time to nurse. The reality was that the very first day we brought Ashley home from the hospital she would not stop screaming long enough for us to sit down and eat. Some friends had brought lunch over for us, and my parents met us at the house, and my mom and dad had to stay in the living room and hold Ashley the whole time we were eating so David and I could sit down with our friends. From that moment on, she cried constantly."

Ashley's crying was due to a severe case of colic (usually assumed nowadays to be abdominal pains, although the medical community still isn't sure), and most of our babies had little trouble with it. But if your baby is a member of the very vocal minority, life can be rough for the first three months or so until she's over it. Chapter 5 gives advice on helping your baby with this problem, although time will be the most effective healer.

Not one of our moms said that motherhood turned out to be what she thought it would. Expectations are tricky things, mainly because they're almost never fulfilled. What you expect to be the most wonderful experience of your life—say, senior prom or your wedding day—will probably disappoint you, whereas something you expect to be the most awful ordeal you've ever been through will likely give you a pleasant surprise by proving you wrong.

Your baby may be easygoing and predictable like Stella's two little girls, or she may have horrendous bouts with colic and cry for hours on end like Chris's daughter Ashley and Trina's little girl Audrey. The reality, though, will probably be somewhere in between. If it comforts you, feel free to expect your baby to be an adorable little angel whose diapers never leak, who cries only when she's hungry and drifts off to sleep in her bassinet without requiring hours of being nursed or rocked. It may happen. But feel free also to turn back to these pages for a little commiseration and advice if it doesn't.

The First Two Weeks

Our moms agree that life as a new mother is much easier if, right from the start, you do as any other sensible person would do upon entering an important profession: Establish priorities and stick to them. Luckily, priorities for the first two weeks or so of motherhood are simple: 1) Get to know your baby, and 2) rest. If you want to be really efficient, do both at once. That's why the Lord invented nursing.

Not long ago a national magazine for new parents did a survey of their subscribers. To the question, "What surprised you most about having your baby?" the most popular answer was not how hard labor was or how messy their baby looked when he or she popped out. The answer thousands of new parents gave was, "We never expected to be this tired!"

Fatigue is the logical conclusion of a long pregnancy, a workout in the hospital that would put Charles Atlas to shame, and being routed out of bed by cries from the nursery several times a night immediately upon arriving home. Even so, it came as a shock to our moms. "Audrey was up every two hours," says Trina. "I was exhausted. Sleep became so precious to me that I would rather have had it than a million dollars. If it hadn't been for my mother's help, I would never have made it."

The maxim, "Sleep when the baby sleeps," has been handed down from experienced mothers to inexperienced ones ever since Eve started giving advice to her daughters. But it can be hard counsel to take unless you have help with the housework, and our moms generally found that even the most helpful husband was no match for a mother or mother-in-law when it came to keeping the house in order.

Stella says, "My mother-in-law did laundry, she cooked, she cleaned house for me, and you'd better believe it was a blessing! All I had to do was take care of the baby. But you've got to have someone who's not going to take over the baby—you have to be allowed to be a mother."

Most of the grandmas who came to help out behaved themselves admirably, but a couple of our moms did have trouble with their supposed-to-be-live-in-helpers. And since your first weeks after childbirth are hardly the time for you to be waiting on houseguests, it's a good idea to spell out what's expected before your help arrives. Have your husband talk to his mother, and you make your needs known to yours. "And make sure that whoever's coming is someone you get along with," says Adrienne.

If you don't have a mother or mother-in-law handy, and if you can afford it, hire someone to come in once a week to help clean the house. (Ways to find household help are covered in Chapter 10.) Or, if you have a best friend who keeps saying, "Let me know if you need anything," take her up on it. Tell her, "Well, my house really needs to be vacuumed . . ." or, "I have this pile of laundry . . ." Sometimes the best baby gift a friend can give is to help with the housework or just come and watch the baby while you take a nap. Don't be afraid to ask. You can always return the favor later, and if your friend has children of her own she'll understand.

Even if grandmas, housekeepers, and friends are all out of the question, there are still things you can do to keep the house from falling apart while you convalesce. Try hard to put things away as soon as you use them, and ask your husband to do the same. (Even the most undomestic husband can manage that much.) And if you possibly can, make several weeks' worth of casseroles before the baby comes and put them in the freezer along with some frozen breads and vegetables. Just doing those two things will keep you from having to worry about making dinner and will at least put your housework on hold until you feel well enough to get to it. Pene used paper plates at mealtime during her first few weeks as a mommy, and she adopted a relaxed attitude about dishes even after that. "I told my husband that the dishes were very happy just sitting there in the sink," she says. "I just walked by every now and then and waved at them."

Adding to your fatigue, in the hospital and at home, will be all the well-wishers who want to see the baby. "I was glad they cared, but I was so exhausted," says Pat. "For the first month or two people just kept dropping by." Visitors are a fact of life when you have a new baby, and according to Patti it's best to adopt an "Oh, well" attitude about them: "When friends come to visit, don't feel bad if your house is a mess. Especially if they have kids themselves, they expect it and they don't care." And if you get caught in your robe with no makeup on, look at the bright side: your visitors are less likely to expect you to run around offering refreshments if you look as if you're really convalescing. Learn to rise with a smile and say, "Thanks so much for coming. Please visit with us again," when you become tired.

No matter how much you enjoy showing off your new baby, drop-in visitors at naptime are no joke, especially if you don't have someone who can help screen them.

Joyce's four children are all grown and most of them are married and gone, but she still remembers how she handled a sticky situation when her first son was a baby: "One of the men in our church who had quite a large family informed my preacher husband that they would be visiting us on Sunday afternoon. My husband passed the information along to me with the added message, 'You'll have to entertain them, because I have to rest after preaching to prepare for the night service.'

"I won't tell you my first reaction! I asked my heavenly Father for wisdom, then made a poster with a picture of a sleeping baby and drew a clock underneath with the hands pointing to four o'clock. The message on the poster read, 'Baby and mother nap until . . . ' I secured it to the front door.

"Sure enough, up drove the big station wagon on Sunday afternoon and out piled all the kids, with Mother following Dad and his guitar. I watched from my vantage point behind the curtain. The parade halted at the front door, the lead child turned back to the car, and all the rest followed. Needless to say our Sunday afternoon rest time was respected from then on. I later invited them over at my convenience, and everyone was happy."

If you have a chronic problem with drop-in nap interrupters, make your clock with movable hands and put it up whenever you and your baby go to bed. Our moms also found that the plug-in telephones being used nowadays are great at naptime. The only drawback is that you have to somehow remember to plug the phone back in when you wake up.

My pediatrician gave me permission to blame things on him during Megan's first few months. He had told me to keep her away from other children until she was at least a month old, so when friends wanted to bring their children over it was fairly easy to say, "We'd love to have you, but Megan's doctor said . . ." It's a real blessing to be able to blame the doctor when people ask why you haven't started feeding the baby solid food yet, or why you didn't bring the baby to church until he was six weeks old, or why you're still breastfeeding.

It may be hard, but try to remember that the advice and interference you find offensive is usually offered with the best of intentions, and it's probably just what another mother is longing for. Patty M. was upset to the point of tears when people constantly wanted to take her baby at church and prayer meetings, whereas Pene would have loved to have someone else hold Aaron while she listened to the sermon. Because of this difference between new mothers, it's essential to your peace of mind that you learn the simple art of the gracious refusal. It will stand you in good stead a few years from now when you're asked to come up with forty dozen cookies for the P.T.A. bake sale.

Getting Back in Gear

It's possible, if you have a lot of household help during the first couple of weeks after your baby is born—and especially if you have help with the nightly feedings—that the real fatigue involved in the daily routine of new motherhood won't hit until after your help leaves. That can be depressing, because just when your mind decides it's time to get the household organized your body decides that it wants to go back to bed and stay there for a few years. We'll talk about the depression in the next section—what this one will tackle is how to gradually get yourself organized without wearing yourself out.

"The thing that went down the most with me was my appearance," says Karin. "Having Matthew was such a change in my life. I had worked as a legal secretary in an office where everyone dressed to the T, and I didn't quit work until the week I had him. I had always been so chic, then suddenly I was wearing nothing but my robe and there was always some kind of mess on my lap or my shoulder. Wayne would come home from work at the end of the day and my hair would be sticking out all over and my makeup hadn't even been washed off from the day before. He would ask, 'What have you been doing all day?'

"I was used to working in an office and feeling productive, so that question broke me down to tears. And it wasn't as if I had just been lying around. The TV hadn't been on, the radio hadn't been on. I'd spent all day feeding the baby, dressing the baby, changing the baby, holding the baby. I just couldn't get into the swing of taking care of another person besides myself. Wayne finally had to set some basic goals for me, because I was walking around like a zombie."

The daily goals Wayne gave Karin for her first six weeks as a mother were as follows: "Getting dressed, making the bed, and cleaning up the breakfast dishes. That doesn't sound like much, but it's a lot when you're a new mother," she says. "Those were my goals—I had to get the bed made, even if it was five-thirty and he was pulling up in the driveway!"

Being a mommy takes time. One reason for this is that most babies like to be held. A lot. "And don't think that holding your baby is going to spoil her!" says Stella. "I don't think you can hold an infant enough. It puts a security into your relationship."

In the last generation new mothers were cautioned against holding their babies when they cried, for fear of spoiling them. Heaven only knows what damage that well-meant advice caused, but today experts espouse holding and cuddling your baby as much as he seems to want it until he's at least six months old and can be encouraged to play with his toys while you get some housework done. "Besides," says Chris, "when he's two or three years old you'll have a hard time getting him to sit still long enough to hug him, so enjoy it while you can!"

Patti has three children and one on the way, so she's had lots of experience with the first few weeks of motherhood. She says, "I tell all my friends who've just had a baby not to have high expectations of what they're going to accomplish during the first six weeks. I got so depressed after my first baby came because I didn't even have time to wash the dishes and fix dinner. So I learned to set one goal for the day—say, to get the dishes washed. Not make the beds, not cook, because maybe dinner was in the freezer. Anything I did above that one goal made me feel good."

After your baby passes the six-week mark, gradually add chores to your daily schedule as your baby's temperament and your own energy permit until you finally feel everything is accounted for. The process will take longer for some moms than for others. Stella's two little girls each took long naps during the day and slept through the night early on. "With that kind of situation," she says, "it's easy to get back into a regular schedule right away." My daughter Megan, on the other hand, had an erratic nap schedule and the strange idea that the way to have a good time was to see how often she could get Mommy up at night, so it was months before life became normal around the Hull house. Marilee agrees: "It depends a lot on what your baby allows you to do. David would sleep for two hours then be up for two hours all day long, and I could do all the housework I wanted to. But then Althea woke up and wanted to nurse every hour and a half, day and night, and it just wiped me out. I didn't get anything done."

"I think it's great to have a written list of goals for the day," says Cheryl, "because as you check them off you can actually see what's getting done. And of course you set priorities in case you don't make it to the bottom of the list—that's just good time management." Our moms warn against setting your goals too high. Cheryl adds, "List whatever will make you feel you've accomplished something. Don't try to be a superwoman; but if you don't have something to shoot for and a way to see what you've accomplished that day, your self-esteem starts to go."

The idea of having your housework all done at once is fantasy for a new mom. When I worked full-time before Megan was born I became accustomed to doing most of my housework on weekends, and during the week I didn't have to worry about much besides dishes and laundry. After she came I kept trying to get it all done in a day. I finally gave up when she was six months old and developed a more practical system that's still in operation at our house.

As many of our other moms have, I have learned to divide my housework into manageable segments. I've found that I'm much more likely to get my work done if it's broken into little chunks, and if I miss a given day's work it's no great disaster—I just make sure I get to it on the proper day the following week. Big jobs, such as cleaning out closets, washing windows, etc., are worked in wherever handy, and daily jobs, such as dishes, laundry, and picking up clutter, get done daily—usually. There's no one day when the house is spotless, but at least this way I'm a little more in control.

Several moms point out that the new mother who wants a spotless house—unless she can afford a maid—not only is dreaming the impossible dream but also has a bad case of misplaced priorities. "Realize that your baby will be little for only a short time," says Terri. "Spend as much time as you can with him. If someone drops in, just say, 'Excuse my house, but I've been playing with my baby.' Maybe she'll be inspired to go home and spend some extra time with *her* children."

Even though it'll probably be a while before your house is spotless again, constant clutter is another animal altogether. Cluttered surroundings are depressing whether they're an office or a home. And the state of your home affects your husband as well. "Keep your house picked up on a continual basis," says Patty W. "Train yourself to put things away as soon as they're no longer needed."

A few additional words on keeping up appearances: If you're like our moms, the days when you drag around in your pajamas with unwashed hair and no makeup are the days when you feel homely and stupid, even if you're really a raving beauty with a Ph.D. But it's possible that. like Karin, you'll have trouble figuring out how to take care of another little person without neglecting yourself. "You have to work your schedule around the baby," says Stella, "and it's hard to fit yourself in. I used to think, 'How can I take a shower? What if the baby wakes up?'"

Most of our moms worked before their babies were born and were accustomed to taking an hour or so to dress in the morning. That became impossible after their little ones arrived. After feeling ugly for a while and deciding they didn't like it, they learned to condense their morning ritual. "What took a half-hour before," says Stella, "I learned to do in five minutes." Instead of slathering your face with foundation, blemish cover, blush, powder, shadow, etc., learn to get a simpler effect with a little blush, eyeliner, brow pencil, and mascara. Home lighting is much kinder than the greenish fluorescent lighting used in offices, so all that extra goop really isn't needed anyway.

Several moms also suggest a change of hairstyle—a cut that can be blown quickly into place or a perm that can be just dampened and combed out. "But do it before you have the baby," says Chris. "If you wait until afterward, you'll be trying to get used to a new hairstyle while coping with a newborn. You'll go nuts." And make sure it's a style that flatters you—quick and easy doesn't count if it makes you feel like a gargoyle.

It will probably come as a rude awakening that all the weight you gained while you were pregnant doesn't fall off while you're in the hospital. But cheer up—about half our moms lost most of their weight during the first three months after their babies were born.

At any rate, the clothes you wear during your first few months postpartum will need to have forgiving waistlines—i.e., elastic. If it's summer, and if you can afford it, invest in some bright, inexpensive sundresses. Or, if it's winter, maybe a couple of bright warmup suits or pants in a size larger than your goal and some flattering but inexpensive sweaters. You'd be amazed at what looking nice will do for your energy level and your general outlook on life. Dawn says, "When I feel sick or tired, getting dressed and putting on makeup makes me feel better. And if when I pass myself in the mirror I know I look good, it makes me feel good about everything else, too."

Cheryl saw a movie that really hit home for her: "In *Mr. Mom*, where the husband stays home and takes care of the kids while his wife goes to work, he did everything the typical new mother does. He let everything go, and he looked awful for a couple of weeks until his wife finally told him, 'You're not taking any pride in yourself. You used to take pride in your work at the office, but you're not taking pride in your work here.'

"That's the way I felt. Just because we're Christians doesn't mean that we can take no pride in our homes or in our appearance and everything will just flow right along. There were times when my self-esteem was low, but I tried to fight it because I felt that if I wasn't the best person I could be I'd be putting temptation in front of my husband to look elsewhere. My attitude would tell him, 'I don't care about you *or* myself.' That's why I made sure I had five minutes to put on a little makeup before Rodger came home for lunch, even if Jason had to cry for a few minutes. I decided, 'I'm going to do this, because it's important to my self-esteem and my marriage.'"

Probably the single most encouraging bit of advice in this chapter is this: IT GETS EASIER AS YOUR BABY GROWS OLDER. Memorize it. If possible, engrave it on a locket and wear it against your heart. It will help get you through the months as you and your baby adjust to each other.

Christian Mommies and the Baby Blues

Before their babies were born, many of our moms regarded "Christian" and "postpartum blues" as a contradiction in terms. "I thought postpartum blues were not something a Christian would have," says Cheryl, "but I had a lot of blue days for a while."

Actually, baby blues can hit Christian mothers even harder than the rest of the populace, because on top of the emotional ups and downs is the guilty notion that you wouldn't be feeling this way if you were really trusting the Lord. That assumption might have some merit if the baby blues had their roots in your spiritual life, but they don't. They hit or don't hit depending on your hormone balance and the fatigue induced by first your pregnancy and then a radically changed lifestyle.

The best advice our moms have for new mothers afflicted with the baby blues is this: Hold on. You will not feel this way forever. We've been through it too, and life is great on the other side. Tell yourself, "I will get through this, and I will not allow it to affect my behavior toward my child and my husband. With God's help, I will emerge from this victorious." If you find yourself completely unable to function, or are still having problems after several months—most of our moms didn't— have your obstetrician check you to see whether you need medical treatment. If not, seek out a qualified Christian counselor who is familiar with postpartum depression and its ramifications.

Below are some of the emotions our moms experienced either before or shortly after the births of their babies. Don't let the long list frighten you—some moms went through just about all of these emotions, but many had just one or two and a few blessed women had none at all.

1) Resentment because of a surprise pregnancy and then guilt at feeling the resentment. Several of our moms had to deal with these feelings long before their babies were due. "I had a terribly negative reaction to my pregnancy," says Chris. "David and I had been married for only five months, and I knew we weren't being too careful, but somehow I just didn't expect to get pregnant. David was thrilled. He knew I had some ambivalence about it, but to this day he doesn't know how badly I *didn't* want to be pregnant. I really had to pray. I went into my room and said. 'Okay, Lord, I know I can't keep feeling this way because it will affect my baby, and I know you have a reason for this or it wouldn't have happened.' I just kept praying until I finally prayed myself through, I guess. By the time I was three months along I had become adjusted to it, and by about six months I was really looking forward to the baby and starting to get the nursery fixed up."

Patti has been through a couple of surprise pregnancies, and what helped her deal with them was simply recognizing the inevitable: "I think it was just a final giving up." She acknowledged that, planned or not, the baby was coming, and she determined with God's help to make his or her life something wonderful.

Nowhere is a person's maturity more clearly displayed than by the way she deals with life's unavoidable inconveniences, and it's sad that our generation has learned to deal with its unavoidable inconveniences by figuring out ways to avoid them. But even though they struggled for a while, our moms showed their maturity by accepting their situation and making the best of it. Chris still has a soft spot in her heart for other women struggling with surprise pregnancies. "Those are strong feelings," she says, "and you can't change yourself when you feel that way. The Lord has to change those feelings."

2) An overwhelming feeling of responsibility—also known as "the mommy jitters." With Pat, this feeling hit as she was on her way to the labor room: "Tears just started running down my face. The nurse looked at me and said, 'Your contractions must be pretty hard now.' I nodded, but that wasn't really what it was. I just got so scared— I thought, 'I'm having a baby!' I had waited so long and wanted it so badly, but all of a sudden the responsibility just overwhelmed me."

The jitters hit Adrienne as she and her husband were bringing Jennifer home from the hospital. "I had never babysat before or anything, and on the drive home I looked at my beautiful little baby, then at my husband, and said, 'Dick, what am I going to do with her?' I started crying—I still get teary-eyed just thinking about it."

Even Stella, who adopted her first little girl, had a brief bout with the mommy jitters. "We'd been waiting and praying for nine years for this baby. But the first night I was weak from the excitement of the day, and I looked at her and asked myself, 'Am I going to be able to handle this?' The next morning the Lord gave me my answer—it was as if I'd had a baby all my life."

Mommy jitters can be compared to the wedding jitters a bride and groom feel just before their marriage—except they're worse. Our society for years has been trying to convince us that if a person isn't happy with her spouse it's perfectly acceptable to take him back and exchange him for a new one, but even the most liberal society doesn't condone doing that with children. When you have a baby you're making a drastic change in your life that can't be undone. And if you haven't had experience with babies, you're stepping into unknown territory no matter how much material you've read on motherhood. The best thing that can be said about mommy jitters is that they're usually very brief in duration, vanishing as soon as you get your little one home and discover that motherhood isn't so hard after all.

3) Confusion and guilt at not immediately falling in love with the baby. With our moms, the division was almost right down the middle between those who fell in love with their babies right away and those who didn't, with the ones who didn't predominating slightly. Chris says, "I had a friend who told me before I had Ashley, 'Now, Chris, when you have that baby in the hospital, don't panic if you don't have an immediate gush of love for that child, and don't think you're a terrible mother. You have to get to know the baby, and you'll learn to love it.' If she hadn't told me that I would have thought I was losing my mind, because when I first saw Ashley I thought she looked about as messy as most babies do, and I wasn't filled with love and awe. I was thinking, 'What am I going to do with it?' She had to grow on me."

Kathy adds, "My sister just had her baby, and she expected this flood of emotion to hit her when he came out. She had been so excited all nine months, but when he finally came she was just numb. I was with her when she had him, and I kept telling her, 'Oh, Nancy, a boy! Look, blond hair! Look at his little fingers! Aren't you excited?' She told me later that she wasn't—the emotions she had expected didn't come. She looked at him, and yet he didn't seem part of her. Not until they brought him to the room and she began to nurse him did that bond start."

With our moms, there was a big difference between the protective maternal bond and the eagerly expected rush of love, the "whatever did we do without this little darling" feeling. The first happened right away and made sure they would protect and care for their babies, but the second sometimes took a while.

Cheryl says, "I found out how quickly the maternal bond takes hold after one full day of being in the hospital. They had done my C-section so quickly that I developed an infection from an unsterile environment. I had a high fever, so there were about thirty-six hours when I could not nurse or see or hold Jason the day after he was born. I have never been as emotional as the day I found out I couldn't hold my baby." (That's saying a lot—Cheryl is the epitome of the cool, unruffled receptionist.)

Marilee and Pene had similar experiences. Pene's first son Aaron had to be in an incubator for his first couple of days, and she found herself going down to the nursery and just looking into the incubator, crying. "I thought, 'This is stupid. Why am I standing here crying and looking at this little baby?'" The reason? Aaron was *her* little baby, and her spirit felt it even though her emotions didn't yet.

An interesting footnote: two of our moms who adopted their little girls fell in love with their babies immediately, a fact that makes our other moms suspect that a big reason for the numbness we felt was fatigue, something adoptive moms don't have to contend with—at least not to the degree that a new mother recuperating from childbirth does.

4) Ambivalent feelings about motherhood during the first few weeks. Our moms who had fairy-tale expectations of mommyhood took a little while to adjust to the hard reality of 2 a.m. feedings, spit-up, leaky diapers, and gas pains. "I was so tired," says Adrienne. "I started to resent everybody—my husband, the baby, myself."

One of the rudest surprises awaiting our moms was that their babies weren't completely under their control. Shock of shocks—they were little people with real minds of their own, even from the very beginning, and they tended to wake when they were expected to sleep, sleep when they were expected to be awake, and cry when they were expected to be quiet. Patti says, "I remember a feeling of helplessness with my first baby. I felt so helpless at not being able to control this child and not always being able to satisfy her."

Chris adds, "When a baby has colic, it seems as if there's nothing positive to make you love her. All there is is constant crying. But you can't take care of someone day after day without starting to love her, even if she's not the most pleasant person in the world. When Ashley was about three months old she started getting cute. She'd go for longer periods without crying, and I started really being able to respond to her. I no longer had to will myself to love her; I couldn't *help* loving her."

I had a similar experience with Megan, even though she had little trouble with colic. Jon and I had carefully planned her arrival, but after she was born the rush of mother love I expected was several weeks in coming. A friend who is also a young mother called me when Megan was about two weeks old and exclaimed, "I'm so happy for you! Don't you love being a mother? I just knew you would!"

My answer was guarded: "Yes, I do, and I'll love it

even more when she starts sleeping through the night."
My love for Megan during those first few weeks was more
an act of mind and will than an effortless flood of emotion.
But the effortless flood did come, and I now shamelessly
tell all inquirers that I'm madly in love with my little
girl.

After having had six children, Adrienne has developed
a stock answer for well-wishers who gush about how
wonderful new motherhood is: "I always tell people,
'Yes, it's wonderful, but the first three months are the
hardest. I love my baby, and I'll be glad when she's three
months old.'" And so, once again, the encouraging note
here is: *It gets easier*. As your baby grows older he'll be
less and less fussy and will settle down to a reasonably
predictable sleeping schedule.

The main thing that helped our moms overcome their
feelings of ambivalence during those first few weeks was
feeding time. A new mother can't expect much from her
baby in the way of love and gratitude since his first social
smile won't make its appearance until he's at least three
or four weeks old, but a feeding baby will give his
mommy some adorable sleepy smiles. (People will tell
you they're caused by gas, but Karin's answer to that is,
"I don't smile when I have gas, so why do people say
babies do?") The closeness of those moments with a contented baby is very special.

5) Shock at the total change of lifestyle. "I didn't understand
the bigness of it all," says Patty M. "I knew that it was
going to be a wonderful experience and that it would
take a lot of love, but I wasn't prepared for just how
much love it would take. I was consumed by my baby's
arrival. Everything changed—there was not one thing in
my life left unchanged. I wasn't prepared for the dramatic

effect her little life would have on me." Stella agrees: "The hardest thing for me to learn was that when you have a child it changes your whole lifestyle. It has to be my living for my child now, not my forcing my child to fit in with my plans."

6) Spiritual dryness. "My spiritual life went down the tubes," says Adrienne, "only because I didn't have the time I'd had before. It was so frustrating to get everything together and go to church prepared for a good sermon, wanting to drink it in because I needed it so badly and having to get up and go outside because the baby was crying."

Even if you're a vibrant, spiritual Christian, the fatigue and hormone changes that come right after the baby is born will probably make God seem far away at times. It's important to realize that the spiritual dryness has physical causes—it's not because you've fallen away and become a terrible person. "The Lord has a special dispensation period for new mothers," says Stella. "God honors you in your motherhood. He gives extra strength, extra hope, extra faith. You may feel as if you're losing out because you're not hearing the Word as much, but there's a spiritual relationship that develops between you and your child too at that time. You just have to relax and say, 'It's okay. The Lord understands, and He will give me strength.'"

It's important, though, as soon as you're able, to get back into a regular devotional time and resume worshiping at church. It's too easy to let your spiritual life slide even after you've recuperated from childbirth. (Chapter 7 covers ways to keep up your fellowship with the Lord.) Motherhood takes a lot out of you physically, emotionally, and spiritually. "And you've got to be filled up sometime," says Adrienne. "That's why your spiritual life is so important."

7) Disappointment if the delivery didn't go as planned. Karin had been all geared up for a natural delivery, but she developed toxemia and had to have an emergency Caesarean section. She says, "I sat there waiting in the hospital while everyone else went home with their babies, and I kept thinking, 'This isn't fair!' You expect the birth of your first baby to be a wonderful experience, but it's not wonderful when everything goes wrong." Karin felt a sense of failure at not being able to go through with the natural delivery, a feeling that Cheryl, who also had an emergency C-section, relates to.

What finally got Karin through it was realizing that if she had been pregnant in the days before C-sections were possible both she and her baby would probably have died in childbirth. "I thought, 'Well, the baby's healthy, and we're both alive.' I kept thanking God that at least everyone was alive." Even a Christian who's trusting the Lord is going to go through some rough emotional waters when her baby's birth doesn't turn out as expected. "Trust God—whatever happens is for the best" rolls glibly off the tongues of those who've never experienced what you're going through.

I was a confirmed S.E.M. who just knew I was going to have an easy time of it in the labor room. My doctor inadvertently supported that attitude by telling me that my above-average height boded well for a fast delivery— and I blew her encouraging words way out of proportion. But evidently my insides were smaller than my outsides, and I ended up pushing for five times longer than the average 30 minutes. The experience shocked me so badly that for several weeks I was unsure whether I ever wanted to go through it again, and I was bitterly disappointed that Megan's birth wasn't the beautiful memory I had wanted it to be. It helped when I finally realized that the big events in my life, such as my wedding and the birth of my first baby, didn't happen in order to give me beautiful memories; their purposes were to get me married and give me a child. The memories are being built as Jon, Megan and I live and love together day by day.

8) Unexplained emotional outbursts. "There were times right after the baby came," says Kathy, "and even while I was still pregnant, when I would think, 'Why did I just get so upset about that? It never used to bother me before.' It was almost as if I didn't understand myself." As Patti explains, "It's like the day before your period starts."

Sonja's hormonal imbalance after the birth of her first child was bigger than most, and it caused some real emotional upsets: "I look back in amazement at some of the decisions I made and the ridiculous hard feelings I caused with my husband and other people I care about. I warned my husband about it the second time around, and he reassured me that he would try to be understanding. I agreed to trust his judgment as the better of the two, even concerning decisions I normally made alone, and it went much better the second time."

9) Irrational fears—also known as "mommy paranoia." This malady goes beyond just checking on your baby at naptime to make sure he's still breathing, and seems to be more connected with the personality of the mother than with hormones. With me it took the form of making me reluctant to leave Megan with anyone, no matter how trustworthy. I finally forced myself to start leaving her periodically to spend an evening out with Jon, and I consoled myself by screening my babysitters extra carefully. It has become easier as time has gone by, and I'm finally able to leave her now with only one page of instructions for the sitter instead of the usual five.

Dawn's fears took a different twist because her baby was adopted: "Every time the phone rang, I thought it was HRS or someone who was going to say, 'I want my baby back.' I knew that the Lord had performed miracles to bring Melody into our lives, but for months I was afraid someone was going to come and take her away."

Sonja had her bout with mommy paranoia before her baby came: "I was afraid that I would have the baby, go home, and then wake up one morning having forgotten all about it, get dressed, and run out the door as usual. I actually had nightmares about it. But when the time came, there was no chance of its really happening—I was so exhausted, sore, and heavy-breasted with milk that I needed no reminders of my responsibility."

For the Christian mother, the solution to mommy paranoia is realizing where the spirit of fear comes from—and it's not from the Lord. "You can get stuck on the fear," says Stella, "and your child will sense that apprehension and become fearful herself. You have to check on your baby and use wisdom, but you also have to be able to rest in the knowledge that the Lord gave you that child, and as long as you're doing what you know is best for her, He can protect her."

Mommies at Home

The new mother who must return to work after her baby is born faces problems of her own, which we'll cover in Chapter 10. One problem she does not face, however, is the sense of isolation and being closed in that a mother who spends all her time at home can develop. Kathy says, "I look forward so much to getting out. I look forward to Sunday school and church because I want to see the people and hear the message. I go into stores sometimes and don't know how to put the outfits together. I'll ask the salesgirl. 'What is everybody wearing nowadays?' I'll be all right for a while, and then it'll hit me again. I talk to my husband about it, but of course he doesn't quite understand because he's out around people all day."

Chris puts the feeling of being housebound high on her list of big adjustments. "Since Ashley was my first baby, I was afraid to take her anywhere for fear she'd catch cold. And because she had colic I hesitated to take her visiting or shopping for fear she'd cry the whole time."

"The solution for me was Grandma," says Stella. "Even though my babies were very good and took long naps, I was housebound because they did sleep so much. Grandparents are a real blessing, and if you have one who will come over and sit with the baby while he's sleeping, it's tremendous. Just go to the store for an hour. Or go for a walk, or visit a neighbor, or do anything just to get out for a little while." Some grandparents adore getting a chance to babysit, but others come to resent it. Have a frank discussion with both sets of your baby's grandparents to find out where they stand. They'll appreciate knowing that you honestly don't want to impose on them.

Cheryl says, "It's easy to get out when your family has two cars, because you can either take the baby with you or find a good Christian day-care center or 'Mother's

Day Out' club. But if you don't, the only thing to do is sit down with your husband and explain to him that you need to have time away from the house. Work out a way to have the car one day a week."

Patty W. agrees: "Treat yourself and the baby to a special outing at least once a week—go to a park, out for ice cream, whatever. And just go out and get some fresh air whenever the weather permits. It renews both of you." It's easy to fall into the habit of staying in the house around the clock, emerging only to check the mailbox. But if you're not careful you can develop a bad case of cabin fever and start resenting your little one for keeping you penned in. "It helps just to find a friend in the neighborhood," says Pene.

Life after baby can become simpler instead of more complex if you let it. Have friends over for popcorn and games instead of going to the expense of a babysitter plus dinner and a movie. Or, during the day, if going window-shopping on a limited budget gives you a case of the covets, walk around a lake or through a local park instead. Use your imagination, and take advantage of the inexpensive cultural opportunities your town offers. There are probably things going on all around you that you aren't aware of.

Unless your baby has severe colic it's no big deal to take him with you, especially if you're nursing and don't have to pack bottles. An excursion every now and then will expose him to all kinds of new sights and sounds and will keep you from getting into a rut. Babies are very portable little creatures if you're equipped with a good stroller or baby backpack. But as nice as it is to get out with the baby, it's even better to go out without him every once in a while. "You need it, and I think your baby also needs it," says Pene. "I've always wanted to be a mother, but there are times when I just need to get away."

I have a helpful husband, and while Megan was little I sometimes told him when he came home from work, "Okay, you keep Megan for a little while. I'm going down to the library (or shopping, or for a walk)." I nursed her right before I left and made sure I was home in time for her next feeding. "David helped me a lot that way, too," says Chris. "He would watch Ashley right when he came home in the evening, and it was so wonderful just to know that even if she cried I didn't have to do anything." Rehearsing with the church choir while your husband watches the baby can give you a ministry outlet as well as an evening out.

Your baby will probably take most of your at-home attention during his first few weeks, but our moms feel it's important to develop some kind of additional creative pastime as soon as you can. You may feel guilty about taking the time for it at first, especially if the house isn't completely in order, but it's important to keep yourself growing as a person. I found that unless I made continual efforts to stretch myself I became very boring; when Jon came home my big, exciting news for the day was, "Megan spat up all over the couch."

"Be sure to take time for yourself," says Connie. "Find something you love to do, and do it often." Trina draws and paints, and several of our other moms do counted cross-stitch, all hobbies with the added advantage of helping them come up with inexpensive Christmas presents for their families and friends. Others of our moms have discovered a love for gardening, which gives them a chance to get out of the house as well as to enjoy seeing things grow. Chris bought an inexpensive intercom at an electronics shop and kept it in Ashley's room at naptime. She kept the receiver with her, and could hear right away when Ashley woke up even if she was outside pulling weeds. Still other moms have developed a love of reading or of good music, both of which relax them and improve their minds at the same time.

Chris gave up on her garden: "It was all I could do to keep it alive until I got four okras out of it! But I love to cook. So when Ashley was little, David would take over with her in the evenings while I went into the kitchen." Other hobbies, such as crafts and dressmaking, can even be the start of a home-based business.

The one hobby our moms do *not* recommend is watching soap operas. "Don't even turn them on!" says Dawn. Constant television watching smothers creativity and robs you of time that could be better spent relaxing, playing with your baby, or doing something stimulating and productive.

The drawback to all these ways of stretching yourself and/or getting out of the house is, of course, that none of them involves spending time with your husband. All our moms agree that you and your husband need to have a date at least every week or two where you go out without the baby—a time to talk and share and relate not as father and mother, but as husband and wife. And that's where a good babysitter is worth her weight in gold. If you've got a couple of sets of eager grandparents close by, your problem is solved. If not, you may have to do a little hunting.

The first place to check is with your friends who have children—do they have a babysitter they've been partic-

ularly pleased with? Or, if your church has a bulletin
board, check it to see if anyone is looking for babysitting
jobs. Or ask your church nursery workers. But be sure
you get ironclad references for any potential sitters from
people on whose judgment you can rely. Patty W. says,
"*Never* leave your baby with someone you don't know,
or who isn't recommended by someone you know and
trust."

Patti and Sonja were both able to figure out ways to
have their babysitting done free. Patti formed a babysitting co-op with several other young mothers, where
points were gained by babysitting for one of the involved
moms and spent by having one of them babysit for her
children. Sonja developed a similar arrangement involving only one other couple: "When our children were four
years and 15 months old, we made arrangements with
some friends who had children the same ages to switch
off babysitting duties with us on alternating Friday
nights. We've been doing it for nine months now—our
marriages have blossomed, and our wallets aren't flat."

No matter who your babysitter is, Patty W. stresses
the need to leave clear *written* instructions on what, if
anything, the baby should eat while you're gone, how
to prepare it, and when to put him to bed. Give a word
of warning, too, if your little one tends to grump himself
to sleep. Also leave a telephone number where you can
be reached, as well as the phone numbers of your pediatrician and the closest emergency room. "If you're
going to be more than twenty or thirty minutes away,"
says Patty, "leave the number of a nearby friend or relative who could get there while you're being called." And
if there's any chance your sitter—especially Grandma or
Grandpa—will need to take the baby out while you're

gone, go ahead and install your car seat in her car and give instructions on how to use it.

After you've done all that, and completely exhausted yourself, go on out and have a good time.

Another problem the mother who stays at home has to face is the guilt she feels, especially when money is tight, at no longer contributing to the family income. When I first quit work after Megan was born I felt a pang every time Jon said he wished we could afford something that wasn't in the budget, even though I was deeply committed to staying home. I finally had to sit him down and tell him, "Honey, I know you don't mean to make me feel guilty, but when you say you want things we can't afford I feel as if you think I should be working and earning money instead of staying home with Megan." He was shocked—that wasn't what he'd meant at all— and he promised to be more sensitive in the future.

Karin says, "I felt bad about Wayne's money. I knew it wasn't *his* money, but when we were both working we earned about equal salaries. I was accustomed to being able to spend money and not think anything of it. Then, after I quit work, I felt guilty if I wrote a ten-dollar check at a discount store." There's a postscript to Karin's story, though: "When I quit work the country was in the middle of a recession, and Wayne had just opened a business. Times were rough, but it's been only two years since then and Wayne makes more money now than we made together back then. I really believe God honored my desire to stay home and take care of my baby."

Stella agrees: "We pulled our belts in and did it, and now, eight years later, I would do it all over again. Our budget was tight but it was worth it. We gave up things we thought were necessities, but they weren't—they were luxuries. My baby was far more important than having all the material things I wanted."

If you're suffering from a feeling of guilt at not contributing to the family coffers, it can be like rubbing salt into a wound every time you write a check in a drugstore and the checkout clerk asks, "Are you employed?" A couple of our moms developed stock answers. Chris's was, "Not me, honey! I stay home with my baby, and I *love* it!" When Karin is asked about her line of work, she answers, "I develop personalities and build morals."

It's easy to feel unproductive when you're a new mother, especially before you develop a reliable daily schedule and get a handle on your housework. There's not much said these days about taking pride in our work as homemakers—our society seems to think that fulfillment and challenge come only from work outside the home. But our stay-at-home moms have grown past that point, and you will too if you keep in mind that you've just done something incredibly productive: you've produced a human being. And you're in the process of rearing him to be a responsible person who is sensitive to his Creator and the needs of the people around him. It's hard to see all that right at first, before your baby's understanding starts to peek through, but every time you show love, every time you come when he's hurting or hungry or just needs to be held, and every time you enforce an established "no-no," you're building his little psyche. And that's worth all the paychecks in the world.

2
...

A Little Behind in Your Housework

Poets and greeting card companies like to use flowery adjectives to describe motherhood: warm, tender, giving, loving. But underneath all the sweetness and light and baby powder, motherhood is something else: *earthy*.

Before long you'll be more familiar with your baby's anatomy than you ever were with your own, and you'll be able to tell what your husband fed Junior for lunch by the color and texture of your child's next dirty diaper. And you'll find, probably to your own amazement, that what was disgusting in the diaper of your neighbor's baby is just a natural part of life when it's your child who's done it. It can even be beautiful—ask any mother who has just seen her baby's first normal dirty diaper after a bout with diarrhea!

And so, speaking of diapers, here are some tips that helped make our diaper duty a little easier.

■ Patty W. recommends disposable diapers for your baby's first three months at least: "Newborns, and especially breastfed newborns, 'go' continually! Disposables are a very practical gift if anyone asks what you need."

■ Most of our babies didn't mind being a bit damp—and those who did, such as Donna's little girl, April, let their mommies know about it in no uncertain terms—so you needn't feel your baby's diaper every few minutes. Before each feeding, at bedtime, and whenever else you notice that she needs changing is enough. And if your child won't tolerate a damp diaper for even a few minutes, take solace in this: Donna is convinced that April's aversion to soggy drawers is what made her potty-training go so quickly later on.

■ Since there's no such thing as a designer diaper, you're the only one who'll know if your baby is wearing discount disposables. "Some store brands are just as good as national brand diapers," says Chris, "and they're much cheaper." *Do* use diapers with elastic around the legs, though. You'll be sorry if you don't, and so will anyone who happens to be holding your baby when she wets.

■ Before Megan was born, I bought a box of each brand of disposables I planned to try. After she came I quickly found out which brands could and couldn't hold their own, and I stuck with the brands that worked well for her thereafter.

■ Linda cut a V in the center front of Philip's disposable diapers during his first few weeks to keep his umbilical stump from becoming wet or irritated.

■ Cheryl discovered that masking tape worked well to reseal Jason's and Brian's disposable diapers. Even though her boys are both toddlers now, she still keeps a roll handy for emergencies—such as when Brian manages to pull the diaper tapes loose. It happens. Julie, mother of brown-eyed, curly-haired Sean, says you've never known true horror until you open your child's door in the morning to find him fingerpainting his crib with the fragrant brown stuff that used to be in his diaper. Megan learned this trick at about fifteen months, and after two or three days of walking in and seeing her grinning at me stark naked from her crib I took my brilliant husband's suggestion to reinforce her diaper tapes with masking tape *before* I put her down for a nap.

■ I found disposable diapers especially useful when Megan had diarrhea, since the super-absorbent pulp in the disposable had a better chance of holding in what would have run right out the sides of a cloth diaper. Diaper doublers or overnight disposables give even more protection against leaks. Of course, your baby's diaper needs to be changed immediately after each bowel movement when he has an intestinal upset. Also, call your doctor for medical instructions and be extra alert for diaper rash at such times.

■ When making cost comparisons between cloth and disposable diapers, consider the fact that a baby who needs eighty cloth diapers each week will probably use only fifty or sixty disposables. "With cloth diapers," says Cheryl, who used both, "you have to change the baby more often. Not only does the wetness stay right next to his skin, but you get a strong ammonia smell if he's at all wet. Plus, disposables hold more, so you don't have to change the baby every time he wets a little bit."

■ A friend gave me a dozen cloth diapers before Megan was born. Even though I used disposables, the cloth diapers were great for putting on my shoulder when I held Megan, for draping her face while she nursed, and for mopping up little messes.

■ If you use cloth diapers, Chris suggests you also use diaper liners, which are available at large discount stores. The liners are made of thin paper, and when your baby has a bowel movement you just lift the liner out of the diaper and flush it. No rinsing! Even if you use disposables, it might be a good idea to use liners so that you can easily flush your baby's bowel movements rather than putting them into plastic bags for the trash collectors. In many areas it's illegal to dispose of human waste in the same manner as regular garbage.

■ Connie kept a diaper pail half-filled with detergent and water in her bathroom. As soon as a cloth diaper left her little girl's behind and she flushed whatever extra was inside, Connie dropped it into the pail. When wash time came, it was a simple matter to carry the pail to the washing machine, dump the contents inside, spin-dry to get rid of the soapy water, then wash.

■ "Don't soak cloth diapers in chlorine bleach," says Cheryl. "It'll eat right through 'em." And that's not the only problem with soaking diapers in bleach—several moms point out that the ammonia in your baby's urine, combined with chlorine bleach in a closed diaper pail, creates dangerous fumes.

■ Most of our cloth-diaper moms washed their children's diapers in detergent and chlorine bleach, then double-rinsed them to make sure no residue was left to irritate their babies' behinds. "Use a wooden spoon to poke the diapers down into the wash water when you're using bleach," says Kristy. "It'll keep your hands from becoming irritated."

■ A friend of Kristy's received sample foil packets of baby wipes when her child was born. After the wipes were gone, she refilled the packets from the large economy size tub on her changing table and kept them in her diaper bag.

■ "Baby wipes are great for trips and outings," says Cheryl, "but if you can't afford them or don't have any on hand, wet a washcloth, wring it out, and put it into a plastic bag. These are essential to have in the car or when you go out."

■ In cool weather, warm the baby wipes between your hands before cleaning your baby's bottom, or use a cloth rinsed out in warm water. The same goes for baby lotion—rub it between your hands to take the chill off before applying it to that warm little behind.

■ It takes just a few hours for a mild case of diaper rash to blossom into a full-blown one, so start treating your baby's diaper area with medicated ointment at the first sign of irritation. With a very bad case of rash, your baby's behind needs as much fresh air as possible in order to heal. Our pediatricians recommend letting children with diaper rash go without a diaper, but that's not too practical if you value your carpet and furnishings—especially with a baby boy. Try putting him into a cloth diaper with no plastic pants and changing him immediately each time he wets.

■ "Don't use alcohol-based baby wipes on your baby's behind when he has a rash," says Mary Ann. "They sting. Use a soft washcloth wrung out in warm water instead." Once when Megan had diaper rash during a visit to Grandmommy's, my mother showed me how to change her diaper without making her cry. While she was wiping the irritated skin, she blew on it gently—no tears!

■ Stock your changing table carefully, since unnecessary items just collect dust and create clutter. If a month or so goes by and you realize that something isn't being used, put it away. And be sure to put such hazardous items as alcohol, lotion, pins, thermometer, etc., in a cabinet out of reach when your child becomes old enough to crawl and climb.

■ Handling their babies' dirty diapers didn't bother most of our moms. All the same, Connie, who did lots of diaper duty with her three girls, feels it's important not to make your baby think he's been bad for filling his diaper— especially when he does it as you're walking out the front door, or, worse yet, all over you. After all, he's just performing a natural function in the only way God gave him to do it. "Sing to your baby and smile while you're changing him," Connie says. (You really *can* sing while gritting your teeth.)

■ As she diapered Zachary and Ashley, Terri pointed out the diaper pins, lotions, etc. Terri says it's also good to get into the habit of explaining, very simply, what you're doing as you give your baby her bath, change her diaper, dress her, or prepare for her feeding. Not only will it be a learning experience for her; it'll help prepare you for the thousands of questions that come when she starts to talk.

■ Megan initiated a contest when she was four or five months old that was still going strong at one year. Her objective was to either sit up or flip off the changing table before I got her diaper fastened; mine was to keep her from falling on her head. I found that keeping a couple of special toys at the changing table helped occupy her attention. A piece of waxed paper worked well when I could keep her from eating it, and she also liked playing with the colored ribbons tied to the open woodwork on top of the table.

■ It's a big help if you can keep your diaper bag stocked so that all you have to do is pick it up with your baby and walk out the door. Here are some things our moms kept in their bags: three or four disposable diapers, a plastic bag for dirty diapers and wipes, a good supply of baby wipes, a pad to change the baby on, a couple of toys, breast pads if you're nursing, masking tape, a change of clothes for the baby, and a cloth diaper for your shoulder. If you're bottlefeeding, add a bottle and bib at the last minute.

■ "I went through three diaper bags before I found one that could hold everything I needed," says Lynda. "I'm the typical overprepared mother. When I take Grant to the sitter, I take an extra pair of shoes, extra socks, and two changes of clothes. In a regular diaper bag, the plastic liner was always attached to the handle, and the weight of everything in the bag would tear out the bottom of the liner in just a few weeks. I discovered that an athletic bag—the type you'd take to the gym—works much better. It's sturdier and holds more."

Graduation Day: Using the Potty

All our moms are emphatic about *not* trying to potty-train a child too soon. Some of their little girls caught on as early as eighteen months—although that was unusual—but the little boys were usually at least two, and often older, before they had enough control. Pressuring a toddler to potty-train too early results in more stress than the Lord ever meant a little child to have to deal with. Chris tells the tragic/comic tale of her little niece waking in the middle of the night sobbing, "But I don't *want* to poo-poo in the potty!" (Her parents got the message and postponed her potty-training for a while after that.) Patti, who successfully potty–trained her children Keva and Joel and is now working on toddler Jonathan, puts it this way: "When they're ready, it's easy. When they're not, it's a struggle."

■ Before you start potty-training your toddler, realize that it's going to take him a little time to get used to this wonderful new idea. "I don't know how I could have been this dense," says Chris, "but I thought that if you waited until the child was ready, she would catch on the first day you put panties on her, with maybe a couple of accidents. So I tried it, and Ashley did not go in the potty *one time* the first day. So, I put diapers back on her for three months. Someone finally told me, 'Chris, it takes a few days.'" Try setting up the training potty in the bathroom and giving your child a few days to become accustomed to its presence before encouraging him to use it.

■ Don't expect your child to tell you when she has to go. By the time she gets around to telling you, it'll probably be too late. Most of our moms used a method similar to the one Chris used with Ashley: First, she showed Ashley the training potty and made sure she understood what they were going to do. "Then, when I got Ashley up in the morning, I asked, 'Do you want to go potty?' Yes. So she sat down; nothing happened. Thirty minutes later she wet her pants. I didn't make a big deal of it. I just said, 'Oh-oh, we didn't make it to the potty,' and changed her pants.

"About thirty minutes later, I said, 'Let's see if you can go to the potty, okay?' I had some miniature marshmallows, and I gave her one if she would just try. If she really *went*, I gave her two or three." With her four children, Joyce used raisins, pineapple chunks, apple pieces—any special treat that your child really likes will do, but be sure that it really is a special treat and not one your child can have any time for the asking. Mary Ann kept a jar of brightly colored jelly beans and let her little boy choose two or three when he was successful.

■ Our moms agree that an important part of potty-training is letting your toddler watch you in the bathroom. Children are great imitators, and it's much easier to persuade them that using the potty is wonderful if they see you doing it. In fact, several of our moms report that their children *asked* to start using the potty because it was something their parents did. Julie, who has two boys, adds: "It's important for little boys to see their daddies in the bathroom. If all they see is Mommy, they'll never understand what's going on." "Jonathan understands what going to the potty is all about now," says Patti, "and he wants to stand up—but he's too short." Kathy solved the height problem for Brandon and Ryan by buying them a short step stool and keeping it in the bathroom.

■ Encourage your child when he uses the potty successfully. Applaud and tell him how proud you are, how proud Grandma and Grandpa will be, etc. Children really do want to please their loved ones.

■ When Chris was first trying to potty-train Ashley, she

had a hard time getting her to sit on the training potty. She says, "Finally a friend told me, 'It's never going to work if you keep wanting it so badly. Just relax. Tell her very lovingly, "Ashley, I don't care if you're not potty-trained until you go to school. As long as you learn before you're six, and when you get into first grade you're not wetting in your seat, it's okay with me." If you'll relax and just keep trying it every now and then to see if she's ready, she'll do it eventually."

What finally got Ashley started was that bane of parents everywhere: peer pressure. "We had company. There were four or five kids her age in the house, and they all used the potty except her. The next day, after they left, I asked her, 'Do you want to start using the potty?' She said yes." Ironically, Ashley in turn inspired another little friend, Tiffany, to potty-train. But be careful that *you* don't pressure your child. Just let her watch her little friends and relatives. She's bound to develop the idea that if they're doing it, it must be fun.

■ Carol is an ex-science teacher with four children. She says, "Instead of asking my little boy, 'Do you want to go potty?' because of the pressure involved there, I ask, 'Do you want to empty your bladder?' It works!" Evidently, some toddlers hear the question, "Do you want to go potty?" as a demand for a performance, with all the fear of possible failure that entails. Carol discovered that asking her child if he wants to empty his bladder has really taken the pressure off him. (Of course it helps to explain very simply to your child what a bladder is.)

■ It was common for our moms' toddlers to take anywhere from a few days to several months to start using the potty for their bowel movements even after they stopped wetting their pants. Just keep allowing your child to practice after each accident and he'll see the light eventually. And try not to be too impatient—for our moms, getting angry didn't help at all. Take note of the time your child usually has a bowel movement each day, and schedule your bowel training around it.

It wasn't uncommon for a child to continue wetting the bed at night for some time, although some stayed dry through the night as soon as they were potty-trained. Nighttime wetting is something your toddler probably has no control over, so don't make him feel guilty for it. Many of our moms found it easiest to continue using diapers at night for a while even though their children were in training pants during the daytime.

An older toddler may continue wetting at night simply because she's wearing a diaper and thinks she's expected to use it. Try putting her into regular underwear (or no underwear) at night and explaining, "Honey, you're not wearing a diaper, so if you need to go potty call me and I'll take you to the bathroom."

■ While she was potty-training Zachary and Ashley, Terri used two pair of training pants with plastic pants over them at outings and at bedtime. This gave them protection against wetting but still let her children feel as if they were wearing "big boy or girl pants."

■ Carol's children were more willing to sit on a sturdy wooden training potty with a plastic seat than on a flimsier all-plastic one.

■ Joyce has some unique advice on potty-training boys: "My older sister discovered that her two little boys liked the noise it made when they 'went' into a tin can," she says. "She also discovered that they were always dry when they first woke up. So if their mother came quickly with the little can, the problem was solved. This worked beautifully for me with my two boys. The little tin potty went with us in the car, too." Be sure to blunt any sharp edges on the can.

■ Patti points out that it's unrealistic to expect your toddler to stay dry through the night if your give him liquids at bedtime: "I give my children their last fluids an hour or two before bedtime, and then have them visit the potty right before bed."

■ The sound of running water helped many of our children to start urinating. And for Megan, the sound of water from the tub faucet was more effective than the sound of water from the sink tap.

■ The most important ingredient to potty-training success, according to our moms, is consistency. "You have to stay on a schedule," says Rita. Standard potty times are: first thing in the morning, a half-hour or so after each meal or snack, before naps, and right before bedtime, with a few extra times in between. Each child's digestive system is different, and it won't take long for you to learn when your toddler needs to visit the potty in order to train successfully.

■ If your child suddenly starts wetting the bed again after having been potty-trained for quite a while, it may be because of emotional pressure. With our moms' children this happened most often when another baby came into the family, but with Scott, Sylvia's little boy, it happened when he started school. "About midway through the school year he began wetting at night," she says. "Now that I look back, I think probably he could see the difference between what he was doing and what the other kids were doing." Scott was later discovered to be dyslexic, and he then received special tutoring. Mary Ann's son Joseph reverted to bedwetting when his baby brother died. In both cases the wetting eventually stopped.

On the other hand, if your child just can't seem to control herself enough to potty-train, don't overlook the possibility of a medical problem. Carol B.'s daughter Kristie was still having trouble when she reached her fifth birthday—and after changing pediatricians was finally diagnosed as having a kidney dysfunction that would have resulted in kidney failure had it been allowed to continue.

Sears' "Wee Alert" or a similar system can probably help an older child whose bedwetting is not caused by a medical problem.

A final word on this subject: When at last your toddler is potty-trained and you're breathing a sigh of relief, don't throw away those diapers. In His infinite wisdom and sense of humor, the Lord designed children in such a way that by the time they're toilet trained they're also just about old enough to start asking for a little brother or sister.

3
•••
Breast and Bottle

When baby formula was first introduced to the general public a half-century ago, it was hailed as technology's best for the modern baby. But in recent years science has realized what many wise moms knew all along: namely, that technology ain't got nothing on God.

Give serious thought to your decision of whether to breast- or bottlefeed your baby. It's more than just a matter of preference, like the choice between using cloth or disposable diapers. God designed every part of your body for a reason, and when you use your breasts to feed your child you're fulfilling the primary purpose for which they were created.

Even the baby formula manufacturers today admit that

breast milk is the perfect food for your baby, and they include a disclaimer to that effect on their labels. Breast milk is more easily digested and less apt to cause stomach upsets than formula. And of course formula contains none of the antibodies present in breast milk, which researchers now claim protect your child from certain viral and bacterial infections, especially in the gastrointestinal tract (i.e., diarrhea). And because breast milk is such a complete food, most pediatricians agree that your baby needs no other sources of nourishment—not even water—until he's four to six months old.

Now, it's only logical that anything *that* good for your baby has got to be hard to do, right?

Wrong.

My paternal grandmother is a smart, sturdy country woman who nursed nine healthy children. She takes pride in the fact that her babies all gulped to keep up with the flow of her milk, and while visiting she paid me the compliment of observing that Megan was doing the same thing. Yet before Megan was born, when folks asked whether I planned to nurse, I would reply, "I really want to. I hope it works out."

Just as I was, most expectant mothers I've talked with are nervous about nursing. Part of it has to do with fear of the unknown. After all, the idea of producing food in your body for someone else is pretty strange. But I suspect that another reason for our nervousness is centered around the horror stories we've been told by mothers who "tried to nurse, but couldn't"—mothers who themselves probably went into nursing filled with fears and misconceptions.

The fact of the matter is, there's just not that much to it. Nursing is much less complicated and requires less effort than bottlefeeding, though it does take more time. Try thinking about it this way: The past couple of generations notwithstanding, nearly every baby ever born has been breastfed. A lot fewer of us would have survived if it were all that difficult.

But all of this is not meant to paint an overly rosy picture of breastfeeding. It's easy to feel like the Lone Ranger while you're nursing, since it's a serious responsibility that no one else can take for you.

Most of our nursing mothers went through an adjustment period of about four to six weeks due to recuperating from pregnancy and childbirth, fatigue, readjusting hormones, and possibly some breast tenderness and nipple soreness. Add to all this an overanxious non-nursing grandma or two, and a baby's first few weeks can be pretty difficult for his new mom. Lynda says, "I was so gung ho about nursing before Grant was born, but when I got home from the hospital everything changed. One of my friends encouraged me, 'Give it at least two weeks.' If she hadn't, I probably would have given up."

Jan is another nursing mother who had a difficult adjustment period: "When Jordan David was a week old, I was so engorged that I could hardly stand having a nightgown touch me, much less a bra or my baby's sucking. There were a couple of times when I cried through the first few minutes of the feeding because it hurt so much. During those crying times I just kept reminding myself of the advantages to Jordan David and me, and that I really wanted that special time with my baby. Everything is going great now—still nursing at six months."

Engorgement can be painful, but it doesn't last long, and it doesn't happen to all nursing mothers. (I know, because it didn't happen to me.) And remember, you would go through some kind of adjustment period or baby blues even if you weren't nursing, and then you'd have to be washing and sterilizing bottles and nipples, boiling water to mix with powdered formula, and warming your baby's bottles at feeding time. The nursing mother has no bottles to wash, no nipples to scrub, no water to boil, no formula to mix. When her baby is hungry, she just plugs him in.

One of the most important benefits of nursing, though—more important than its ease and lack of necessary paraphernalia, more important than the fact that nursing is much, much less expensive than formula—and nearly as important to our moms as the nutritional superiority of nursing over formula—is the sense of oneness it gives you with your baby. Without exception, our nursing mothers (even Jan and Lynda) feel they developed a closeness with their children through nursing that nothing else could have given them.

Getting Started

Read everything you can about nursing. It will help take the mystery out of it. And along with reading, it's very important to ask questions. "Ask anything," says Cheryl, "even if you think you're supposed to know the answer already." Your local chapter of the La Leche League is a great place to call for encouragement or information. It can also be a tremendous help to find a friend who nursed successfully and ask her to serve as your mentor.

■ Elementary as this sounds, a newborn needs help finding the spout where the milk comes out, so make sure you get your baby plugged in at the right spot. Kristy laughs about her experience with this now, but it was very *un*funny to her at the time: "They brought my baby in for her first nursing at about nine at night. Everyone was gone, and the room was dark. I was so naive—I stuck the baby up there and thought everything was fine.

"But it *hurt*, so I pushed the beeper and the nurse, a big Southern black woman, came in. I was crying, and I told her, 'This is killing me!' 'Let me check it,' she said. She pulled the baby away, and she hadn't even been on the nipple. She exclaimed, 'Child, that baby's done sucked a blood blistah!' Sure enough, there was a big ol' hickey on the side of my breast!"

■ Sometimes, retracted nipples or some other irregularity can make nursing difficult for your baby. Cindy recommends asking your obstetrician before your baby is born whether you need to work on drawing your nipples out to help your little one nurse more easily. "I was having trouble nursing Lindsey in the hospital," she says, "but I didn't realize there was anything abnormal about my nipples until I saw the girl who shared my hospital room nursing her baby." With a little patience, Cindy overcame her problem and was able to nurse Lindsey without further difficulty.

■ Nipple soreness can be at least partially prevented by taking some toughening-up measures during the last trimester of your pregnancy. One standard exercise is to rub your nipples briskly for a couple of minutes each morning and evening with a towel or washcloth. And since your expanding bosom will make new bras necessary anyway, go ahead and buy a couple of nursing bras and wear them with the flaps down underneath your clothing as much as possible. The constant rubbing against your clothes will help toughen your nipples.

If you do have a problem with sore nipples, try the method Michele used with little Sarah Danielle: She let her nurse through a rubber nipple shield. She recommends, though, that you use it on only one breast per feeding, and alternate breasts. This will break your nipples in gradually while keeping your baby accustomed to their taste and feel.

■ Having a little person sucking on your breast eight to ten times a day can produce another painful problem: nipple dryness and cracking. To prevent it, use nipple cream after each feeding during your baby's first few weeks. Cleaning your nipples with soap or alcohol will dry them out and make them more likely to crack, so just keep them clean with clear water.

■ Our nursing moms found that after their milk came in one breast usually leaked while their baby was nursing from the other, so take breast pads and an extra nursing bra to the hospital with you. You'll probably need to wear breast pads constantly during your baby's first few months, and several companies make disposable ones. Chris, though, made her own reusable pads from cloth diapers, and Terri made inexpensive emergency breast pads by cutting up a disposable diaper. She got about twenty pads from each diaper, and the plastic backing kept her milk from soaking through to her clothing. Linda used thin terry washcloths as breast pads. She just folded them and tucked them into her bra cups.

■ Several of our nursing moms discovered that when they felt their milk letting down while they weren't wearing pads they could stop the flow by crossing their arms in front of their breasts and pressing in firmly. In fact, when Megan was a few months old I eliminated my need for breast pads, except at night, by pressing in on one breast for a minute or so while she began nursing from the other.

▪ During your first few weeks of nursing, carry a cloth diaper or a receiving blanket in your diaper bag when you go out in case you soak through your breast pad. More than once, having a blanket to drape over my shoulder saved me from acute embarrassment.

▪ You'll need to help your husband understand that all nursing mothers leak at times. It's the way God designed them. Especially during your first weeks of motherhood, stimulation of the nipple is what triggers milk letdown— whether it comes from scratching an itch, your baby's sucking, or your husband's caresses.

▪ Julie wears a front-closing underwire bra instead of a nursing bra. It gives her more support than a regular nursing bra, and is easier to unhook discreetly. "Plus, it's a whole lot easier to get back into," she says. "You don't have to reach all the way up to your shoulder to rehook it."

▪ Nursing babies need to be burped between breasts and at the end of the feeding. I gradually learned that when Megan started to squirm during a feeding, chances were she either 1) needed to be burped, 2) was filling her diaper, 3) was taking a play break (as she grew older), or 4) was full.

▪ It has already been mentioned that an anxious new grandma without nursing experience can make your early days of motherhood more difficult. One of our moms, who shall be nameless for the sake of family harmony, says, "I wouldn't leave my baby with my husband's mother,'cause I was scared to death she would feed him." Our nursing moms agree that having a husband who supports you in your decision to nurse—and isn't afraid to say so—is essential if you're to withstand opposition from other family members.

Jan adds, "It helps to make a joke of it—you know, 'Now, Mom, he's only a week old. He doesn't need that piece of pizza!' "

"With my first baby," says Patti, "I was really uptight about everything Grandma did. But I finally realized that the baby won't die if she gives him a bottle, and if it makes her feel better, it's okay—especially since Grandma sees him only once in a while." And take heart. Once Grandma sees that your baby really *is* thriving on breast milk, she'll relax.

■ Several moms suggested this method of keeping track of your baby's weight between checkups: Weigh yourself, then step back onto the scales holding your baby. The difference between the two weights is your baby's weight. Do this only every couple of weeks, not every day. Babies gain weight in small increments, and worrying day by day about whether your baby is getting enough nourishment can make your milk production go down. Call your pediatrician if you feel your baby isn't gaining weight normally.

■ A wise mother warned me before Megan was born that there would be days when I seemed to do nothing but nurse, and she was right. Breastfed babies eat more frequently than formula-fed ones—as often as every two hours at first, and sometimes even more often than that. But if you keep your priorities clear, your nursing times become God-given opportunities to relax and cuddle your baby, not interruptions.

Jan says, "I feel breastfeeding is God's way of slowing Mommy down. Sometimes I do absolutely nothing while Jordan David is nursing but watch him. Other times I read the mail or a book, pray, watch TV, or jot down a 'things to do' list." Joining your local library is an inexpensive way to keep yourself supplied with good books.

■ Jan warns that just because your baby wants to suck doesn't necessarily mean he's hungry. "I nursed Jordan David for two hours straight one night and he still wanted more. I called my husband's cousin, who's a doctor, and he told me, 'You've overfed him, and his stomach probably hurts. Give him a pacifier and let him suck while you hold him.'" If your little one won't take a pacifier, cut your nails short and let him suck on the end of your finger.

■ Nursing even the lightest baby without support will make your arm feel as if it's about to fall off. A thick pillow underneath your elbow will keep your arms and back from becoming tired.

■ "Breastfeeding mothers are told that our milk flows better when we're relaxed," says Cheryl, "but it's hard to relax when your baby is tense and crying. I found that if I took a minute before I picked Jason up and took some deep breaths, put on some quiet music, and said a quick prayer, I could immediately unwind a little."

■ Long before your baby starts teething, he may bite down and arch his back, pulling his head away—and your nipple with it. That's an easy habit to nip in the bud, though. Julie did it by tapping Ian on the cheek; Megan responded to a gentle thunk on the back of the head. "Anything to break the baby's concentration," Julie says. "You have to explain to him that your nipple isn't portable; it stays with Mommy."

■ Several of our nursing mothers, including me, learned the hard lesson that a baby who becomes too accustomed to feeding from only Mommy may refuse to take a bottle at all, which makes it very hard for you to leave her with Grandma or the sitter for an evening out with your husband. To keep that from happening, let your husband give the baby a bottle of expressed milk or formula several times a week after your baby is three or four weeks old. If you're desperate for sleep, ask your husband to do his feedings at night while you rest. Be careful not to rely on bottlefeedings too much, though, or your milk production will go down.

■ If you've already gone too long between bottles and your nursing baby refuses to take one, try offering it to her at the beginning of each feeding, while she's hungry. Be persistent—it took Chris a month to retrain Ashley this way. Kathy breastfed her three children, and she says they took their bottles more easily when she rested her hand against their cheek as they drank.

■ Megan flatly refused a rubber nipple but would drink at age six months from the hard plastic sip tips that are an intermediary between bottle and training cup. The tip fits into the nipple ring on the bottle and should be available in the baby section of your supermarket.

■ Don't buy a bulb-type breast pump—not one of our nursing moms had success with it. Hand expressing is much easier. The technique takes a little practice, but, according to a nursery worker of my acquaintance, babies who refuse to take a bottle of formula from a stranger will often gulp down their mother's milk. Your obstetrician or his nurse can show you how to express.

■ Expressed milk will stay fresh for a day in the refrigerator or for several months in the freezer below zero degrees Fahrenheit. If you're expressing for long-term storage, keep the bottle you're filling in the freezer, tightly capped. Express into a sterile bowl, then pour the milk immediately into the bottle and put it back into the freezer, where it will freeze in layers and stay fresh. I found that expressing an hour or so after a feeding yielded more milk for storage and still allowed me plenty of time to produce milk for Megan's next meal. Or, try expressing from one breast while your baby nurses from the other.

■ Nursing is more difficult if you must return to work full-time, but it's not impossible. Lynne did it this way: She breastfed baby Michael during the weeks she took off after his birth, but gave him a small bottle regularly to keep him accustomed to it. When she returned to work, she was still able to nurse Michael for his morning, evening, and latenight feedings, and she expressed several times during the day to keep her milk production up and to prevent her breasts from becoming too full. "Take extra breast pads and a cloth diaper to work with you," she says. "No matter how neat you are when you express, you're going to drip." She also stresses the importance of having a refrigerator nearby if you plan to save your expressed milk for your baby's midday feeding the next day, since breast milk goes bad quickly when it's not refrigerated.

■ One of the most common arguments against nursing is that it's too restrictive for the mother, but it has been my experience that the nursing mom can go just about anywhere the bottle mom can. All it takes is a little planning. True, you can't leave your baby with Grandma for the weekend while you're nursing, but I was able to leave Megan with my parents and go with Jon to Disney

World's Epcot Center for a full twelve hours by freezing four feedings in advance and expressing several times (which took only five minutes or so each time) while we were there.

■ Taking your nursing baby with you makes getting out of the house even easier. But you'll need to revamp your wardrobe in case you have to nurse while you're out. The general consensus of our nursing moms is that the best blouses for nursing are pullovers and sweaters that you can lift from the bottom. Your baby's face and the folds of your blouse cover your breast, and your baby's body hides your exposed midriff.

■ By the way, *all* (yes, even the most modest ones) of our nursing moms nursed in public at one time or another—and usually no one knew it except the person they were with. Julie says, "You *can* nurse in public. Just take a shawl with you to put over your shoulder and drape the baby's face. And when your baby is older, use a safety pin to attach the shawl to your shoulder, since older babies love to pull it off." Our moms have used this method to nurse discreetly in movie theaters, crowded restaurants (booths seem to work best), and friends' living rooms.

Do be sensitive, though, about nursing in mixed company where everyone will be aware of what you're doing. Husbands whose wives have nursed are usually very comfortable around other nursing mothers. But single men and husbands who've never been around nursing mothers can feel intense discomfort just knowing that a woman in the room has a baby at her breast.

■ Give your baby the freedom to play at your breast. Feedings are great times for building your child's self-esteem and establishing a healthy liking between you. If your baby likes to pull on your necklaces, try stringing some brightly colored wooden beads and hanging them around your neck for her to play with at feeding time.

■ A word of warning: Don't depend on nursing as a method of birth control unless you want another baby right away. Several of our moms learned this by experience.

■ If your little one suddenly starts waking up ravenous in the wee hours after sleeping through the night for a while, it may be time to ask your pediatrician about giving him some cereal for dinner. This happened with Megan at about four months, and will probably depend on your baby's weight.

■ There's no set rule on when a child should be weaned. The experts are now saying that one year is the earliest a baby should be completely weaned to a cup, but there's no reason why you can't keep nursing long past that deadline if you want to. Let your child, your pediatrician, and your own wishes be your guides. Karen H. nursed Josh, now a two-year-old he-man, for eleven months and wishes it had been longer. "Nurse your baby for as long as you can," she says. "Those are very special times."

Bring on the Bottle

This book is unabashedly pro-breastfeeding, and indeed most of our contributing moms are breastfeeders, although it wasn't planned that way. But there's no need to feel as if you've failed your baby if you can't nurse for some reason. Many of us "baby boomers" were raised on formula and did just fine. Too, even the most devoted nursing mother will probably praise God for the invention of the bottle every now and then.

Bottle mommies are, however, faced with a temptation from which the nursing mother is spared: namely, to prop a bottle in their baby's mouth while they take care of something "urgent"—like housework. Don't do it! The Lord designed your body so that you'd have to cradle your baby in your arms while nursing him, and bottle-feeding needs to approximate this posture as closely as possible. "That time is very important for both of you," says Rosemary, and Wanda recommends that you continue holding your baby during feedings for as long as he'll let you: "That closeness is great, and they grow up way too fast!"

■ Powdered formula is less expensive than premixed formula, but it takes more time to prepare. Connie made things easier for herself by mixing enough formula for 24 hours at a time and refrigerating the extra bottles.

Some baby bottle manufacturers don't recommend using a microwave to heat formula because of the need for extra precautions. If you decide to use one, be cautious. Avoid overheating the bottle, and remove the nipple to keep the bottle from exploding (as it will if the formula becomes too hot). Also, avoid glass bottles—which can shatter if the chilled formula is heated too quickly—and microwave for only five seconds at a time until you reach the desired temperature. Shake the bottle and test the temperature carefully before feeding the baby. Warn your husband and any babysitters to do the same.

As your baby grows older and no longer needs to have the water for his formula sterilized, pre-measure a couple of days' worth of powdered formula at a time into individual bottles. When feeding time comes, just add warm water and shake.

■ "A newborn needs to be burped gently after each ounce

or so of fluid," says Connie. "Drinking too much at once can cause her to spit up, usually on you." Air bubbles can also give your baby a tummyache, which will in turn give you an earache. Connie found that the best position for burping her little girls was to set them on her lap facing left. She gently supported the baby's chin with her left hand while tapping her back with her right. Remember to keep a cloth diaper handy in case your baby spits up.

■ After your baby is a month or so old, you may not need to sterilize his bottles and nipples and the water for his formula. Ask your pediatrician; a lot depends on the water in your area.

■ Cow's milk was meant for baby cows, not baby humans, and it can lead to problems if you feed it to your child too soon. Ask your pediatrician before switching over from formula.

■ Many of our babies refused to drink water, preferring milk or juice. Vicky solved the problem by diluting Lauren's juice with an equal part of water. A couple of bottles of this each day gave Lauren the equivalent of one bottle of juice and one bottle of water.

■ Most of our bottle mothers are emphatic about not putting a baby into bed with a bottle. "It's bad for his teeth, causes ear infections, and makes it harder to get rid of the bottle later," says Chris. Wanda adds, "It's the hardest habit to break."

■ Before taking Jordan David out to run errands, Jan measures powdered formula into a bottle and puts it into her diaper bag. "After I've shopped for a couple of hours, I just drive through McDonald's and ask for a cup of hot water, and maybe order a soft drink for myself. I pour the water into the bottle and shake it, then let it cool while I relax and have my drink." If your baby won't wait while his bottle cools, take along a separate container of water. "Sean liked his formula just as well at room temperature as he did heated," says Julie.

▪ Don't feed your baby in a moving car, especially when the two of you are alone. If he starts to gag you could cause an accident trying to stop and help him, and the bottle itself could injure him if you're involved in a collision.

Breaking Away

Several of our moms were surprised at how easy it was to wean their babies. In fact, some, like Stella's little girl Dina, weaned themselves. For our bottle mothers, weaning was usually easier if the toddler wasn't accustomed to taking a bottle to bed and if weaning was accomplished at or shortly after a year old, before the toddler had time to start looking at the bottle as a security blanket.

▪ Both bottle and breastfeeding moms usually followed a similar procedure: Long before they were ready to wean, they acquainted their little ones with the training cup by allowing them to drink water and juice from it. Then, when Mommy decided the time was right, she very gradually started substituting a cup of milk or formula, one feeding at a time, for the breast or bottlefeeding. This gradual method worked especially well for our nursing moms, since it allowed their milk production to dwindle slowly.

▪ Cheryl allowed her boys an occasional bottle until they were two years old, but eventually the time came to break with it completely. "The best way I've found to break any habit," she says, "is to encourage the behavior I do want. We gave Jason a cup when he was a year old, and praised him when he drank from it without spilling. As he approached his second birthday we were preparing to toilet-train him, so we told him, 'You're really getting to be a big boy now—you're almost two years old! You're going to learn how to go potty all by yourself, and you're not going to need a bottle anymore.' With his birthday, that was it—no more bottle. It was fairly easy."

■ Patty W. recommends putting only water in your toddler's bottle if he refuses to give it up: "He'll be more willing to part with it, since most babies aren't too crazy about water."

■ Giving up the last feeding before bedtime can be hard emotionally for both of you—especially if your baby is accustomed to being nursed to sleep. It helps to substitute a new bedtime ritual for the breast or bottlefeeding. Megan continued to enjoy and ask for her "nurse and night-night" right up until I weaned her at two years old, and I delayed weaning her several times, fearing that it would be traumatic for both of us. But Chris, Ashley's mom, gave me an idea that made Megan's weaning almost painless.

For her second birthday I bought her a small cassette recorder designed especially for children. I showed her how to push the buttons, and it was such a novelty that she wanted to carry it around the house all day.

But an hour or two before naptime and bedtime, I loaded the recorder with a cassette of Christian nursery rhymes, put it into her room and told her, "We'll listen to the recorder later when we go night-night."

When bedtime came, I cuddled her and sang to her for a few minutes, then turned the recorder on with the volume low and put her to bed. She was so eager to listen to the recorder that she hardly noticed the fact that we hadn't nursed. By the time the recorder's novelty wore off, she was no longer accustomed to being nursed to sleep.

If you don't want to spend a small fortune on prerecorded cassettes, buy some blank tapes and record your child's favorite stories, songs, and nursery rhymes.

4
...
Solid Food:
The Adventure Begins

Your baby's entrance into the fascinating world of solid food is one of the first signs that he's growing up. It's also one of the first places where his budding personality will start to shine.

Jennifer Joy showed herself to be a fastidious young lady who hardly ever misplaced a drop of food—a trait that Patty W., her mom, says mercifully carried over into the months when she began eating finger foods and feeding herself. Kimmie, on the other hand, sucked her thumb furiously after each spoonful of cereal, using it as a plunger to ram the food down her little gullet and squirting cereal out the sides of her mouth in the process. Still other babies used mealtimes to assert their independence, refusing to take food while Mommy was holding the spoon and insisting on feeding themselves at the ripe old age of eight or nine months.

Starting Out

The first solid food your pediatrician will probably tell you to give your baby is rice cereal mixed with formula or breast milk, to which you will gradually add pureed fruits. There are a couple of ways to make preparation of these meals quicker and easier. If you have a microwave, mix enough cereal for a day or so at a time and keep it in the refrigerator, either in clean baby food jars or else in a container from which you can ladle out enough for one serving at a time.

As with bottle manufacturers, some baby food companies are reluctant to recommend using microwaves to heat baby food because of the need for caution. So again, if you choose to use a microwave, be careful. Because cold glass can shatter if the contents are heated too quickly, it's best to heat in very short (five-second) bursts, stirring the food each time. Also, stir the cereal and test the temperature before spooning it into your baby's trusting little mouth. Such caution is necessary because microwaves heat those tiny jars of food very quickly and may heat them unevenly, causing hot spots that will burn your baby's mouth.

Here's an alternate method for non-microwavers: Measure enough cereal and powdered formula for one serving each into clean baby food jars. When mealtime comes, add warm water and fruit.

■ Most of our moms occasionally had trouble getting their children to sit still and look up during feedings.

Babies would much rather examine their belly buttons, or grab the spoon, or stick their fingers into their mouths and then anoint their heads with cereal. At such times a jangling set of keys or a noisemaking toy can be a great distraction. "I held the toy up in front of my baby and jangled or squeaked it," says Connie. "While she was occupied with looking at the toy, I spooned the food in." For Julie, the time-honored tradition of turning a spoonful of food into an airplane or train still serves its purpose: "It works. Ian's attention is so distracted by what I'm doing that the food could taste like soapsuds and he wouldn't care. He opens his mouth and I shove the food in." On the other hand, from Patti: "I tried that with Jonathan, and he shoves it back out."

■ When your baby's doctor prescribes vitamin drops, put them into her juice or cereal each day after it has been warmed. Megan refused to take her vitamins straight. They dribbled down her chin and all over her clothes. By the way, the same method can be used to give medication when your baby is ill, but do check with your doctor or pharmacist to see whether there are any foods with which your child's medicine should not be mixed.

■ If your baby tries to grab the spoon while you feed him, try giving him something to hold while he eats—a teething ring, a simple rattle, another spoon. Just make sure it's something that washes easily and that you don't mind getting messy.

■ Your baby's bib needs to cover him from his shoulders to his lap. I prefer terrycloth bibs that can be thrown into the washer to plastic bibs that have to be wiped clean. The terrycloth has the extra benefit of absorbing spills and dribbles instead of letting them sit on top where they can be smeared around by exploring little hands.

■ Most babies hate having their faces wiped, so try making it a game. I dabbed playfully at Megan with a damp paper towel while making funny noises, then followed up with several quick, gentle wipes. I was usually finished before she had a chance to become upset.

■ If you're going to have to feed your baby while you're out, you can keep her cereal from spoiling by measuring the cereal and powdered formula into a plastic cup and adding water just before serving. If you're not sure whether there's a water supply at your destination, take along another container with the right amount of water. At mealtime, dump the cereal-formula mixture into the container and stir.

■ If your baby makes frequent visits to Grandma's house, buy extra baby food, along with a spoon and bib, to leave there. You'll have less to pack each time you go.

■ When your pediatrician gives you the go-ahead to start feeding your baby vegetables and meats, you'll have fun watching your little one's expression as you spoon green beans into his mouth when he was expecting peaches. Debby, who has three girls, says that when her babies were reluctant to try a new food she put a bit of an old favorite, such as the aforementioned peaches, on the tip of the spoon. The little girl would taste her favorite food first and eat the whole spoonful.

■ Introduce new foods one at a time, leaving a gap of several days between each one. That will make it easier to pinpoint the source of any food allergies.

■ Never give honey to a child under twelve months old. Its use has been linked to infant botulism, a potentially fatal form of food poisoning. For this reason it's best to check with your pediatrician before adding honey to your child's diet.

■ I was surprised to find that making your own baby food, when it involves meat, Is not less expensive than buying commercial baby food. At the time of this writing, a 4½-oz. jar of turkey and vegetable dinner can be bought for between 21 cents and 25 cents, depending on the brand. The same size serving of homemade chicken vegetable dinner costs about the same and possibly a bit more, depending on how you adjust your ingredients.

I still preferred to make Megan's food, though, for a couple of reasons: It gave me control over which ingredients, and how much of each, went into her tummy, and it tasted much better than the bland, unidentifiable chicken pudding sold by the baby food companies—even though it contained no added fats or seasonings. The recipe calls for chicken, but as I began to make baby food on a regular basis I found it much easier to bake a large turkey, skin and bone it, make broth from the carcass, and freeze the meat and broth separately in two-cup batches to be used either in her food or in casseroles.

And so, without further ado, I submit to you my recipe for Hull House Baby Stew, which Megan loved and which I began feeding her at around six months, as soon as her pediatrician okayed meats and vegetables.

Hull House Baby Stew

1 2½-lb. chicken (or 2 c. chopped turkey meat)
4 c. water (or 4 c. turkey broth)
1½ c. chopped carrots
2 10-oz. pkg. frozen green peas
1½ c. rice cereal

Rinse the chicken and put it into a large pot. Add the water and simmer covered until tender. Remove and cool the chicken, discard the skin and bones, and cut the meat into one-inch pieces. Strain the broth and skim off the fat, then use the broth to simmer the vegetables until tender. Add the chicken, and puree the mixture in batches in a food processor or blender, using more water if needed to make it blend smoothly. It's important that this mixture contain no lumps to make your baby choke, so check it carefully. The puree should be a bit soupy. Add the cereal, and mix thoroughly. Adjust the consistency by adding more water or cereal as needed.

Baby stew can be frozen several ways: in ice cube trays (when frozen, pop the cubes out and store in plastic bags), in clean baby food jars (leave room for expansion at the top, and check the lids after the stew is frozen to make sure they're still tight), or in plastic containers. Do whatever works best for you. As your baby grows older and his digestive system matures, you can vary the recipe by using a pound of stew beef instead of the chicken, and green beans with the strings removed or broccoli instead of peas. Use your imagination. For an older baby with a good number of teeth, process the mixture more coarsely, use less broth, and substitute chopped, cooked noodles for the rice cereal.

■ Plain meat pureed in broth was too grainy for Megan to swallow, so I learned to smooth the texture by adding rice cereal and a little extra broth.
■ Freezing vegetables for your baby is simple. Just cook until tender, puree, and freeze in ice cube trays or baby

food jars, smoothing the texture with a little rice cereal and cooking liquid if necessary. Sweet potatoes, carrots, squash, green peas, green beans with the strings removed, and broccoli are all easy to prepare this way. If your vegetables turn out to be stringy, strain them through a sieve.

■ If you decide to freeze pureed fruit for your baby, you can keep it from turning brown by adding about a tablespoon of lemon juice to each quart of fruit. Apples, pears, bananas, and peaches are good fruits to preserve this way; a little corn syrup can be used to sweeten them if need be, and straining them will remove any strings. When Megan grew old enough to eat bananas as a finger food, I kept from wasting the ones that became too soft by mashing them, adding a little lemon juice, and freezing them in half-cup portions. She loved eating them half-thawed as "banana ice cream."

■ Instead of freezing Jonathan's food in advance, Patti fed him pureed table food. "With my first baby, feeding seemed like a real challenge," she says, "but by my third, I was just giving him spoonfuls of whatever we were eating. I just took some out before I added the spices."

■ Several of our moms caution against adding seasoning or fats to food destined for your baby's tummy. They're not needed, and they could give him a stomachache.

■ When Ashley began eating finger foods, Chris put an old beach blanket underneath her high chair at mealtimes. "After she finished eating, I just picked up the blanket and shook it outside. It saved me from having to sweep and mop the floor after each meal." Patti, though, has the ultimate solution for messy floors: "We have a dog."

■ Our moms hailed finger foods as a real blessing. "Finally, Mommy can have a hot meal," says Julie, "since the baby can eat while you eat." Cheerios were the A #1 favorite of moms and babies alike. They're easy to pick up, don't make a mess, and are extremely portable. They're also easily gummed into mush by babies who are late sprouting teeth. (Megan was so late that we thought about having her fitted for dentures.) As their babies cut more and more teeth, our moms started feeding them fish sticks, American cheese, vanilla wafers, pieces of banana, pear, or apple, chopped seedless grapes...

As you may have guessed, finger foods are another area where you can use your imagination. Just about any food that's not too spicy and is firm enough for your baby to hold, yet soft enough for him to chew easily, can qualify. But proceed with caution when you start your baby's journey into the marvelous, messy world of finger foods. Cut the food into small pieces to lessen the danger of choking, and never give your baby a round food, such as grapes or banana or hot dog slices, without first cutting it into halves or quarters. And even more importantly, never feed nuts to a young child or let him eat unattended. Of course if you give your baby a Cheerio and she gags, fish it out. She's not ready yet.

■ Until your baby is at least a year old, Cheryl recommends double-checking with your pediatrician or a baby health-care book before giving new foods. "Some foods that seemed like good, healthful snack ideas to me caused real problems," she says, "—like serious diarrhea."

Depending on how many teeth their children had, most of our moms began feeding them table food at about a year.

■ "I insist that my kids eat at least one bite of a new food," says Patti. "If they don't like it, I don't make them eat it. After all, I don't eat foods I don't like."

Many vegetables have a similar vitamin content. If your child won't eat peas, maybe she'll like green beans, or vice versa. Patti found that sometimes, though, the dinner table became yet another area where her toddlers tested their disciplinary limits: "If my 2½ year old says, 'Yuck, I don't like that,' none of the others will eat it, so I've had to be very strict about their commenting on my delicious cuisine."

If your child is a really picky eater, you may want to check with your pediatrician about giving her a vitamin supplement.

▪ Wanda's daughter Michelle has been intolerant of sugar and allergic to artificial color since birth, which has prompted Wanda and her husband, Dennis, to do some in depth research on sugar and additives. "Artificial color, we discovered, was in everything from medicine to shampoo, both of which affected her," says Wanda. "We learned a lot through trial and error, and now have a built-in radar for food, drinks, and snacks." Something else Wanda and Dennis discovered: "Any juice made from concentrate may have sugar in it—concentrate is made with an allowable amount of sugar. The company doesn't have to state 'Sugar Added' unless it exceeds those limits." Some juice concentrates are now being marketed that claim to contain no added sugar. Just to be sure, check with the company before giving them to your child.

For older toddlers who need to avoid sugar, Wanda recommends these snacks: "Natural applesauce, raisins, cheese, dried or fresh fruit (stay away from pineapples and oranges, since they have a high natural sugar content), natural juices, and natural peanut butter. Michelle loves to make 'smashed banana jelly' for her sandwiches." Smashed bananas also make good "butter" for toast.

"Natural juices or plain yogurt mixed with fruit can be frozen in popsicle molds as a nice summer treat; you can also make 'jello' from natural juices and an envelope or two of plain gelatin." ("Natural" in this context means without sugar or other additives.)

5

Crying, Teething, and Other Fun Things

It's a puzzlement why otherwise tenderhearted, sensitive Christian parents take such glee in scaring their friends who are about to enter parenthood, but they do. And if your baby hasn't yet made her grand entrance, your friends who beat you into the baby business are probably having a great time terrifying you with stories of how their babies screamed for hours on end with colic, or how two-year-old Hilary *still* isn't sleeping through the night, or how little Joshua had diarrhea all over Pastor Sternhagen. When they really want to be cruel, they tell you how much a good pair of walking shoes cost and then twist the knife by pointing out that a growing baby needs new ones every two months.

Terror, though, is usually just fear of the unknown or

unfamiliar, and the best remedy for it is finding out what to do about the situation. So here, in this chapter, you will learn What To Do about any number of circumstances, along with practical advice on some miscellaneous topics.

Hush, Little Baby

There are several things all babies do regardless of their color, cuteness, or socioeconomic bracket. Four of them are eating, sleeping, burping, and going to the bathroom. Can you guess what number five is? That's right—crying.

No matter how sweet and placid your baby is, she's going to cry occasionally. It's the only way God gave her to tell you she needs something. "If I had just one piece of advice to offer new mothers," says Stella, "it would be, 'Relax!' The more relaxed you are, the more relaxed your baby will be." Our moms have all experienced the frayed nerves that come from having a baby who continues to cry for a reason only she knows but can't tell, but they've also learned that getting upset does more harm than good. When the unexplained crying times come, just take a few deep breaths and ask the Lord for wisdom, patience, and—above all—love.

You'll be relieved to know that colicky babies were in the minority among our children. Less than a third of our moms reported significant problems with it. Your relief will be short-lived, though, if your baby proves to be among the vocal few. But don't despair—since colic is generally supposed to be caused by abdominal pain, there are, to a certain extent, things you can do about it.

■ Wanda's daughter Michelle suffered from colic until she was four months old. Her problem was aggravated by an underdeveloped digestive tract and a severe intolerance of the sugar in her baby formula, a condition it took several doctors to uncover. "She cried for hours at a time," says Wanda, "and when you have a baby in pain you try to learn quickly what makes her feel better." One of the things that worked for Michelle was a warm bath: "I supported her on her tummy in her little tub, with her head resting in my palm. As she lay there, I rubbed her tummy gently. I suppose it relaxed her stomach muscles and helped the pain go away." Of course, don't try this until your baby's umbilical stump has fallen off. Something else that helped Michelle was for her mommy to walk her or rock her while singing softly. "Even when she was tiny, songs about Jesus watching over her and loving her soothed her more than any others," says Wanda.

■ "When Ashley had colic," says Chris, "it sometimes helped for me to lay her on her stomach across my knees and pat her back. And occasionally just riding in the car would calm her down—we did that in the middle of the night a couple of times."

■ "I breastfed one of my babies and didn't breastfeed the other, and they both had colic," says Kristy, "so I couldn't blame it on the way they were fed. What helped me most was remembering the phrase from Scripture, 'And it came to pass...' A child is in one phase or another until he's married, but whatever he's in now is going to pass. It won't last forever." True enough—colic usually goes away by the time a baby is around three months old. Do check with your pediatrician, though, if your formula-fed baby is having trouble with colic. A change of formulas could help.

■ I found nursing to be a wonderful pacifier, especially when Megan was very young. The warmth, closeness, and ability to suck nearly always soothed her, and usually put her to sleep. The few times she had colic she seemed to feel better when I nursed her while reclining, with her tummy pressed against mine. I spent a couple of nights that way, in fact.

■ Cheryl found fresh air to be the best way to calm her little boys when they were colicky or fussy: "Walking settled both baby and Mommy, and the exercise didn't hurt either."

■ If you're pretty sure your baby doesn't have colic, but he's still crying even though he's been fed, changed, and burped, the time has come for Mommy to play detective. *How long ago was his last nap?* Many babies become cranky when they're tired. *Has he been overstimulated by too many visitors or strange surroundings?* With several of our babies, it helped to take them to a quiet, darkened room and rock or nurse them when this happened. The hum of a fan helps to mask outside noises. *Could his clothing be causing discomfort?* Grant, Lynda's usually placid little boy, cried nonstop during a visit to his aunt's house until Lynda took off his shoes. When his daddy had dressed him that morning he curled up his toes, and his foot had gotten stuck in that position inside his shoe. *Have you introduced a new food to his diet that could be causing gas? Or, if you're a nursing mother, have you eaten a spicy food that could be causing the problem?* If your baby's crying is due to gas, try one of the colic remedies already mentioned or try laying him on his back and gently bending his legs several times so that his knees touch his tummy. "It helps release the gas," says Cindy. *Is it possible that your baby is bored, or is just plain having a grumpy day?* If so, diversion is probably your best bet, and Chapter 6 is full of diversionary tactics. *Is your baby ill?* If your child's crying is accompanied by a temperature above 100 degrees Fahrenheit, diarrhea, vomiting, pulling on the ears, or other abnormal symptoms, call your pediatrician for instructions. *Last, but probably first, does your baby simply want to be held?* If so, hold him.

■ When Megan was tiny, on the rare occasions when she was overly tired or too wound up to nurse, I discovered that if I put her into her crib and let her cry for a few minutes—say, ten or fifteen—she would release enough tension so that when I picked her up again she would nurse and fall asleep. A few times she even fussed herself to sleep before the time limit was up. "If a baby is fed, dry, and healthy, it won't hurt her to cry for a little while," says Rosemary. Our other moms agree. Keep a sharp eye on your baby if you're letting her fuss, though—Megan once rubbed a blister on her toe and popped it while kicking in her crib. Also, burp your baby when you pick her up, since she's probably swallowed some air.

■ "Don't think you're not a good mother if your baby has a fussy time of day," says Chris. "Sometimes your baby will cry no matter what you do, whether you hold him or not." Cheryl adds, "Start preparing dinner early in the day so you won't have as much to do during your baby's fussy period, which will probably be in the early evening." Sure enough, most of our moms report that their babies were grumpiest during the late afternoon/early evening hours.

For mommies who can't think that far in advance, Julie

recommends the cloth baby backpacks that snuggle the baby against your stomach or back while you work. If you plan to use a cloth baby carrier, be *very* careful working around hot foods, and start using it while your baby is still very young. Several of our moms found that their little ones wouldn't tolerate the unaccustomed confinement because they had waited too long to try it. Make sure the carrier you choose gives your baby's head and neck adequate support.

■ Babies have a strong sucking urge that isn't always satisfied at the end of feeding time, so some of our moms encouraged their children to use a pacifier. When Connie's baby girls refused the rubber nipple, she made it more acceptable to them by putting a dab of corn syrup on the end at first. (Remember what we said in Chapter 4: never give honey to an infant.) Chris didn't separate Ashley from her pacifer until she was almost two, but when the time came she used an interesting method that was completely untraumatic for Ashley: "I cut off the tip bit by bit, a little more each day until it was down to a nub. She didn't even notice when I finally took it away."

■ Carol has this comment about babies crying in public: "There will be times when you're halfway finished buying groceries and your baby will start screaming, and none of your distractions will work. Grin and bear it— it's part of being a mother." LeEtta adds, "Most people have had a child in that situation, though, so they understand." And if they haven't, they'll understand when they do get around to having children.

■ The last resort in crying remedies comes from Kristy: "If all else fails," she says, "try cotton." She explains,

"You gently put the baby into his crib, then you go into your room and put the cotton in your ears."

Lullaby and Good Night

For your baby's first few weeks, unless he's very unusual, he'll be paging you nightly to come and open up the 2 a.m. buffet—or, more likely, the 10 p.m., 2 a.m., and 6 a.m. buffets. He has to—his little tummy can't hold enough yet to get him through an eight-hour stretch. And besides, he has no way of knowing that you've been sleeping through the night ever since you were eight weeks old and don't just love coming into his room for a visit and a snack two or three times a night.

■ Steel yourself mentally to get up at least once a night for your baby's first couple of months. That way you'll have a wonderful surprise if he starts sleeping through the night earlier than expected. And don't get your hopes too high when your baby finally does sleep through for the first time. Nearly all our babies went through phases when they slept through the night for a week or so and then began waking again.

■ When their babies were small, most of our moms either nursed them to sleep at naptime and bedtime or rocked them to sleep in their wind-up swings. If you're going to let your baby take naps in his swing, Cheryl points out the need to make sure you get one that will recline. Some don't. And of course keep a close eye on your child if he's sleeping in his swing.

As their babies grew older, their naptime habits changed—both in length of the naps and in going-to-sleep methods. Ashley's favorite method of going to sleep was for Chris to rock her. Grant played quietly in his crib until he became drowsy and then nodded off. Megan preferred to be nursed at naptime until she was about nine months old, when suddenly she refused to take naps unless I just put her into her crib and let her grump her way to dreamland. To quote the editors of *American Baby* magazine, "It's not uncommon for a baby to cry himself to sleep. The crying seems to rid him of tensions that otherwise prevent his transition from waking to sleeping."

So don't be thrown off-balance or frustrated by the sleep phases your baby passes through. They're just another sign that he's growing and changing, and they're common to all of us. "Every time I thought I finally had Philip's schedule figured out," says Linda, "he changed."

▪ If you can, put your baby to bed as soon as she starts acting sleepy. Believe it or not, becoming overly tired can result in your baby's taking shorter naps, not longer ones.

▪ Keeping a very dim nightlight in your baby's room will let you check on her without turning on any other lights. But if she refuses to go to sleep try extinguishing all the lights, including the nightlight. At about seven months, Megan wouldn't sleep with a light on in her room. The light gave her too much to look at.

▪ All our moms checked their sleeping babies to make sure they were still breathing, but some of their little ones breathed so softly that it was hard to hear them. Several moms solved the problem by gently holding a mirror in front of their babies' lips when they wanted to check on them. The baby's breath fogged the glass, and Mommy's mind was set at ease.

▪ If your little one just can't sleep, try turning out all

the lights and walking or rocking him in a completely quiet room. That way there's no visual or audible stimulation to keep him wound up. Walking him will keep him from trying to stand up on your lap, which can become a problem as babies pass their first few weeks.

■ As her two little boys passed the age of six months, Cheryl found it best to try to have their naps at the same time each day. "It helped me develop consistency in discipline and scheduling," she says, "but it also made naptime a special time." She recommends loving firmness as a way to get this schedule started: "Tell your child it's time to rest, and perhaps rock him and nurse him, or read a story or sing, or lay him down and massage his back, or, as he gets older, say a little naptime prayer. But then say good night, close the door, and let him go to sleep. This will give you the time you need to nap, do housework, have devotions, or do whatever else you need to do."

■ "At only a few weeks," Glenda warns, "our baby could roll off a double bed, even with pillows surrounding him. After a real scare, we learned to put him on a mattress on the floor when he wasn't in his baby bed."

■ A baby won't necessarily sleep in the same position forever. Megan was a tummy sleeper from birth, but when she reached five months she began going up on her hands and knees the instant she touched the crib mattress. I started putting her down gently on her back instead; the problem was solved. If your baby starts crying the instant she hits the crib no matter what her position, she may just not want to be left alone. A soft bear with a wind-up music box inside helped Megan at such times.

■ Lynda keeps toys in Grant's crib so that he can play quietly if he wakes in the night. She says, "I figure that sometimes I wake up in the middle of the night and have to read until I get drowsy, and this is pretty much the same thing. Grant usually plays with his Busy Box for a while and then goes back to sleep."

■ Almost inevitably, there will come a time when you'll have to start letting your baby fuss himself back to sleep when he wakes up in the night. I resisted the thought when other moms warned me about it and didn't become desperate enough to try it until Megan began waking every two hours when she was eight months old. I was petrified. I wanted to do the right thing for Megan, but I also desperately wanted to start sleeping at night and feeling like a human being again.

So Jon and I prayed for wisdom, and that night, when she woke only an hour and a half after I had put her to bed, we let her fuss. When she realized I wasn't coming she became very upset and cried hard for about twenty minutes. Then, suddenly, silence. "Oh no," I told Jon, "she's choked to death." I tiptoed to her door and peeked in. The wail started again and I backed off. After about five minutes, more silence. Ten minutes later she resumed crying, but it was only a minute or so before she finally gave up and slept the rest of the night. The next night she again woke a couple of hours after I had put her down, but cried for only ten minutes or so before giving up. The third night she let out a single "Yaaa!" before settling back down, and she's slept through the night ever since with the exception of a few bouts with the flu and other childhood illnesses—which brings us once again to the cardinal rule of motherhood: *Be flexible.* Even after your baby starts sleeping through the night consistently, there will be times when he needs you to offer some nocturnal solace—when he's sick or having teething pain, or during those fun-filled nights when he has learned to stand up in his crib but hasn't yet figured out how to get back down, or when he's older and has obviously been frightened by a nightmare. The trick is to know when the problem has been solved, then go back to your policy of no after-hours service.

Some psychologists recommend the following method of convincing an older baby to sleep through the night: when she wakes and begins to cry, go in and say gently, "It's okay. Mommy's here, but it's time for you to sleep." Perhaps pat her on the back for a minute, then leave quietly. Don't turn on the light, don't pick her up, and don't stay longer than a minute. Repeat the procedure every five to ten minutes until she goes back to sleep.

She'll probably cry for quite a while the first night, but the crying spells should become shorter and shorter each night until they stop completely.

▪ "When your toddler reaches the size and age where he's inclined toward and able to climb out of his crib," says Patty W., "he's probably ready for a child's or twin bed. If you have enough space, put the bed in the same room with the crib and use it for naps at first, then gradually nights as well. And do buy a guardrail. They're very inexpensive, and your child will fall out of bed without it. It'll make him feel more secure just to know it's there." A few of our moms started out by letting their toddlers sleep on the mattress on the floor with the guard rail, adding the box spring a few weeks later, and the frame a few weeks after that.

▪ After all this advice on putting your baby to sleep, here's some from Connie on waking him up: "When you need to wake your child," she says, "do it gently with soft words and an easy rub on the back rather than by flipping on the light and announcing, 'Time to wake UP!' The way you wake your baby can determine his mood—calm and happy versus jumpy and irritable."

Time for a Bath

After seeing hundreds of pictures in catalogs and advertisements of babies happily splashing away in bathtubs filled with rubber duckies and toy boats, it comes as a shock to new mothers that newborns don't enjoy their first baths. The little ones usually cry from fear and cold—especially since their bodies can't be immersed in warm water until the umbilical stump falls off. Sofie's husband Paul, a pediatrician, has some advice on making those initial bathtimes less traumatic: Wrap the baby in a receiving blanket and gently sponge-bathe one part of his body at a time with comfortably warm water, keeping the other parts covered. Remember not to bring the wet blanket into contact with your baby's umbilical stump.

■ Gather all your bath supplies before you undress your baby for her bath, and keep a firm grip on her as you transfer her from the bathtub to the dressing area. Wet babies are slippery!

■ For the first few months, a molded bath sponge is wonderful for your baby to lie on in the tub. It supports her head up out of the water, leaving both of your hands free to bathe her. After your baby is old enough to sit up, a rubber bath mat or a thick towel will keep her from sliding around in the bathtub.

■ New moms tend to be petrified of the soft spots (fontanels) on their babies' heads, but there's no need to be.

The skin covering the fontanels is very tough, and washing your baby's hair thoroughly won't hurt him. In fact, if you don't, and allow dead skin and oils to collect on his scalp, your baby can develop a crusty skin condition called cradle cap.

■ A cotton swab dipped in alcohol works well to clean your baby's ears, but don't do any deep cleaning with it. It's unnecessary and dangerous to stick a swab down inside your child's ear. Unlike what your mother always taught you about housework, "Just clean what shows" is a good rule of thumb here.

■ As your baby grows older and graduates to the family bathtub, hang a mesh bag in the tub for her toys. When bathtime is over, rinse the toys off and put them into the bag to drain. This will keep the rest of the family from tripping over them in the shower.

■ Cover the bathtub faucet with a spout protector or a washcloth secured with strong cord to keep your baby from bumping her head, and make a strict rule against standing or crawling around in the tub.

■ Connie recommends blunt nail scissors to trim your baby's fingernails, since nail clippers can pinch and biting the nails off can leave a jagged edge or pull the nail off into the quick. Lynda keeps blunt-tipped scissors on Grant's changing table. She says, "Every few days, I check his toenails and fingernails while I'm changing him." "I did it while my boys were sleeping," says Cheryl. "They slept right through it." I usually found it easiest to trim Megan's nails while she nursed. If I did it while she was up and active, she stood in grave danger of losing her fingertips along with her nails. I supported her head on a thick pillow, which left both of my hands free.

Keeping Up Appearances

The havoc that can be wreaked in a family room by a six-month-old baby who's just beginning to crawl is one of those things you have to see to believe. And believe me, you will.

As your baby grows older and even more mobile, his potential for strewing toys from one end of the house to the other increases dramatically. So, unless you want to spend your child's toddlerhood up to your neck in toys, it's important to have some kind of system whereby the clutter gets put into its proper place at the natural breaks in the day—i.e., naptime and bedtime, and before meals and outings.

■ "We have a couple of small laundry baskets that we keep in the rooms where the boys play," says Cheryl. "At naptime, or when I receive news that unexpected company is on the way, I just carry the basket around the room and toss the toys in, to be put away in the boys' bedroom or in their big toy chest at a later time. Now that they're toddlers, Jason and Brian enjoy helping me put the toys into the basket."

■ When Megan outgrew her yellow plastic bathtub, I kept it to use as a portable toybox since it matched her bedroom and slid easily underneath her crib. When we took it out into the family room she liked to unload all the toys and sit in her little "boat"—and I've even been known to use the tub as a spare laundry basket when the need arose.

■ With the great room concept in homes becoming more and more popular, fewer families have a separate family room or playroom where the children can keep their toys.

If you're particular about your decor, get a big, covered wicker basket or a pretty wicker clothes hamper to use as a living-room toybox.

■ Keep only about ten toys in your living-room toybox, since the number you have in it is inevitably the number your toddler will drag out. And keep four or five books on a low bookshelf, the rest out of reach. Rotate the toys and books every week or two.

■ "Watch the wall about two feet off the floor once your child starts crawling and walking," says Cheryl. "Handprints there are easy to miss since they're not in your line of sight. And if your baby manages to get hold of a crayon or pen and marks the wall with it, a plastic scouring pad will sometimes clean what a cloth or sponge won't. An art gum eraser will take care of pencil marks."

Teething Isn't Fun

"When I cut my wisdom teeth," says Virginia, "I finally understood why teething made my babies so grumpy." Your child will be teething off and on for most of his first two years, so it's important to come up with ways to soothe his itching, painful gums. Our babies liked many of the following teething ideas better than commercial teething rings.

■ Terri says, "A washcloth wrapped around an ice cube and tied with strong cord worked well for Zachary and Ashley. The cloth absorbed the water as the ice melted along with any drooling from the baby."

■ Cold vegetables and fruits were favorite teething tools for our little ones. Several moms found that a peeled, refrigerated carrot was a good soother for their babies' sore gums. Jan let Jordan David teethe on celery sticks; Julie gave Sean and Ian thick, cold cucumber slices with the seeds removed; and Wanda used thick apple slices as a sweet way of soothing Michelle's gums. Make sure any pieces of fruit or vegetable you give your baby aren't small enough to fit all the way into his mouth, though, or he may choke.

You baby will probably go through a transition period when he has enough teeth to gnaw off a chunk of food but can't yet chew it up. To avoid the danger of choking, don't let him teethe on food during that time. Linda came up with a really unique way of helping her teething babies: frozen bagels.

■ "Even a soft children's toothbrush can be rough on your baby's gums," says Patty W. "When he first starts cutting teeth, put a dab of toothpaste on a damp washcloth and rub his teeth gently with it once a day. When it's time to switch to a toothbrush, make it fun. Buy a cute children's toothbrush for your baby, and let him brush his teeth along with you when you do yours. Times like that create a feeling of togetherness."

Of course, you'll need to help your child brush his teeth for several years, since a toddler doesn't have the manual dexterity to do a thorough job. And never let a child climb or run with a toothbrush in his mouth.

Safety Always

The best safety device you can give your baby is a constantly vigilant mother. True, it takes quite an effort to make sure your baby is always within either sight or earshot and to buckle him in every time you go out in the car, even if he cries, but it's well worth it.

It would be impossible in a few pages to give warning of all the predicaments babies get themselves into, and even after reading this incomplete listing you'll probably wonder how any babies manage to grow up at all. Don't let these potential horrors cause you to live in fear. Your responsibility as a mother is to do your very best to make your child's world safe and to trust God for the things you can't foresee.

As diplomatically as possible, insist that your baby's grandparents read and follow these safety tips if you let your child spend much time alone with them. The safest home in the world won't help your baby if Grandma's house is full of hazards.

■ Starting the day you bring your baby home from the hospital, USE A CAR SEAT. This is vital to your baby's safety, but for some reason many otherwise good mothers don't see the need to buckle their babies in *every* time they go somewhere in the car, even though many state laws now require it. If you feel you can't afford a car seat, try to borrow one or check with the Salvation Army or your local sheriffs department. Your child is too precious to risk losing.

■ Patty W. says, "If you don't have a cloth cover for your car seat, put a towel or small blanket over it when you have to leave the car—it can get pretty hot in the sun." Wanda remembers a friend whose baby cried every time he was put into his car seat until finally Wanda noticed that the hot straps were making angry red marks on his shoulders. Also, if at all possible, get a quilted cloth seat cover to keep your baby from sweating against the warm plastic.

■ Babies' actions are largely reflex at first. Your child

can grasp the side of his changing table and flip himself off before you know it, so don't turn your back on him for even an instant while he's on the changing table. If he does manage to flip off, don't panic, but do call your pediatrician. He or she can give you danger signals to watch for if your baby has had a fall. Many of our moms' children fell off a bed or a changing table at least once and recovered just fine. That's why they're called "bouncing babies."

■ Never, *ever* leave your baby while he's in the bathtub, even if he's lying on a bath sponge. Ignore the phone and the doorbell; otherwise, take your wet little one with you to the phone or door.

Several of our moms have bathroom horror stories, all of which occurred because they left their babies or toddlers alone to go take care of something "urgent." Donna says, "One day when April was two years old, she was playing in the bathtub when I had to leave the room for a second. My husband had left the blow dryer on the counter by the sink. April got out of the bathtub, got the blow dryer, plugged it in, got back into the bathtub, and turned it on. Praise the Lord, she did not drop that thing into the water. I ran in and jerked the plug out of the wall."

Linda left eighteen-month-old Philip alone in the bathroom for a moment only to be summoned back by blood-curdling screams. Philip had gotten out of the tub and grabbed the hot end of Linda's curling iron.

So, the moral of the story is, don't leave your baby or toddler alone in the bathroom, especially not when there are small appliances in the room.

■ The time to babyproof your home is when your child first shows signs of creeping. Cheryl got down on her hands and knees when babyproofing for Jason and Brian to give herself a baby's-eye view of her house. "It gave me a better idea of what tempting things were in their sight range," she says, "and showed me small items in the carpet or under the chair or sofa that I would otherwise have missed."

■ Babies, especially teething babies, put everything in their mouths and are fascinated by small objects, so keep the floor well picked up once your little one is old enough to creep. If you sew or do handcrafts, be meticulous about picking up dropped pins and buttons. They can be deadly if your baby manages to get one into her mouth.

■ The most important babyproofing Julie and her husband Larry did was to put plastic plugs in the electrical outlets. She says, "An accident can happen so easily. Those little wet fingers that the baby just took out of his mouth or that little tongue that does most of his exploring can find the wall outlet, and you may not even notice that your baby is near the outlet until it's too late." Also, I noticed when Megan began roaming around in her walker that the electrical outlets were just about at her eye level. Put plugs in the outlets above your kitchen and bathroom counters, too, against the time when your child learns to climb.

■ Before allowing your baby to play with a new toy, examine it for sharp edges, pointed tips, or loose parts—eyes, ears, nose, tail. Stay away from cheap toys made with brittle plastic—which can break into sharp pieces—and toys with small parts on which your little one can choke. Most toys nowadays carry labels that indicate what age level the toy is made for. No matter how brilliant your baby is, stick with toys at his age level.

■ Dolls with yarn hair can be a problem for teething

babies. Megan had a Raggedy Ann doll she played with constantly, until one day I discovered a wad of red yarn in her mouth.

■ Hanging your baby's pacifier around her neck with a ribbon sounds like a cute, handy idea, but don't do it. She can be strangled or seriously hurt if the ribbon becomes caught on something.

■ Once your baby is old enough to push up on his hands and knees or sit up by himself, take his crib mobile down and don't tie anything across the top of his crib or playpen. Otherwise he could become entangled and hurt himself.

■ When your child starts to crawl up to tables, dressers, etc., and pull himself to a standing position, a well-padded playpen is a good place for him to practice standing up and sitting down. Remove most of the toys from the playpen, leaving only ones that won't hurt your child if he falls on them.

■ Know the names of your houseplants, and call your local poison control center or county agricultural extension office to find out whether any plants within your baby's reach are poisonous. You'd be surprised how many common houseplants are. Sooner or later your baby is bound to grab a leaf and put it into his mouth, and you can save him from illness or death by eliminating hazardous plants until he's older.

■ Terri suggests using a twist tie to corral electrical appliance cords. "A small baby can reach a lot more than you think," she says. Patty W. goes even further, suggesting that electrical cords be taped to the back of table legs. She says, "It's so easy for a crawling baby's legs to get caught on a cord and pull a lamp over."

■ "Make sure you know what your baby is doing all the

time," says Karen H., "especially if things are quiet.
Babies get into things you'd never dream of."

■ Keep the doors closed to rooms you don't want your
baby wandering into, especially bathrooms. Toilets are
fascinating to older babies and toddlers, and, believe it
or not, children have been known to fall in and drown.

■ Secure the cords of curtains and venetian blinds to the
wall or drape them over the curtain rod out of reach.
Babies have been known to accidentally strangle themselves while playing unsupervised with long cords.

■ Donna stresses the importance of child-proof latches
on drawers and cabinets that contain medicines, cos-
metics, pesticides, cleaning supplies, and sharp objects.
Even better, put such items in high cabinets, and then
put latches on those cabinets in case your little one learns
to climb up and reach them. "Especially now that I have
two children," she says, "I can't have my eye on both of
them all the time. While I'm with one, the other child
can get into my cabinets before I know it."

■ Buy a small bottle of ipecac syrup in case you ever
need to induce vomiting after an accidental poisoning.
Or purchase a bottle of activated charcoal, which can
absorb poisons a child has swallowed and give you time
to get to the emergency room. (One brand name is Super
Char, from Gulf Bio-Systems, Inc., in Dallas. This is
not the kind of charcoal used to grill steaks.) Check with
your pediatrician or poison control center for instructions
on how to use these medications. According to Megan's
pediatrician, a leading source of accidental poisonings is
the medicine in Grandma's purse or Grandpa's coat
pocket.

■ Cook on back burners whenever possible, and keep
the handles of pots and pans turned to the back of the

stove. Also, don't allow your baby to play near a hot stove, and never lift a pot of hot food or liquid over your baby. Always go around him.

■ A baby in a walker can reach further than you might think. Don't leave sharp objects like knives or glasses that can shatter near the edge of the counter, and make the stove knobs a strict no-no.

■ Keep all plastic wrap and plastic bags out of your child's reach, and don't leave them in your wastebaskets when she becomes old enough to crawl around.

■ Patty W. recommends keeping your ironing board either put away when not in use or in a room where your baby isn't allowed. "Even a cool iron will hurt your baby if she pulls it off onto her head," she says.

■ Also from Patty W.: "When your baby starts walking, make it a habit that he always holds your hand when you go out together. If you make exceptions, your little one will take advantage of it. They're faster than we think." To give Michelle a feeling of freedom, Wanda used a baby harness and leash on walks and shopping trips. "I got some nasty comments from people who told me I was treating my little girl like a pet animal," she says, "but I always replied, 'Well, I love my child too much to let anything happen to her.'" Having the courage of your convictions is a great help at times like that—and a good-sized stubborn streak doesn't hurt either.

■ Terri says, "When your toddler is big enough to pull doors open, tie bells to the ones you don't want her to touch. That way you'll know when to come running."

■ Patty W. says, "As early as possible, teach your toddler his first and last name, his parents' names, city, and street name, if not his street number and phone number. No mother wants to think about her child's getting lost, but precautions can't hurt." It's a good idea, as soon as your child can understand, to teach him not to get into a car or go with anyone Mommy or Daddy hasn't certified as okay. Sad though it is, a child playing outdoors should be either in a fenced-in yard behind a locked gate, or within a supervising adult's sight range—preferably both.

■ Don't dress your toddler in clothes embroidered with his name. A stranger coming up, calling his name, and saying, "Your mommy told me to come and get you," is very convincing. There are a number of simple storybooks available dealing with such problems as kidnapping and sexual abuse. One example is *The Danger Zone* series from Word, Inc. Use these resources to teach your child to protect himself.

Holiday Hazards

■ Keep your carpet free of dropped Christmas tree needles, which when dry are as sharp as pins. Also, make sure none of the hooks used to hang ornaments become stuck in your rug.
■ Keep glass ornaments high on the tree, with only safe, soft ones within the baby's reach.
■ It's generally best never to leave your baby unsupervised in the room with the Christmas tree. Its bright colors make it irresistible, and your child can pull it over on himself in an instant.
■ Holly and mistletoe are poisonous, so put them up out of reach or avoid buying them until your baby is older.

The Well-Dressed Baby

■ Experience with her four children taught Sofie this lesson: "Never, never, *never* buy clothes that fit perfectly. I always buy clothing that I have to hem up a few inches or that needs to have the button moved over."

■ The age sizing used on babies' clothes isn't standard from manufacturer to manufacturer, so our moms learned to ignore it and go by their children's height and weight instead. For example, at four months, Megan was wearing twelve-month sleepers.

■ Terri and Connie were both proud mothers of little girls with no hair. They made sure everyone knew their children were girls by sticking bows to their peach fuzz with double-sided tape. Keep an eye on your little one, and take the bows out when you're at home. Your baby can choke on a bow if she manages to pull it off her head and stick it into her mouth.

■ If your baby's shirt won't stay in, use a piece of masking tape in the front and back to stick his shirttail to his disposable diaper or plastic pants. Keep a roll at your changing table and in your diaper bag, since the tape sticks to disposable diapers so well that you may have to change it each time you change a diaper.

■ Chris started a habit when Ashley was born that's still yielding benefits now that her little girl is three: "Any time I dress Ashley to go out," she says, "I change her back into play clothes—i.e., clothes that already have identifiable stains on them—as soon as we get home. That way if I feed her or give her a drink it doesn't get on her good clothes. As a result, I hardly ever have to wash most of her nice outfits." This keeps Ashley's good clothes from wearing out prematurely.

▪ Chris found that a good way to keep Ashley's shoes tied—especially as she began to stand and toddle around—was to tie the laces in a bow, then tie the loops of the bow in a knot.

▪ I went through Megan's closet and dresser when she was about six months old and weeded out the clothes she had outgrown. I was amazed at how many there were and how much extra storage space I ended up with. When you do this, the outgrown clothes can be given away or saved in plastic bags for your next child. Repeat the process a couple of times a year.

▪ "Since children's clothes are small," says Lynda, "we had Grant's closet made with shelves for stackable clothes above, and the rack for hanging clothes about halfway down." Having the shelves on top keeps Lynda from having to stoop while putting Grant's clothes away or finding an outfit for him to wear. Although Lynda had Grant's closet custom-made when she and her husband were building their new house, it would be simple to adapt an existing closet with wooden or plastic-coated wire shelves. Such customizing yields so much extra storage space that a dresser in the baby's room isn't necessary. Kristy also points out that the low rack for hanging clothes makes it easier for you to teach your toddler to hang up his own clothes later on.

▪ If you're like most of our moms, birthdays and Christmas are the two times of the of the year when your baby's wardrobe will receive its biggest boost. "When people ask what your baby needs," says Patty W., "ask them to consider department store gift certificates. That way you can buy the things your baby really needs, in the right sizes. And ask them to limit dressy clothes. Sleepers, playsuits, and undershirts are much more practical."

■ Several of our moms have found yard sales and consignment shops to be good places for finding children's clothes, especially dressy outfits that are usually worn only once or twice before they're outgrown or play clothes that must fit but don't need to look brand-new.

■ Pene's skill at sewing keeps her children in inexpensive clothes: "Especially when they're little, it doesn't take much material at all to make a pair of shorts or a sundress."

■ Check carefully for quality when buying everyday play clothes, especially once your baby starts crawling. An outfit isn't cheaper if it has to be replaced before it's outgrown. Chris says, "You can buy good clothes at discount stores, and you can buy shoddy clothes at expensive department stores. You just have to look carefully at what you get. Check the seams and the fabric to make sure clothing is made well." Make it a habit to check the clearance and sale racks before looking at higher-priced clothes.

■ Our moms are all for getting good children's clothes as cheaply as you can no matter where you find them, but they're not willing to compromise in the area of shoes. "A cheap shirt can't hurt your baby's body," says Chris, "but a cheap pair of shoes can ruin his feet." Luckily for our pocketbooks, though, babies don't need shoes as soon as the shoe manufacturers would like us to believe they do. Until your child begins to stand and try to toddle, shoes are merely for decoration and warmth unless your pediatrician has told you that your baby needs corrective shoes. And even when he starts walking, the best shoes for your child to wear while he's at home are none at all. In cold weather, a footed sleep/playsuit with nonskid rubber pads on the feet will do just fine, with maybe a pair of thick socks underneath for extra warmth.

When your baby is old enough to walk outdoors and in public, high-topped shoes or good quality sneakers are a good way to start, and our moms insist that nothing can take the place of a professional fitting. If you find that your baby is a standard size you can then feel free to buy his play and dress shoes at discount stores.

■ Before their babies began to stand and walk, several of our moms got away with buying their children's shoes too big and letting their feet grow into them. But that was no longer possible when their little ones began to toddle. Shoes that are too big don't give a baby the stability he needs, and they can rub blisters on his feet. If your budget won't allow for new shoes every couple of months, buy them *slightly* larger than needed and let your baby wear thick socks until he grows into them. Feel the toe and sides of his shoes every week or so, and buy new shoes the minute the old ones start to become tight.

■ Patty W. says, "To help your toddler learn to put his shoes on the correct feet, put a small piece of colored tape on the bottom of his right shoe."

God's Name Doesn't End in M.D.

Children's health care is far beyond the scope of this book, but our moms do have some definite ideas about dealing with your baby's doctor.

Your pediatrician may someday literally have your child's life in his hands, and the yellow pages are not the place to find him. Ask for references from your friends with children or from your obstetrician.

Even after you've chosen a pediatrician you respect and trust, remember that he or she is human. If you suspect that something is wrong with your baby, go with your instincts. "You live with that child every day," says Carol. "The doctor doesn't." You may never have to face this situation, but don't hesitate to get a second or even a third opinion if, after you've thoroughly discussed your concerns with him, your pediatrician can't seem to identify the problem or insists that there isn't one. "Even if you turn out to be wrong," says Chris, "at least you'll know!"

A hearing problem with Rita's son Brian, a severe foot problem with Vicky's daughter Lauren, and even a life-threatening kidney dysfunction with Carol B.'s little girl Kristie went undiagnosed by the first doctors to see them. Lindsie, LeEtta's little girl, went untreated with bronchitis for three months because her doctor kept saying she'd get over it. LeEtta says now, "I'm not going to be so sentimental about my pediatrician next time. If I don't see results, I'm going somewhere else."

Our moms are much in favor of finding a good, comprehensive children's health care manual to refer to when problems arise. "I have several medical books," says Carol, "and I try to read up as much as I can when there's an illness. Then, when I take my child to the doctor, I can point out the symptoms. Believe me, it helps." Obviously, you should never try to diagnose and treat an illness at home, with the possible exception of a head cold. The purpose of a health care manual is to help you communicate with your child's doctor—not to replace him.

And most important, of course, is to trust the Lord for your baby's health and ask Him for wisdom if she shows unusual symptoms. Hard as it is to conceive, He loves her more than you do.

6

A Busy Baby
Is a Happy Baby

We'll begin this chapter by bursting yet another
bubble: We're not going to tell you how to
make your baby occupy himself all day long
so you can go about your business and not spend time
with him. Even if that weren't impossible, it would be
awful for his development. A ten-year-long study guided
by Dr. Burton L. White, author of *The First Three Years
of Life* (Prentiss-Hall), indicates that the most important
factor in your baby's intellectual development is the
amount of time he spends interacting with you, his
mother. It's absolutely essential that you talk to him,
play with him, cuddle him, read to him, explain things
to him, and provide new experiences for him—especially

during the crucial time between the ages of eight and eighteen months.

Having said all that, we'll now add that it's not necessary for you to entertain your baby all day long. He learns much by playing alone and by watching you go about your daily activities, and in this chapter are some tips our moms used to keep their little ones occupied and happy at home and abroad.

■ Beg, borrow, or buy an infant swing if you haven't received one as a shower gift. It's a great invention, and our moms found that their babies were much more willing to sit and watch Mommy work if they could swing at the same time. They often took naps in their swings as well.

■ Let your baby sit in his swing or infant seat and watch while you do dishes or unload the dishwasher. He'll enjoy touching the dishes as you put them away—cool, smooth glass, rough wooden spoon, shiny metal pan. Tell him the name of each item. "I put my little girl's swing in the kitchen while I worked," says Carol, "and gave her gadgets that didn't have small parts and weren't pointed—a metal tea strainer, plastic measuring cups, everything possible, to let her touch and feel them."

■ Tear off a sheet of aluminum foil and hold it in front of your baby. You can't let him have it, of course, but you'll have fun watching him react to his reflection and to the noise the foil makes when he bats it.

■ A friend of mine claims he'd be a millionaire if he could invent a toy as fascinating to babies as a paper bag, but more durable. Infants love the crackly noise paper makes, plus the fact that a small paper bag is light enough for them to wave around. Watch your baby carefully when she plays with paper, though. She can quickly gum a piece off and swallow it.

■ Vicky's daughter Lauren loves soap bubbles. "I used to blow bubbles for her in the kitchen while she sat in her carrier," says Vicky. "Now I do it while she's in the bathtub. She loves it! She tries to pop them."

■ Put your baby in her infant seat and carry her around the house with you. She'll enjoy watching you work, especially if you talk and sing to her while you do it.

■ "Make sure your baby has plenty to look at in his crib and playpen," says Lynda. "Grant loves to look at his Busy Box or listen to his wind-up musical crib toys." Babies also love mirrors, and there are some good unbreakable ones for the crib and playpen on the market. Your little one will have fun looking at the mirror and trying to figure out who the other baby is.

■ Sofie learned by hard experience that it's important to start using the playpen *before* your baby is old enough to creep. If she becomes too accustomed to the wide, open spaces, she may refuse to stay in it. Our moms warn against depending on the playpen too much, though. "A playpen can be bad if you constantly use it as a baby-sitter," says Carol, "and if you don't keep stimulating toys in it. You know your baby is bored if she stops crying when you take her out and put her on the floor." It's best to use the playpen only when you really can't keep a constant eye on your child for some reason.

■ Don't clutter your baby's playpen with too many toys. They make it hard for her to maneuver, and she can play with only one or two at a time anyway. Just put two or three interesting toys in with her and set the rest aside. Change the toys every few days. I did find an exception to this rule. When Megan reached the age of six months or so she became very interested in putting one item inside another. Every now and then I would put a whole box of toys into her playpen with her and she occupied herself for long periods of time taking all the toys out of the box and then putting them all back in.

■ When babies are about six months old they learn what is to them a delightful game called "Mommy Pick-Up." They drop their rattle or toy again and again and expect you to pick it up each time. You can help short-circuit this by tying the toy to your baby's highchair with a short piece of strong cord (not yarn, which your baby will gnaw through). Remember to supervise any play involving cord to make sure your child doesn't become entangled.

■ Many of our children love playing with balloons, especially if the balloon has a short cord (about 5″) so that it can be dragged or held. "I have a whole bag of balloons in my kitchen," says Carol. "They do pop, and it scares me but not my children." Any balloon play should be closely supervised by Mommy, and popped balloons should be confiscated immediately. Also, never allow your toddler or young child to try to blow up a balloon. It's too easy for him to suck in at the wrong time and inhale it. Vicky says, "My brother choked badly on a balloon when he was about two. I still remember it."

■ Some of our moms have finally discovered a use for junk mail. They give it to their babies to play with. Megan's favorites were the crackly cellophane window envelopes, colorful flyers on card stock, and catalogs—especially those with pictures of children. The best part of this play idea is that it's free, and it renews itself daily. It is still important, though, to supervise your baby when she plays with paper, especially if she's teething.

■ When their babies became old enough to crawl around and explore, several of our moms gained peace and quiet as they worked in the kitchen by giving their children their own special kitchen cabinet filled with plastic cups, bowls, lids, and unbreakable plastic cookie cutters. "Ashley loves those plastic bowls," says Chris. "She takes them all out and stacks them inside each other and sees which lid fits on which bowl. She's learned a lot about sizes that way."

Carol uses the plastic cups in her children's cabinet to teach them independence: "My three-year-old can go and get his own cup and water, because our refrigerator has a spout for cold water on the front. Even the neighbor kids do it now when they come to visit."

■ When Megan was about eight months old I bought her some children's books with animal pictures. Within a couple of months she had learned to imitate most of the animal sounds, and by the time she reached the tender age of fourteen months she and her books were inseparable. Her library had expanded to include books with pictures of mommies, daddies, babies, trees, and flowers, and I was often treated to the sight of her sitting by her toybox "reading" to herself. I heard mostly nonsense words, punctuated every now and then with a "Ball!" "Arf-arf!" "Meow!" "Baby!" "Duck!" or "Ribbut!"

I was amazed at how quickly her vocabulary grew because we took the time to sit down with her and her little books. She made the fascinating discovery that every time she and Mommy or Daddy opened a book she learned something new—a new sound, a new name— and she loved it. I believe a big factor, too, in her love of books is that Jon and I are both avid readers and she often sees us with a book in hand. Often now when I'm sitting on the couch reading she will get a book, climb up, and join me.

■ "Zachary has his own little photo album," says Terri, "and I give him all my seconds whenever I get two prints. He's played more with pictures than with any other toy I've invested in." When Megan was fifteen months old I got an inexpensive photo album with clear plastic pages and filled it with pictures of her grandparents, uncles, aunts, cousins, and of course Mommy and Daddy and Megan. It rapidly became her favorite picture book. She enjoyed being able to recognize the people she loved, and it was also a good way to acquaint her with her relatives who live out of state.

■ Thirteen-month-old Lindsie's favorite game is for LeEtta to teach her the parts of her body. "I ask her, 'Where's Mommy's hair?'" says LeEtta, "and she thinks it's so funny to reach up and grab it. Sometimes she'll just come up to me on her own and start pointing at my nose, or ears, or eyes, and now she's doing it with everybody—even strangers." This game is a good way to keep your child occupied while you change her diaper.

■ Wanda recommends keeping two boxes of toys—one for your baby to play with now, and one to put away for the time when he tires of the toys that are out. This way your child can have new toys from time to time without your having to pay for them. In fact, it's a good habit to put away one of your baby's old toys each time he receives a new one. By the time he tires of the new toy, the old one will be interesting again. Wanda also suggests a rainy-day play box of toys, games, and craft ideas for when your child is old enough to chafe at being kept indoors by bad weather or illness.

■ "Remember," says Terri, "you're not too old to get down on your child's level and play games and just be silly." Wanda's daughter Michelle puts in a word here: "It makes me feel important when Mommy and Daddy take time to play with me."

■ Our moms generally found that the best toys for holding their toddlers' attention were creative ones— i.e., toys with multiple uses such as building blocks, dolls, and even cardboard boxes. Carol says, "Play-dough is great for a toddler who's finished teething— say, three years old. We keep some in a jar on a low shelf so our little boy can get to it, and it keeps him busy for a long time. He loves crayons and paper too— just very basic toys."

■ When rainy weather keeps them inside, Janice gives three-year-old Brock and his big brother, Brandt, an old catalog and a couple pairs of rounded-tip scissors. "They'll cut out pictures for hours," she says.

■ Our moms are strong believers in the idea that the best way to persuade your toddler to let you do your housework is to let him in on the act. "Let your child help you in everything possible," says Patty W. "It takes longer to get things done, but it's worth it because you're also making memories and building your tod-dler's confidence and sense of self-worth. At two, Jennifer helps wash dishes, fold laundry, and make beds. She loves it!"

"When I'm baking," says Terri, "my little boy is sitting on the counter and my little girl is in her highchair beside me. One gets to put in the baking powder and the other gets to put in the flour. And I tell you, at four years old Zachary right now can probably cook better than my husband. He wants to be right there doing whatever I'm doing, and since I've taken the time to teach him to help I've found that he doesn't have much interest in television."

Julie's three-year-old son Sean also loves to help out around the house: "Right now," she says, "it's more fun for him to help Mommy than to play." An excellent side benefit of letting your toddler participate in the housework is that it builds good work habits for the time when he'll have daily chores to do by himself, and it can still be yielding benefits years later when he's married and is sharing the housework with his working wife or helping out after the children arrive.

■ Donna stresses the need for children to get fresh air and physical exercise by playing outside and taking walks. When Megan began walking we got into the habit of taking a stroll around the block right before naptime when the weather was nice. She toddled along, holding onto Mommy with one hand and picking up leaves and grass with the other, constantly asking "Zat?" She especially loved it when we took along a small paper bag that she could fill with her treasures. She learned much about the world around her, met some new friends, and got tired enough to take a long nap and give Mommy a break when we got home. Virginia's children loved to play in their sandbox when they were little: "I stayed with them for a few minutes at first to give them some ideas about making little mounds and cakes," she says. "Then I sat on the back porch where I could watch them while I relaxed and read. They played sometimes for hours. When they finished, I picked them up and took them straight to the bathtub, and after their bath they were usually so tired that they went right to sleep."

Out and About

▪ Our moms generally found it best to feed their babies just before they went out to dinner until their children were old enough to eat table food. This kept them from becoming hungry and cranky while their parents ate. It's also best to avoid going out when it's almost naptime or when your baby is obviously getting tired and grumpy.

▪ The trick to peaceful restaurant meals is keeping your baby occupied. It's only natural that he should become bored during an evening out—after all, he's already eaten his dinner. Here are some possible attention keepers: a piece of waxed paper or a colorful greeting card, peeled carrots that have been kept cold in a cup of ice water, a bottle of water or juice, a special toy, or a cloth or vinyl book.

▪ The moms who discovered this trick thought they had done something unique until they got together with our other moms who had done the same thing: quite a few of our babies like lemon wedges. "Ian loves them," says Julie. "It's hysterical, because when we give them to him in a restaurant people just stare. He makes the worst faces, but he won't quit. The sour taste seems to keep him coming back for more."

Carol B. made the same discovery: "Kristen would be happy through the whole meal as long as we kept handing her lemons. We just made sure there were no seeds." Megan loved them too—in fact, for a while our biggest problem when we went out to eat was persuading her to give up her lemon wedge at the end of the meal. We found that squeezing the lemon wedge and then dipping it into our iced tea or water before giving it to her kept it from being too sour.

You probably shouldn't try this until your baby is at least four months old. Also, when your little one starts cutting teeth you'll need to watch to make sure she doesn't chew off a hunk of the rind. And make this a rare treat because constant exposure to the acid in a lemon wedge can erode your baby's tooth enamel.

■ LeEtta was surprised to find that not all restaurants provide highchairs. If you're taking your child out to eat at a new place and aren't carrying your own baby seat, she recommends that you call first.

■ "Unless your baby or toddler is naturally quiet and contented," says Patty W., "don't take him to a formal restaurant where everyone will be made to feel tense and uncomfortable if he decides to fuss. Until he matures enough to understand what's expected of him in social settings, confine your family meals out to family restaurants, where baby noises are not out of place."

■ When Vicky takes Lauren shopping, she takes along a bottle or cup and a packet of Gatorade. She says, "I just stop at a drinking fountain and add water, and I always have something for her to drink." For older babies, a plastic container of crackers can also work wonders to keep you from wishing you'd never left home.

■ When Terri's toddlers become restless in church, she keeps them quiet by hiding coins between the hymnal pages. Zachary and Ashley love looking for them, and this quiet game keeps them occupied for quite a while. Of course, this game shouldn't be played with a teething toddler, who might put the coins into his mouth.

■ "In children's church and other places where I was supervising several small children," says Glenda, "we played the 'silent game' to see who could be quiet the longest. They loved it, and it gave me a welcome rest."

■ Our moms agree that it's your responsibility to supply the toys to keep your child entertained during visits to friends' homes. Carol B. says, "We had a little garbage pail with a lid, and we filled it with inexpensive toys, books, and a doll or two and just picked it up by the handle and took it with us whenever we went anywhere." Carol adds, "And if you accidentally go out without the toys, you can always ask your friend for a few plastic bowls and measuring cups."

Over the River and Through the Woods

■ We took an extended car trip when Megan was four months old, and we saved our sanity and kept her entertained by stringing a 1'-wide strip of elastic between the windows in the back seat and using it to hang toys in front of her car seat. We made sure the toys hung just low enough for her to touch, bat, and tug on them, but not low enough to smack her in the face if we hit a bump. A knot tied in each end of the elastic will keep it from slipping out of the closed car window, and it's a good idea to change the toys frequently.

■ "We always bought small, inexpensive, safe new toys when we made a long car trip," says Glenda, "and we never gave them all to them at the same time. Just one or two would keep them occupied for quite a while." Wanda still assembles a vacation box during the weeks before a long trip even now that her daughter is ten years old. She includes inexpensive toys and games, books, coloring books, and whatever else she thinks will help the miles go by faster for Michelle. Patty W. adds, "With a toddler, it's especially important to take along a favorite blanket or stuffed animal to help her go to sleep."

■ "As our toddlers grew older," says Glenda, "we played games while traveling, such as counting trucks or cars or cows or certain types of signs. It kept them occupied for a long time and taught them to be observant. We also sang songs together and did word games. These things were fun and educational."

■ Remember, too, that your little one needs a chance to get out and stretch every now and then, even if you don't. Make frequent rest stops where you can unstrap your baby and let him crawl or toddle around and get some fresh air.

7
...
Never Too Little
for Jesus

The first step toward raising a child who has a vital relationship with Jesus, according to the mothers in this book, is to be a mommy who has one of her own. For better or for worse, our moms acknowledge that you are the first image of God your baby sees: the omnipresent giver of food, help, and solace; the omniscient being who always manages to catch him when he's about to turn the knobs on the stereo or eat the magazines, even if he was sure you weren't looking. The child whose parents shower him with love and affection and are patient with his childish mistakes—while dealing firmly with direct disobedience—probably isn't going to have too much trouble grasping the concept of a God who is also loving, yet just.

"Children's perceptions of God are affected by their parents," says Marilee. "If a child's parents are very lenient, he may get the idea that he doesn't really have to obey God or anyone else. On the other hand, if his parents are overbearing, quick to punish, and never say 'I'm sorry' when they're wrong, the child may get the idea that God is just waiting around with a baseball bat to knock him on the head when he makes a mistake. We are the examples of God to our children. If we're not walking our Christianity right, they're going to get a distorted view of what He is like."

It has already been mentioned that children love to imitate, a trait which can be both delightful and scary. The first time your little prodigy says "Mama!" is wonderful and precious; the first time you see your toddler echoing an attitude you thought was well hidden may not be. But our moms believe that children's natural gift for imitation is vital to their spiritual training. "The Bible says that we are imitators of Christ," says Cheryl, "and until our children reach the point where they can understand that, they are imitators of us."

Where It Begins

Now that you're thoroughly frightened, let's talk about where spiritual training starts—our moms insist that it begins long before your child is able to understand the words you use as you pray over a meal. "It starts even before you conceive the child," says Adrienne, who, with six children, is perhaps the professional mother of our group. "You tell God you want a baby, and then all through your pregnancy you pray for the child and for your wisdom as a mother." Virginia adds, "We started praying beside the crib when our children were babies. Even though they may not understand, children sense your prayers."

But please don't despair if your baby is already here and you're getting a late start. Nancy was one of several moms whose interest in spiritual things was reawakened with the births of her children. Mothers in general are more willing to do things for the sake of their little ones than for their own good, and reconciling with the Lord is no exception. But Nancy's renewed walk with God became more than a dull, dry church attendance for the sake of her family; it grew into a beautiful, vital relationship. As she puts it, "My husband and I learned right along with the children."

Our moms recommend that you pray daily not only for your child but with him, even while he's still tiny. Aside from the blessed fact that God will hear and answer, your child's understanding will grow in time and a habit of prayer interwoven in daily life will have been formed. Also, several of our moms began reading Bible stories to their children while they were still infants. Reading to a young baby may consist of nothing more than pointing to the characters and telling him their names, or telling nursery rhymes in a sing-song voice while trying to wrestle the pages from his grasping little hands. Again, though, his understanding will grow with time, and if you make his story times fun you'll have the added benefit of a child who loves books and who will probably be an early reader. *The Christian Mother Goose Book* by Marjorie Decker is wonderful, by the way.

As Time Goes By

Ideally, you should pray with your little one so often that prayer becomes second nature to him. "If you'll pray with your child about small things," says Connie, "he'll learn early to turn to the Lord in everything. I prayed with Lisa on one occasion for a hurt finger when she was about two years old. She said, 'How God gonna heal it? God gotta Band-Aid?' She thought Band-Aids could fix anything. But now, practically every day as she leaves for school, she says, 'Pray for me today, Mother. I have an English test (or a math test, etc.).'"

With that in mind, here is a list of ways to build your child's prayer life:

■ *As soon as your toddler begins putting words together into simple sentences, teach him to repeat short prayers after you.* Always explain what you're doing, making sure he understands what you're asking or thanking God for.

■ *Stay away from formula prayers.* Pray simply and sincerely about the needs of the moment. "God bless Mommy, Daddy, Grandma, Grandpa, etc." can be included but shouldn't make up the whole prayer every time.

■ *As his understanding grows, ask your child to pray for you.* "We have asked Mary, who's three, to pray for us many times," says Adrienne. "Her prayers are short and to the point—sometimes just, 'Dear Jesus, help Mommy to feel better,' but we know that Jesus hears them." Karen H. says, "When Randy or I don't feel well or have an 'ouchie', Josh prays for us. You'd be surprised how often his childlike faith gets prayers answered." Teach your child to pray for his little friends, too.

■ *Let him see the answers to his prayers*. "Tell him when you feel better and thank him for praying," says Cheryl, "or if you were praying for money and the Lord provides, tell how He provided and then have a prayer of thanksgiving. Prayer is real. It works. Let your child see it work." Dana agrees: "Bryan had a little friend at the end of our street who had an asthma attack. When his mother told me about it on the phone, I said, ' Bryan, why don't you and I pray for Chris?' We prayed, and that night when I called Chris's mother she told me that he was much better and was playing outside. Bryan's faith grew by leaps and bounds."

■ *Teach your child to give thanks*. Our moms agree that by the time a toddler is two and a half or three he can answer the question, "What are you thankful to Jesus for?" or, "What are you happy that Jesus gave you today?" Thanking Jesus for Mommy, Daddy, grandparents, food, trees, flowers, etc., helps your little one understand that these blessings are not owed him; they are indeed gifts from a God who loves him very much.

■ *Finally, don't force your child to pray aloud if he doesn't want to*. Keep offering the opportunity, but don't push it. After all, aren't there times when you don't feel like praying? On the other hand, Rita points out that a child who declines to pray because of bashfulness may need some encouragement. "Brian never wanted to pray at the dinner table because he was shy," she says, "so when I saw him in the kitchen after dinner I would tell him, 'Brian, that was a beautiful prayer.' That bit of encouragement really bolstered him. Now, if anybody hesitates when we start to pray, Brian jumps right in."

While your child is small, our moms agree that it's best to simply incorporate spiritual training into daily life rather than enforcing a structured devotional time, although some toddlers love to sit down to a Bible story and short prayer before Daddy leaves for work in the morning. "When a child is hungry," says Marilee, "that's when you feed him. When his mind is off somewhere else is not the time to force him to sit down and listen to a Bible story. It won't sink in then anyway.

"Capitalize on the times when he asks about things during the day. Sometimes, all of a sudden, my little boy will ask something like, 'Mommy, why does that man smoke?' Then I tell him very simply about habits. I tell him how sometimes when you start something it's hard to stop and that smoking hurts our bodies, and Jesus gave us very special bodies and He wants us to take care of them. Just about any question he asks during the day can be turned into a simple spiritual lesson."

"I think that's more what 'training a child up' is all about rather than sitting down and trying to teach," says Cheryl. "Christianity is not a part of your life; it *is* your life. Spiritual training is not so much what you say, but what you're living." Most of our moms agree with Kristy that "as long as your child is getting spiritual input from both parents, you can save the more structured time for when he's older,"—maybe when he enters nursery school or kindergarten.

If mornings are too rushed in your house, a before-bedtime Bible story and prayer is a good way to get Daddy involved. Marilee says, "Jeff always makes sure he goes in right before our little boy goes to bed. He tells him a story about Moses and Pharaoh or David and Goliath, since those are the things we want him to go to bed thinking about. At the end of the story, Jeff always turns it around and tries to apply it to our lives. For instance, with David and Goliath, he teaches that Jesus helps get rid of the giants in our lives—like lying and stealing."

Our moms found that Bible stories are great to use throughout the day as well. "My boys would much rather hear about Noah or David and Goliath than something like Hansel and Gretel," says Cheryl. "I just keep the books on hand, and when they want a story I say, 'Okay here's a story about Noah,' rather than telling them, 'Sit down. It's time for Bible study.'" She recommends reading only as long as your toddler's attention holds, since forcing a child to sit still while you plow through to the end is one good way to make him dread Bible story time. "Start skipping pages when you feel yourself losing him," advises Adrienne. "He won't notice if you come to the end sooner than usual."

Virginia made hand puppets from paper bags and used them to populate her stories. "Even when my children were only one or two years old, those puppets got their attention," she says. "As they grow older, they like to help make the puppets, too," adds Wanda.

In the absence of puppets, some kind of pictures are necessary when telling stories to a young child. "They need the pictures because they don't know how to imagine yet," says Adrienne. "The things they picture in their minds are not always in the story. A friend of mine was reading a story to her little boy, and she came to a part where it said, 'Suddenly his eyes dropped to the floor.' The little boy got very upset and didn't want to hear any more of the story. When she finally got him calmed down and asked what was wrong, she realized that he thought the character's eyes had really fallen onto the floor!" Fortunately, there are many good illustrated Bible story books, children's Bibles, Christian storybooks, and devotional books for children on the market now.

When you decide to start having a regular family devotional time, our moms unanimously offer this bit of advice: Keep it short and gear it to the child. You and your husband can always have a more adult devotional time together after your toddler is in bed. "Don't sit down and read the King James Version to a little child," says Kristy. "He'll become bored and resent your family devotions." Most of the children's devotional books our moms use have a picture, a short Bible story, and a couple of questions on each page. *The Bible in Pictures for Little Eyes* by Kenneth Taylor (Moody Press) is a classic example.

Our moms found that children learn best and have the most fun when they can get involved, whether the involvement is asking and answering questions about a Bible story, praying for Mommy and Daddy, or something a little more active. Virginia began teaching her children Bible story songs with hand motions before they were a year old. At first all they could do was copy Mommy's gestures and babble along, which they loved, but they gradually learned more and more of the words. "It was something happy and joyful that they could do," she says. "They learned a lot that way." Your church nursery should be a good source of these songs.

For older toddlers Scripture songs were a wonderful way to learn Bible verses, but our moms had other ways of teaching their children God's Word as well. "When Ashley was born," says Chris, "a friend gave me a pillow with her name and a Bible verse for each letter of her name embroidered on it. When she was about fourteen months old, I started reading it to her every morning while I made her bed. At eighteen months she could say the last word of most of the verses, and at two years old she could say almost all of every one of them—not by herself, but with just a little help."

Terri's four-year-old son, Zachary, has a set of 26 cards with a Bible verse for each letter of the alphabet. Terri says, "Zachary loves to memorize those cards. He has a wallet-sized set he takes almost everywhere he goes, and a big set at home. I wish I had gotten them sooner—he was already four when we started, and he had no trouble at all learning one a day." Of course, be sure you don't push your child to learn too much too quickly. Let him proceed at his own pace—after all, you want this to be a good experience. Terri recommends offering lots of encouragement and praise as each verse is learned. Making Scripture memorization fun for your child will pay off not only in spiritual benefits as you explain the verses to him, but in self-discipline and the self-esteem that comes from accomplishment.

Our moms make no apologies for using flash cards and pillows to help their children memorize Scripture. "Call it a gimmick, call it what you will," says Dana. "It's a learning tool, and it works." Adrienne, who was the friend who made Ashley's pillow, adds, "When you use the child's name, you give her Scriptures to grow up with. Those become her special Scriptures. I didn't just put those verses down at random for Chris's little girl. I really thought over them and tried to pick ones a small child could grow up with. I wanted her to be able to say, 'God meant that verse for me.'"

Answering the Great Questions of Life
(In 25 Words or Less)

Children have a matter-of-fact way of asking questions that have stumped wise men since Creation. "Where did God come from, anyway?" demanded Kristy's little girl Jennifer. "Did He crack out of an egg, or what?"

Janet's three-year-old son, Derek, had just been acquainted by his babysitter with the term "Jesus' house" for church, and as they prepared to go to services that Sunday Derek was very excited and kept telling his mommy that he was going to see Jesus at His house and sing Him a song. On the way there Janet asked Derek, "Do you want to practice the song you're going to sing for Jesus?" "No," he answered, "I'll just wait till I get to His house."

Later, as they were leaving church, Derek had a troubled look on his face. "Mommy," he said, "I didn't see Him. I didn't see Jesus." At that point Janet knew it was time for Derek's spiritual training to go a step further. "Jesus is everywhere, Derek," she told him. "He's in the car with us." Derek was fascinated by this bit of news. "And on motorcycles?" he asked. "And in the sky? Up there in those clouds?" He accepted Mommy's answer without hesitation, which small children do most of the time, to the great relief of their parents.

As you teach your child to pray, he'll inevitably come up with requests—unreasonable requests, or requests for unnecessary miracles—that you know God won't grant. Those are the times when Mommy has to do a little fast thinking. "My little boy Bryan had some mosquito bites the other night," says Dana, "and he was scratching and scratching. So when Bridget prayed that night, she prayed that God would take away all the mosquitoes so Bryan wouldn't get bitten anymore. How do you explain that when he comes up with another bite?" Actually, this might be a good time for a little biology lesson about how God has a purpose for every creature and that mosquitoes lay eggs in the water for the fish to eat. I can't think of any other purpose for mosquitoes.

"We've had bad situations happen because of carelessness," says Carol B., "and our daughter Kristie will pray and pray and not see an answer. That's when we share that sometimes God uses these situations to help us grow and learn to be good stewards of what we have."

Sometimes, though, God chooses not to grant a child's valid request without giving a clear explanation. A composite answer our moms use at such times goes something like this: "Jesus hears you when you pray, just as Mommy hears you when you ask for something. But sometimes Jesus has to tell you no just like Mommy sometimes has to say no. We don't always understand why He says no, but we do know that He loves us and always does what's best for us."

The most important thing about answering these heart-stopping questions, according to Nancy, is not to over-explain. "Give a child only what he asks for," she says. "I found that worked so well with my four little ones. When you've satisfied the child's curiosity, stop right there." For example, if your child asks where God came from, keep it as simple as possible: "Well, God has always been here. Nobody made Him, but He made us."

"If all else fails," says Adrienne, "it's not bad to say, 'I don't understand it either. I choose to believe it, though, because the Bible teaches us that it's true.'" Pointing to the Bible is not a cop-out. In a world where millions of things are unexplainable, it teaches your child to have faith in the ultimate authority of God's Word.

Above and beyond all, our moms recommend praying for wisdom when the questions come but waiting to explain life's great mysteries until your child is old enough to start asking about them. In Adrienne's words, "For goodness' sake, don't look for trouble. These things are hard enough for *us* to understand!"

When Mommy and Daddy Blow It

There are probably few people who wouldn't like to be thought of as perfect—or at least almost perfect. And it's tempting to allow our children to put us on pedestals and look at us as gods instead of just grown-up people who were once little like themselves and who make a mistake every now and then. The problem is, your child is bound to discover the truth sooner or later, and our moms insist that letting her in on the secret from the beginning can prevent emotional scars for everyone involved.

"It's important for your kids to see how you handle it when you make mistakes," says Adrienne. "So many people grow up thinking a Christian has to be a perfect person. If your child grows up thinking you're a Christian and you're perfect, when *he* makes a mistake he's liable to feel as if it's not worth it to try anymore. If he sees that you make mistakes along the way and sees how you handle it with God, he learns that it's okay to make mistakes. God forgives you."

Another of our moms shares, "I can't remember my parents ever admitting to me that they had made a mistake. I grew up thinking they were perfect. One of the biggest problems I had when I was growing up was condemning myself because I couldn't be like Mom and Dad; yet somehow I never saw the areas in their lives where they were inconsistent. I've often thought that my kids will never grow up with the mistaken idea that their mother is perfect. I've let them know time and time again that there are ways I've failed, and yet that God still loves me and is willing to take my heart and wash it clean. My children are so open now to saying at night when they pray, 'Lord, I blew it.' It's a protection against the feeling of condemnation that comes when a child does wrong and thinks, 'Mom never makes a mistake. I must not be a Christian.'"

"Let them hear you pray, 'Lord, help me to be a good mother. Give me wisdom,'" says Kristy. "I pray that in front of my children every day." As your child sees you leaning on Jesus, she learns that He is strong enough to hold her up as well.

It's also important to ask your child to forgive you when the situation calls for it. "If you've done something that has hurt your child," says Wanda, "even if it was unintentional, you need to ask her forgiveness." Not only does seeking your child's forgiveness heal your relationship and prevent resentment from creeping in, it also teaches her that it's okay to apologize and that it's important to be sensitive to the feelings of others.

Now that we've covered transgressions against God and against your child, what about disagreements between Mommy and Daddy? Our moms feel it's best not to inflict your more serious arguments on your child. "But if she sees the disagreement," says Cheryl, "She should see the forgiveness and reconciliation too. All of that is a part of her spiritual training." Several moms also point out that a child who has witnessed a parental argument should be reassured that although Mommy and Daddy disagree sometimes, they love each other very much. If there are serious marital problems, a child will need frequent calm reassurance that the trouble is not her fault.

Helen, whose children are now grown and serving the Lord, feels it's not a bad thing for children to witness minor parental differences of opinion as long as you and your husband can disagree agreeably and not let it get out of hand: "It's good for them to know that their parents have separate ideas about some things. That gives the child an opening to say eventually, 'I'm an individual too, and I can have my own thoughts.'"

The Great Santa Claus Debate

Whether or not you allow your child to believe in Santa Claus and other fairy tales is a very personal decision, and even our moms weren't able to come to an agreement about it. Most of them were against telling a child point-blank that Santa is real, because, after all, he's not. But, aside from that point, we had a wide range of opinions.

Some of our moms' children chose to believe that Santa was real even without the encouragement of their mommies and daddies, and their parents made no effort to burst the bubble until the children were old enough to ask. "When they ask, though," says Adrienne, "tell them." Other moms were adamantly opposed to letting their children believe something that wasn't true and taught them to smile indulgently when misguided store clerks and relatives asked what they wanted Santa to bring them for Christmas.

Cheryl is one of the moms who decided to let Santa stay in the picture as a fun pretend character while keeping the focus on Jesus' birthday. "Since he was two or two and a half," she says, "Jason has had no problem understanding that Santa is a fun pretend person just like a cartoon or something you see on TV. To him, Santa is just like a Smurf or a big character at Disney World."

Megan was two and a half when she began receiving the Santa messages that were coming at her from all sides. Try as I did to explain that the man in the red suit was just somebody's nice grandpa, she couldn't understand. She would smile brightly and answer, "He's coming to my house!"

After some frustration, I finally realized that fantasy and reality were still one big, happy jumble to my little girl. For Megan, Donald Duck and Mickey Mouse were real, Big Bird and Kermit were real, and so was Santa. I decided simply to smile when she talked about Santa, to explain things as she was able to comprehend them, and to keep the focus on Jesus' birthday as much as possible. (Letting her play with a molded plastic nativity set was a big help in that area.)

Even the moms who chose not to allow their children to believe in Santa Claus rejected the idea that a child whose fantasies about Santa are dashed will question whether Jesus is real. Since the Santa conflict is a fairly recent development, most of our moms believed in him when they were little. Not one can remember being confused as to whether Jesus was real because Santa was not. However, I have heard of a few cases where that did happen, and in my opinion it's not worth the risk.

Terri says, "The Christian influence in my family was so strong that the Santa issue didn't bother me. My own little boy *knows* that Jesus is real—we live with Jesus every day. We don't live with Santa Claus. I know that deep down inside Zachary knows Santa isn't real, but he's really into pretending right now." Cheryl agrees: "If Jesus is part of our everyday experience and we're talking to Him and teaching our children about Him every day, they have no trouble distinguishing between Him and Santa Claus. Now, with families who go to church only on Christmas and Easter and don't recognize Jesus the other 363 days of the year, that could be a problem."

Something that hasn't yet been mentioned is the danger you run of being lynched when your little one tells a neighbor child that Santa isn't real. Wanda made Santa's pretend status an especially fun family secret that was never to be breathed outside the home walls. "I explained to Michelle that it might ruin Christmas for the other children if we told them," she says. Some of our other moms initiated fun family traditions focusing on Christ's birth that their children could tell their friends about. We'll talk about them and other holiday ideas in Chapter 11.

Marilee makes the point that a parent who lets her child believe that Santa brings the presents is allowing him to shower love and gratitude that rightfully belongs to Mommy and Daddy on a pretend person. Dana adds, "When grownups ask my kids, 'What did Santa bring you?' they say, 'Santa didn't bring me anything. My mom and dad gave me presents because they love me very much.'

"The same thing goes with other myths, like the Tooth Fairy—these occasions can be used as tools to build a relationship with our children. When Brian or Bridget lost a tooth, the money I put under their pillows was always accompanied by a special little note just for them from me. Those notes meant more to them than the Tooth Fairy possibly could have. These are great opportunities! We need to be using them as tools to cement the love between us and our children."

Visiting Jesus' House

While your child is an infant, our moms agree that church is primarily for you, not the baby. They're divided on the issue of using the church nursery, though. As a first-time mother, I hesitated to leave Megan in the nursery. I was sure she would be traumatized by my departure, and I just knew that the other babies would beat her up. Also, Megan ended up with a cold several times after being left in the nursery with all those runny-nosed kids.

By the time she was a year old, I was desperate enough to risk an occasional cold. Worship services had become ordeals, with Jon and me juggling Megan between us, alternately stuffing Cheerios into her mouth and half drowning her with bottles of water. She seldom cried, but, being a friendly child, she had the habit of peeking over the back of the pew and saying "Hi!" and "Oooo, whazzat?" making it hard for the people behind us to pay attention to the sermon. Jon always ended up taking her out of church before the service was half over. "It comes to the point where you have to say, 'What am I going to church for?'" says Dana. "Sometimes you have to put your child into the nursery so that you can get some spiritual food from the sermon to take home with you."

Of course, in some churches whether or not to use the nursery isn't an issue, simply because there isn't a nurs-

ery. Several of our moms found themselves in that situation, and they learned to make the best of it. Taking
along an infant seat kept them from having to juggle the
baby back and forth quite so much; and quiet toys,
Cheerios, and a bottle went a long way toward leaving
them free to hear what was going on. Also, they found
that their child's personality was a big factor in deter-
mining whether or not he did well in worship services.
Cheryl says, "Jason would work up to a cry, so I could
see it coming and slip out. Brian didn't. It was just 'Yaaa!'
and there he was for the whole congregation to hear. Our
church had a nursery, and as soon as he was a couple of
months old that's where he went."

Trading off take-out duty with your husband or a
kindhearted friend or relative can help you get more out
of the service. Or, you can try the solution Marilee and
her husband Jeff found: During David's first few months,
they traded off going to services alone—one week Marilee
went to Sunday morning service while Jeff stayed home
with the baby, then she stayed home while Jeff went to
the Sunday evening and Wednesday night services. The
next week they switched. True, this isn't a good long-
term solution, but it can help you stay spiritually fed
while waiting for your baby to grow old enough to go
into the nursery.

Even after your child reaches the toddler stage, the
spiritual training he receives at church isn't going to affect
him a fraction as much as the training, negative or positive, he receives at home. His in-church time will be
three or four hours a week at most—and that's counting
Sunday morning, Sunday night, and Wednesday night.
You've got him the rest of the time. As Lois says, "If
you neglect the training at home, I don't care where you

take 'em—they're not going to get it. They'll think, 'Well, that's good enough for the preacher, but it's not good enough for Mommy and Daddy.'"

Church is important, though, and it needs to be seen in its proper role as a special place where we meet with other people to worship the God we live with every day at home. To that end, several moms chose to take their toddlers into the service with them at times rather than always leaving them to play in the nursery. "There were times when I took my kids into services because I wanted them there," says Virginia. "I made sure they didn't distract other people; I carried them out if they got rowdy and I taught them how to behave in church. They learned to sit still and be quiet, and they sensed the Spirit of the Lord even though they didn't understand a lot of what was going on."

"Children need to know why Mommy and Daddy go to worship services," says Cheryl. "We worship God at home, and we love Jesus all the time, but when we go to church we're worshiping with other people at God's house. I have to tell Jason why he can't wear his jeans on Sunday—and it's not because I care what other people think. It's because church is Jesus' house, and Jesus is the King. When you go to visit a king, you want to get all dressed up and be on your best behavior, so we don't goof around like we do when we're playing outside. It's important to make church special to children rather than just taking them along for the ride."

Our moms feel a child should be allowed her little occupiers—dolls, Bible story coloring books, and other quiet toys—until she reaches kindergarten or her first grade year at least. "By then, children are in a more regimented schedule at school," says Dana. "That carries over to help them sit still and listen in church. Bryan is eight now, and he doesn't write in church anymore. With him it was a gradual thing, a transition from childish things to, 'I don't do that anymore. I'm grown-up now.'"

Taming the One-Eyed Monster

The American public in general and Christians in particular have a love-hate relationship with the one-eyed monster in the family room. We know much of what we watch is bad for us, but we find it nearly impossible to give up the effortless leisure of lying there staring at the screen for the sake of something more wholesome, such as a game or a good book. The problem is, this kind of junk food is doing something worse than killing our bodies; it's killing our morals. And it's addictive.

"TV is the hottest issue in our family right now," says Carol. "Last summer our set was hit by lightning and we didn't get it fixed. We had an old-fashioned summer— we played games, we read. It was wonderful. But when football season came my husband got another TV, and now we have one in the bedroom and one in the family room. I've had to learn to turn the TV off, no matter what, when there's something on we don't want our children to see. It's hard—we have temper tantrums sometimes, because the kids get addicted to it. The more TV they get, the more they want. This summer we may have to put it into the closet."

As they monitored the available children's programming, our moms were horrified to realize that Saturday morning cartoons are often very little more than a combination of advertisements, violence, and occultism. Even the heroes of some cartoons are witches and wizards. It's especially difficult for a Christian mom to teach her children that these things are wrong when TV portrays them as good and all their little friends are copying them.

Lois recommends, though, that if you decide to make certain shows off-limits to your child you make sure he understands why. "Don't make arbitrary rules," she says. "If he's at a friend's house and a forbidden show comes on, he needs to be able to say, 'Uh-oh, that's about witchcraft. I'm not supposed to watch it.' He may not like the rule, but at least he'll know why it's there."

The consensus among our moms is that the least painful way to keep your child away from programs you don't want him to watch is simply never to introduce them to him in the first place. Terri says, "Zachary doesn't know about any of the popular TV shows, with maybe a couple of exceptions, and I want to keep it that way. Since we've never had these shows on in the first place, he just doesn't realize he's missing anything. He's allowed to watch TV with his friends at their houses, but he doesn't seem to miss it at home."

Our moms agree that kids need to be able to curl up occasionally and do nothing, just as adults do. And there really is a fair amount of good, wholesome children's programming available, especially on the cable networks—some of it even Christian—but it's just another variation of Murphy's Law that whenever you or your child want to sit down and unwind in front of the TV set the airwaves are bound to be cluttered with junk. For the families who could afford them, videotape recorders offered a way out. Terri says, "I record the shows I want Zachary to see. He's at the age where he wants to do things over and over, and he's even started reading a little bit from watching 'Sesame Street' again and again."

Lois injects this point: "It's important to have a balanced life. TV can be an easy babysitter, and to allow a child to sit there for six to eight hours a day, even when all the shows are good shows, teaches him no balance at all. He doesn't learn to appreciate reading, he doesn't go out to play, and he doesn't learn how to occupy himself. The TV monopolizes all his time." For a young child, an hour a day of TV watching is probably more than enough.

It makes sense that if you limit your child's television viewing, the time that would have been taken by the TV set has to be filled with something else. Many of our moms have a strong desire to instill a love of reading in their children, but they've found it takes self-discipline to sit down and read with them when there is housework that needs doing. "You have to make yourself do it," says Carol. "You have to take the time. The dishes won't go anywhere." *The Read-Aloud Handbook* by Jim Trelease (Penguin) is a rich source of book ideas for children of all ages. (For other non-television ways to occupy toddlers, see Chapter 6.)

The Chef Eats First

A new mom can't expect to be the best spiritual trainer since Charles Wesley's mother if she's starving spiritually herself. Susanna Wesley had the right idea. She knew that in order to give her children a good spiritual foundation she had to spend time alone with God, and if *she* could find the time, back in the days before automatic appliances, so can we.

Society is so fast-paced today that it's easy to feel guilty just for sitting down when there is work to be done. But, come to think of it, things haven't really changed that much in the past couple of thousand years. Jesus' friend Martha was the type who had to make sure the house was in order and dinner ready to be served before she would sit down with the Lord, with the result that she probably never did sit down and really listen to Him. Her mind was most likely running ahead to the meal's next course, worrying about whether the Lord would like it or whether the new servant girl would trip and spill it on His lap. Mary's room may have been a bit messy and her meals a bit late, but I'm willing to bet she never went a day without her personal devotions.

"You just have to set your priorities and do it," says Kathy. "You can't let all these other things get in the way." Carol, like most of us, learned this lesson the hard way: "I wasn't fellowshiping with the Father, and I was getting off track until a dear friend came to me and said, 'Carol, you've lost your joy.' The idea that you don't have time is an attack of the enemy. If you leave that time out, Satan gets in."

"And boy, does your family feel it!" adds Lois. "When you're going through a stressful time or a difficult experience, you need even more time alone with God. I know that by experience. Habakkuk says that the joy of the Lord is our strength. I was walking by a Christian bookstore the other day and saw a plaque with the Scripture. 'In Thy presence is fullness of joy.' I thought, 'Aha! so *that's* where you get the joy of the Lord.' It's not a ha-ha happy feeling, but a deep-seated, peaceful joy that comes only from being in His presence."

It's a paradox that those difficult times when we need God most are usually the times when we're least inclined to seek Him, but our moms agree that maintaining our relationship with the Lord is vital to both our own spiritual health and that of our children. As Kathy says, "You can't live the life in front of them unless you have that special time yourself."

While your baby is small, your best bet for uninterrupted devotional time is probably during his naps or while he's nursing. "But as he grows older," says Lois, "It might be wiser to make sure you don't do it while he's napping. He's got to learn that time alone with God is important. Just say, 'I'm going to have my private time with Jesus. You go into your room and have your private time, too.'" She also points out that having your quiet time while your toddler is awake teaches him to respect your privacy.

Lois and Kathy are firm believers that when a child sees his mother go to the Lord with her problems, he learns that he can go to Him with his own. Lois went through a rough family time when her children were small, and she says, "I sometimes just sat my children on my lap while I was praying, because they got scared if they saw me cry. I told them, 'Come sit with me, but you can't talk to me because I'm talking to Jesus.'" Joyce adds, 'It's important to reassure your children and say, It's okay—Mommy's talking to Jesus, and Jesus is going to help her feel better.'"

"Mommy, Why Won't Daddy Go to Church?"

It's sad but true in many families that while one spouse is trying to train the children the other is undoing the lessons, passively at least. But as hard as it is, our moms caution against making your child's spiritual training a marital battleground. "Be as submissive to your husband as you can," says Cheryl, "and ask the Lord to open doors during the time when you're alone with your child."

A mother who is home all day can still read her child Bible stories, pray with him, and sing little songs. A mother with a full-time job has more difficulty. A Christian day-care center or babysitter can help, and few spouses are sufficiently anti-Christian to keep their wives and children from attending church. (Chapter 10 shares more ways a working mother can make the most of her time with her child.)

"Children understand more than we give them credit for," says one of our moms, whose husband played the Christian role for a while but eventually left her for another woman. "My kids love their daddy, but they know he needs Jesus in his heart. He may not support prayer at bedtime or meals when they're with him, but they know about the things of God because I've taught them."

According to Adrienne, the bottom line in one-parent spiritual training is this: "You do the best you can, whenever you can, and trust God to take care of your child." And, after all, that's all any Christian parent or set of parents can do. A child will encounter countless anti-Christian influences as he grows, and his ultimate spiritual welfare is between him and God. "God doesn't say, 'Okay, here's your child. You have to make him love Me,'" says Adrienne. "That child has a choice, just as you do. You have to teach him that he has that choice, and that your choice for God has been good for you, and that you know it will be good for him too. You can't say, 'You must be a Christian.' Pray that he will choose to love God, but don't force it down his throat. Forcing him is the best way to turn him off."

Making the Decision

Stella encouraged Shauna to accept Jesus as her Savior when she began asking questions about the lessons she was learning in Sunday school. She says, "I know she'll come to have a deeper realization of what sin is and why she needs the Lord as she grows older, but that doesn't mean these early decisions aren't valid and important." Chris agrees. She bought Ashley a Christian storybook in which the child protagonist learned the gospel story and asked Jesus to come into her heart. "When we finished reading, I asked her. 'Would you like for Jesus to come into your heart too?' She said yes, and we prayed together right then."

It's important to realize that your job as spiritual trainer is not finished when your child makes a decision for Jesus; it has only begun. A solid Christian walk is built one brick at a time, day by day, year after year, as you and your child live, love, pray, laugh, read, worship, and learn together.

"I used to worry about how we could be sure we were doing the right things with our girls," says Connie. "How could we make sure they would turn out right? I finally decided to do the very best I could and leave the rest to God."

8

Who's in Charge Here, Anyway?

Have you ever noticed how dogmatic people are about the way other people's children should be raised—especially when they have none of their own? Few are so virtuous that they can see a toddler running amok in a department store without forgetting all about Jesus' guidelines for throwing stones and saying in their hearts, "If that were *my* kid . . ." Chances are you've done it yourself. I know I have.

Our pomposity comes home to roost, though, because even rarer than an understanding bystander is the toddler, however well-disciplined, who has never embarrassed the daylights out of his mother—or at least tried to. And if you were to take the aforementioned toddler's harried mom aside, she wouldn't tell you that her aim in life is to produce offspring with no self-control or regard for the rights and property of others. She'd say without hesitation that she wants her child to be well-disciplined. She has one of two problems, though: Either 1) she doesn't know how to go about disciplining him, or 2) she knows how, but isn't doing it. In this chapter, it is our moms' intention to deprive you of Excuse # 1.

An Up-Front Word About Spanking

Spanking is a controversial method of discipline that is often misunderstood and just as often misused. For that reason, we need to take a moment right away to clarify our stance on the subject.

The mothers in this chapter were chosen specifically because their children are thriving and well-adjusted, yet every one of these mothers advocates the judicious use of spanking, when appropriate, as a disciplinary tool. The reason is not because we enjoy hitting our children, or even because we believe that spanking is always the best way to discipline a child. We recognize that there are some children, particularly hyperactive children, adopted children who have previously been abused, and other children with special needs, for whom spanking may not be a good idea. We also recognize that as a child grows older there are other disciplinary methods that work as well or better depending on the situation. We'll elaborate on that subject later in this chapter.

The reason we feel so strongly about spanking is that it is one of only three disciplinary measures that work with older babies and young toddlers, the other two being distraction—offering an alternative for the forbidden object—and physical removal from the tempting situation.

Mommy's "No" carries no clout unless it is followed by one of the above three measures when the transgression is repeated, which it most likely will be.

When you take away a mother's right to deliver a swat on the hand or the fanny, you sentence her to endless frustration as she turns her persistent ten month old away from the stereo for the fortieth time and chases him frantically around Grandma's house offering alternatives for the porcelain figurines. You also increase the likelihood that she will finally vent that frustration on her child in the form of verbal or physical abuse.

In recent years, some psychologists have made the ridiculous claim that a parent who spanks her child is teaching him to use violence to solve his problems. Perhaps this is true with the parent who lashes out in anger at her child, but it is purely false when the spanking is done thoughtfully and lovingly, with the child's best interest at heart.

When it becomes necessary to spank your child, as our moms believe it almost definitely will, it's vital that you do it right. Because of this, a fair amount of space in this chapter is devoted not only to the physical mechanics of spanking and other disciplinary methods, but to the parental attitude involved as well.

An interesting sideline: I noticed that the mothers in this chapter have a tendency to be assertive, at least where their children are concerned. It's not that they're domineering; they just know what kind of behavior they want from their children and how to go about getting it. They respect their children and expect their children to respect them in return—and they're not mealy-mouthed about enforcing established rules.

They also tend to have a strong sense of fair play and

to be very affectionate, traits which probably help prevent them from becoming authoritarian.

And now, on with the chapter.

Cardinal Rules

Discipline of a small child is fairly simple, but its effects, positive or negative, snowball in a way that makes your child and the people around him feel its repercussions all his life. Do it well, and you establish in him a loving respect for your parental authority that will make it easier to discipline him in later years. Do it poorly or don't do it at all, and you set up a host of people for heartache: your child, his future teachers, employers, friends, spouse—and yourself most of all.

Our moms believe there are certain unshakable tenets in the great art of childrearing that can be followed from the time you give your baby his first "No!" until the day he goes off to college, although of course other factors will come into play as he grows older. (For example, spanking a teenager is a definite no-no.) These cardinal rules are:

1) Hug your child often. "Be sure to administer *at least* as many hugs as you do spankings," says Dana. Our moms believe it's important to ingrain in your child, right from the start, the knowledge that although you may not love certain types of behavior you always love *him*—a variation on God's policy of hating the sin, not the sinner. Even before he begins to walk, make a habit of taking your baby in your arms and kissing him after you discipline him, saying, "Mommy loves you very much, but when she says no, she means no."

2) Plot strategy. Our moms strongly recommend that

as the time to start disciplining draws near, you and your husband hold a strategy meeting to decide what the no-no's in your house will be. Talking about it beforehand will keep your husband from coming home in the evening and disciplining your baby for touching something you had certified as okay, or from letting her play with something you had made firmly off-limits. "Come to an understanding with your husband about acceptable and unacceptable behavior," says Patty W. "Do it privately, and never argue about it in front of your child."

Chris has gotten into the habit of turning Ashley's discipline over to David when he comes home from work. She says, "When he's there, I don't reprimand her at all unless she's doing something dangerous. She's learned now that when Daddy is home, he's the authority. I'm in charge while he's gone." Now, that doesn't mean Chris saves up Ashley's transgressions throughout the day and dumps them on David when he walks in the door. She handles discipline problems as they arise, but when Daddy comes home, it's his turn. This practice keeps her from becoming the heavy in Ashley's eyes.

It's vital that a child not see one parent as the disciplinarian and the other as "safe." Glenda says: "I may not quit disciplining entirely when Joe comes home, but my kids know that if their dad is home, he's the authority. What he says goes."

3) Don't discipline for behavior you've never made clearly off-limits. Believe it or not, children aren't born knowing not to stick their fingers into electrical sockets, hit their playmates, climb up onto the kitchen counter via the dining room chairs, or run through the pile of leaves Daddy just spent two hours raking. Karin says, "One day Matthew climbed up onto our boat, and Wayne just took him down and spanked him. Matthew was heart-broken. He kept crying and asking, 'Why?' That was when I realized children need to understand the rules before they're spanked for breaking them. We should have taken him down and warned him, 'Don't climb up on the boat, because you could fall down and hurt your-self.'"

It's important also to make sure your instructions or warnings have been heard and understood. "Tell your child clearly what you expect," says Patty W., "and then watch until it's carried through."

With a baby who is just entering the wonderful world of discipline it's a good practice to go over to her, touch the object, look her in the eyes, give her a firm "No!" and move her away—and no smiles, please. You know she's gotten the message if she starts to touch a forbidden object, then glances over to see if you're watching.

It's sometimes hard to know whether your child has understood you or not, but Glenda says, "Even at a year old, you can explain, 'When Mommy says "Come here," you must come here.' Just get right in front of her, lock eyes with her, and explain it so that she's listening in-tently to what you're saying. Then, in the future, if you're sure you called loud enough to hear, immediately go and get her. She has to know you mean business." Chris adds, "When you get a child to look into your eyes, you break her concentration. And the older they get, the easier it is to tell when they're deliberately tuning you out."

4) Encourage good behavior. This is much more effective than simply punishing bad behavior, and tangible re-wards usually aren't necessary. A smile and a sincere thank-you or "Very good!" when your child obeys, together with a hug, can work wonders.

5) Don't phrase as a request what you mean as a command. As a parent, you have every right to give your child reasonable commands and expect them to be obeyed. God gave you that authority in the Bible so you could teach your little one how to get along in the world. Denying a parental command is disobedience, but the freedom to deny a request is one that should be allowed the youngest of human beings. The ability to say no to nonessentials, such as, "Would you like some more bananas?" or, "Would you like to kiss Uncle Fred?" encourages independent thought without encouraging rebellion. Teach your child the difference right away.

6) Don't cry wolf. Our moms believe that the mother who says no, gives a command, or threatens to discipline without being prepared to follow through is asking for trouble. "Don't say no unless you mean it," says Connie, "and whatever you say you'll do, keep your word." Dana says, "Lots of no's or wordy explanations or threats to discipline will only confuse your baby and teach him that you're stalling and he can get away with his disobedience a little longer. Follow through after one warning, and he'll learn that you will not allow his disobedience." Karen H. adds, "Always follow through with your promises—whether for discipline reasons or for fun things. Your child will learn quickly whether you keep your word or not." Teaching your baby to heed your "no" the first time you say it does more than save you from the exasperation of having a child who doesn't listen. It may keep him from pulling the iron down on his head or running out into a busy street someday.

7) Discipline in love, not anger. "When it becomes necessary to spank your child," says Stella, "you have to keep in mind why you're spanking. A child should be spanked for disobedience, not because Mommy's upset and angry at what he did." Try to keep in mind, when your child pulls a whole row of books out of the bookcase, or when he hits the off switch on the TV two seconds after you tell him "No!", or when he runs away when you tell him to come, that he's not doing it to insult you. He's testing his limits to see how far they stretch, and it's up to you to calmly but firmly give him the answer.

Stella says, "Your attitude has to be, 'I still love you, but you're going to be spanked because you disobeyed and brought this upon yourself.' You'll find that when you spank with that attitude you hate to do it, because you're not angry or upset and it's hard to spank when you're not angry and upset. But you know you're doing it for your child's good, out of love, and he feels that love."

Remember, too, that "discipline" and "spanking" are not necessarily synonymous, and that this rule applies to other methods of discipline as well. When your toddler is old enough to be isolated for rambunctiousness or deprived of privileges for shirking his responsibilities, those means should be employed to help him learn appropriate, responsible behavior—not to torture him for irritating you.

An excellent reason for following through with discipline after one warning, aside from the fact that it teaches your child to obey right away, is that it doesn't give you time to become upset and exasperated. The parent who finds herself losing control while spanking, gaining satisfaction from hitting her child, or inflicting physical injuries on her child should seek out a qualified Christian counselor, who will help her bring her emotions under control while still recognizing the importance of discipline. It's better to just put your baby or toddler into his crib and walk away for a few minutes than to risk taking your anger out on him.

8) Let the punishment fit the crime—and the child. "There are no cookie-cutter kids," says Dana. Some of our moms' little ones were so tenderhearted that a firm "No!" was enough to turn them into paragons of obedience. Others required several spankings for the same transgression before realizing Mommy meant what she said, and a few seemed to take spankings as a personal challenge, their little eyes flashing as if to say, "I bet I can last longer than you can!"

We'll cover alternative methods of discipline in the section on older toddlers, since, as we've said, the only disciplinary methods that work with a baby or young toddler are distraction, spanking, and having Mommy physically remove him from the tempting situation. But the basic idea is to make sure you are never guilty of trying to swat a fly with a sledge hammer. That is, don't use a harsher form of punishment than needed, but at the same time make sure the form of discipline you choose is one that will motivate your child to obey. "Every child in a family has a different personality," says Glenda, "and you have to use the measures that work best for him as an individual."

9) Be consistent. This is probably the hardest rule to follow, but our moms believe it's also the most important. One reason it's so hard to be consistent is that there are so many areas of discipline where consistency is vital: the objects and behaviors that are off-limits, your methods for dealing with disobedience, and the hugs, kisses, and talks that follow after.

Good discipline is predictable. Discipline that is dished out arbitrarily is worse than none at all. Your child must always know, beyond a doubt, what the results of his actions will be. Otherwise he'll never learn to avoid misbehaving in order to avoid the consequences. "Set specific boundaries and hold to them," says Patty W. "What's not okay today must remain not okay tomorrow."

"Your consistency in discipline lays the foundation for self-discipline," says Marilee. "Younger children learn to catch themselves before they do something unacceptable because they don't want to be disciplined; in later years they become able to keep from doing unacceptable things, or to make themselves do necessary things, simply because of the sense of right and wrong that has been ingrained in them."

Consistency means following through at Grandma's house and in public, too. Glenda says, "Many times in a new place the child will completely ignore you, thinking, 'Maybe if I keep on going she won't say anything.' Even if he knows something isn't permitted at home, he'll test you in public to see if you follow through." "Every kid has tried that," adds Virginia. As your baby enters toddlerhood it'll probably be easier on you to step into the ladies' room or out to the car or around the corner rather than spanking him before dozens of disapproving eyes. All the same, it's essential that your child not discover that there are places where he's immune to discipline.

10) Don't yell. In view of rule # 7, this rule may seem a bit redundant. It would seem only logical that discipline without anger would be discipline without yelling, but with some moms yelling seems to be the standard way of communicating with their children. The problem is, toddlers learn to deal with maternal yelling the same way most people deal with any other constant, meaningless noise: they tune it out. When you try to discipline your child by turning up the volume on your vocal cords instead of following through, you show him you don't mean what you're saying, no matter how loudly you say it. Cheryl says, "I don't like to yell, because it puts me in the position, in front of my child, of losing both my dignity and the battle."

Besides, yelling does a poor job of conveying love. "Show your love in everything," says Dana. "Even when you say, 'Pick up your toys,' the tone of your voice will convey an emotion to your child. Let your voice say, 'I love you lots!' even when you're having to discipline him. I heard a speaker once who put it like this: 'In everything my mother said to me, her *attitude* said, "I wish I had a hundred little boys just like you!"'"

When I began to discipline Megan, my goal—and I reached it when she was about a year old—was to be able to say, "No, Honey," in a loving, gentle tone, and have her obey me. The reason she obeys me, though, is because I started out by saying it in a no-nonsense tone of voice and following through consistently with the appropriate disciplinary measures. Yes, I had to continually reinforce this lesson as she approached two years old. (And yes, during that phase I blew it and lost my temper more often than I care to admit.)

Off to a Good Start

Our moms believe that the purpose of discipline for an older baby or young toddler is to protect him from his environment (and in some cases, his environment

from him) while at the same time establishing respect for
your authority. And, tender though this age may seem,
they began seeing the light of understanding in their little
ones' eyes during the second half of their first year—
which, interestingly enough, was also the age when their
babies began crawling around and getting into mischief.
A baby that young can't yet understand the *word* "no,"
of course, but he gets the general idea by your facial
expression and the tone of your voice.

"It's good to begin early with enforcing obedience,"
says Dana. "When he starts touching things he's not
supposed to touch, make him look you in the eye and
give him a firm "No!" If he goes right back to it, proceed
to physically discipline him by turning him away or giving him a swat on the hand. That way he'll learn quickly
to obey."

It isn't always necessary to discipline your baby for
onetime no-no's. If he starts reaching for the pretty break-
ables at a friend's home, get to him quickly and distract
him with a safe alternative. If it works, you're home free.
If not, give him a firm "No!" and follow through if he
disobeys. At home, though, your baby has to be made
to understand in no uncertain terms which permanent
fixtures are off-limits—and if you do it right the first few
times you won't have to be constantly nagging him, erod-
ing the love between you and your child. If turning your
child away from a forbidden object several times is
enough to make him leave it alone, that's great. But if
not, don't be afraid to administer a mild swat to emphasize your point.

Before their babies began to toddle, most of our moms
just smacked their child's hand lightly with their own
when he touched an item that he had been warned was

a no-no or did the same with the back of their baby's leg when he tried to climb over the couch or stand up in the highchair after having been told "No!" Babies' memories are very short. In order for a spanking to be effective it needs to catch your little one in the act if at all possible, since a delay of even a few seconds can make your child wonder why you're spanking him.

Karin, along with most of our other moms, has strong feelings about the need to pick up your baby after a spanking to reassure him of your love. She says, "I've heard people say you shouldn't pick a child up while he's still crying—that you should let him cry it out first— but I disagree." I do too, and I agree with Karin that the child whose mother spanks him and then walks away is not only going to feel that he's been disciplined, but that he's been rejected as well. When Megan reached the age when discipline became necessary I made it a practice always to pick her up and console her after a spanking, saying gently, "Mommy loves you very much, but when she says no, she means no." She rapidly got to the point where the first thing she did after a spanking was hold out her little arms for me to pick her up.

According to Dana, an unaffectionate family background gives you no excuse to be an unaffectionate mommy: "You've got to learn to be one, that's all," she says. Several of our moms came from undemonstrative families and have felt a lifelong yearning for the physical closeness they missed with their parents. One of them says, "It's important to hug your kids, and it's important for your kids to see you and your husband hug. I never saw affection between my mother and my father, and now my husband says I'm a cold person. It's funny—

I'm affectionate with my children because I really want to make up for what I lost with my parents. My husband says I give them more intimacy than I do him."

Getting back to the basics of your baby's first few months of discipline: Don't hesitate to babyproof your home as thoroughly as you can. There will inevitably be a few things left down that you can use to teach him the meaning of the word no—the TV controls, a bookcase, a magazine rack, piles of folded laundry on laundry day. "If something is pretty and is going to catch a baby's eye," says Cheryl, "natural curiosity is going to make him want to touch it. If it's going to break, it should be put away." "A baby needs plenty of room to explore," says Patty W. "Try not to frustrate him."

Our moms like for their children to be curious. "How else can they learn?" asks Donna. Whenever possible, close the doors to all the rooms you don't want your little one to enter and let him roam, keeping a sharp eye on him, of course, because babies can get themselves into predicaments that would never occur to their mothers. Several of our moms even found a way to let their children explore the no-no's by allowing them to sit on Mommy's lap and handle, taste, and touch each item before Mommy put it back up out of reach.

Most of us were guilty, at least a few times, of reacting with a knee-jerk "No!" when our babies touched something they hadn't played with before. "Think about what you're saying," says Marilee, "and only come down on your baby for the things that are important. If it can't hurt him and he can't hurt it, let him play with it. It's a learning experience for him to taste, feel, and touch."

Offer alternatives for no-no's whenever possible. Megan knows that the magazines under the coffee table are forbidden, but she's had plenty of opportunity to explore the fascinating properties of paper because I give her my daily junk mail before I throw it out. Chris does the same thing, and she says, "Even a nine-month-old baby can be made to understand that she can have only the magazines Mommy gives her." Adrienne suggests giving your baby her very own little magazine rack or box filled with outdated catalogs, pamphlets, and colorful flyers. As your baby grows a little older, she can learn that it's okay to crumple and tear junk mail, but not her little storybooks because those are special. Along the same lines, Megan knows she can't play with my piles of folded laundry, but she's welcome to wade through the heap and drag clothes through the family room before I get to it. It gives me an incentive to do my folding quickly!

Even in the very first weeks of your baby's discipline, consistency is vital. A nine month old is usually too young to exhibit much rebellion, but the mom who isn't consistent to discipline for disobedience from the very beginning arms a time bomb that will go off in her face when her baby reaches full-fledged toddlerhood at one and a half or two years old.

Dana objects to the fact that many children mind their fathers better than they do their mothers: "That shows a lack of consistency," she says. True, Daddy is bigger than Mommy and has a deeper voice, and he's not home as much. But several of our moms believe the real reason why children often mind their fathers better is they've learned that Mommy doesn't always follow through, whereas they haven't made that discovery about Daddy. Familiarity unfortunately *does* breed contempt unless your child knows you unerringly mean what you say. "Saying, 'No, don't do that' over and over again is nagging," says Marilee, "and your child will just ignore you after a while because he knows you don't mean it. Mean it when you say it, and take care of it right away. If you do, and you make your child feel the consequences of his disobedience, you won't have to nag all the time."

Learning to Share

According to our moms, you can begin teaching a child to share as soon as he's old enough to crawl around and appropriate other children's toys—which is a good reason to get together regularly with your friends who have babies his age. Your child will be well into toddlerhood before he really understands what sharing is about, but that doesn't mean you can't start ingraining good habits early. "Sharing is a learned skill," says Cheryl, "and children don't learn it just by watching. It's something the parents have to take an active part in teaching. Now, at four years old, Jason understands when I tell him, 'You need to share that toy.' But at nine or twelve or eighteen months is the time to actively teach sharing when they're with other children."

Our moms recommend calm mediation—after all, it's silly to reproach your one year old for not sharing when he's never been taught how—and Cheryl says it's best to actually help your child hand over a toy: "Let's let Brian play with the truck for a while. Thank you! It's good to share our toys. Now, what can we find for you to play with?" Make sure each child has ample time to play with a favorite toy, and give lots of short explanations, all variations on, "You played with this for a while; it's Brian's turn now." Cheryl adds, "Be sure to hug your child when he does share. It should definitely be rewarded, so he can see some benefit from sharing—that it's not just a chore, but that it's a nice thing to do, and you're pleased with him for doing it." And don't be disheartened if your little one sends up wails of protest at first. It's only natural.

Glenda says it's possible to acquaint a first child or an only child with the idea of sharing by teaching her to share with Mommy and Daddy. "Even small children can learn to share their cookies, or whatever," she says, "but do use the word 'share' while you're doing it." When Megan began eating finger foods at around eight months I began teaching her to share her Cheerios, asking, "Will you share with Mommy? Will you give Mommy some?" At first she leaned toward me with a piece of cereal in her little fingers, but jerked back as I was about to take it. Then once, probably by accident, she let go and it dropped into my hand. I said "Thank you!" and popped it into my mouth with a funny noise, and it was clear sailing from there on out. Little did I know I was creating a monster—soon not only did she want to put the Cheerio into my mouth herself, but she wanted me to stick out my tongue so she could make sure it was in there.

Playing On Their Own

Several of our moms taught their older babies and young toddlers to play by themselves for short periods (with emphasis on the word "short"), breaking them of the habit of constantly wanting Mommy's attention. But it wasn't easy. Chris says, "You have to just sit the child down and say, 'Mommy has to work, and you have to play with your toys. Mommy can't hold you right now.' Then give her a hug, and put her down with her toys.

Ashley cried a lot for the first couple of days, but after a while she got the idea and became interested in other things besides Mommy. We finally got to where after breakfast she would get her toys and play by herself, checking up on me from time to time."

A Word of Caution: Small children need a lot of love and attention, so make sure you don't abuse this method to get out of the time you need to spend with your baby. Glenda says, "Your child needs to know how to play by herself when you really have to get something done, but you also must realize when you're overdoing it and need to stop and spend time with her." Virginia believes too much disciplining is done on a selfish basis—what Mommy is really saying is, "Go away, kid, ya bother me." "I see it in so many families I know," she says, "and it tears my heart out. The mother will say, 'I have something I want to do, so you have to get out of the way.'"

Much misbehavior, with children of all ages, is a bid for attention that occurs because the child is left at loose ends, with nothing to occupy her mind or her hands. Dana recommends taking some creative toys to each area of the house where you work to give your child the security of being able to play in the same room with you rather than being stuck in a playpen in the living room while you're working in the bedroom. And as soon as she's old enough, let her "help" with whatever you're doing.

Toddling Along

Once your child passes the baby stage, discipline becomes more than just a choice between spanking him and changing his geographical location, since toddlers are ca-

pable of doing much more than just touching something
Mommy said no about. They can also run through the
house or be otherwise undesirably rowdy; they can take
toys away from other children; they can be openly de-
fiant; they can neglect to do assigned tasks—the list goes
on and on, and it grows as time goes by. But don't panic—
they can also hug and kiss and say "I love you, Mommy,"
and the intellectual, emotional, and spiritual growth that
takes place during toddlerhood is nothing short of amazing.

Your toddler's personality plays a big part in the
method of discipline you choose, as does the nature of
his transgression. Don't fall into the rut of spanking every
time your child does something you don't like. There are
times when other methods are more effective, and we'll
discuss them at the end of this section.

Our moms believe a toddler deserves an explanation
when an object or a behavior is made off-limits. Karin
says, "My little girl, Meagin, is not quite a year old, and
I already explain things to her. If you just say, 'Don't
touch the stove,' a toddler is going to reach over and
touch it to try to figure out why it's forbidden." Even a
young toddler can usually understand a simple explanation, although she may need to hear it several times.

Patty recommends dramatizing your explanations with
lots of emphasis: "I told Jennifer, 'Don't touch the stove,
because it's *hot* and it will hurt *very much*.'" You can even
put your hand next to the stove, then jerk it back and
say "Hot!", or teach your baby the meaning of hot by
blowing warm air from the blow dryer on her hand, or
letting her touch a warm jar of baby food. But *never* hold
your baby next to a hot burner; if she panics at the

realization of what "hot" is, she could slip and land on it.

Explanations are just as important after your child has committed an offense as they are before. He needs to know that he's being spanked, or made to sit still, or whatever, because of something he did and not because he pushed Mommy past her limit. Just be sure to keep your explanations short and to the point to avoid confusing him. "I always explain before I discipline," says Cheryl, "because my boys have to know what they've done wrong."

Karin says Matthew clearly understood her explanations when he was about eighteen months old. "That may seem awfully young," she says, "but I think children understand more than we give them credit for." She adds that giving a reason for saying no, rather than just dictating to him, has actually made Matthew act more responsibly: "It makes him feel good that we trust him with the information."

When it came time to start actual spanking, as opposed to just swatting their baby's hand when he touched a no-no, the majority of our moms warned the child about spanking the first time they caught him in a transgression, then spanked the second time around. And most moms opted to use a paddle. They gave several reasons, not the least of which is that Mommy's hand didn't always produce the desired effect on her toddler's sturdy behind. Cheryl found herself with that problem when Jason was three, and it was Jason himself who offered the solution: "He told me one day, 'You need a paddle.'—Evidently they had one in the nursery he attended. So we went to the store and he showed me what to buy. I'm sure he thought his brother was going to get it more often than he was!"

The most popular paddle among our moms is a light, flat paddleball type, although several use the flat end of a lightweight wooden spoon. They recommend the buttocks or the back of the leg as your primary target, since both locations have plenty of natural padding and no protruding bones. Remember, a spanking is just to remind your child who's in charge. It's supposed to sting, but it should never injure your child or leave welts or bruises. Try out your technique a few times on the back of your own leg to make sure you're not too heavy-handed before using it on your toddler, and have your husband do the same. (On *his* leg, not yours. There are limits to motherly sacrifice.)

Many of our moms believe that a paddle offers more advantages than simply being more effective than a hand. "The nice thing about a paddle," says Cheryl, "is that you have to actually go and get it—you don't just haul off and smack the child when you've reached the point of anger. And now that Jason's four, sometimes I'll tell him to go and get the paddle. That gives me a minute to cool down, and gives him a little time to contemplate his sins."

Karin agrees: "I try to always do my disciplining in a set way so that Matthew will always know how he's going to be disciplined. He doesn't have to worry whether he's going to be slapped across the face. He knows he's been warned, and it's time to be spanked with the paddle."

At the beginning of this section we mentioned some of the ways toddlers get themselves into trouble. We'll now go down a list of behaviors our moms ran into and show ways they handled them:

■ *Budding Independence.* This is not the same thing as rebellion, but it can look suspiciously like it at times.

My darling daughter's first complete sentence, at age 18 months, was, "Megan do it!" Suddenly she wanted to do everything herself, from putting on her shoes and climbing into her car seat to not wanting to hold my hand while we walked through crowded stores.

It was comforting to talk with other mothers involved in this project and learn that their experiences as their children approached age two had been almost identical to mine. As I did further research I found that our children's you-say-yes-I-say-no behavior was a well-documented toddler phase called negativism. This, I discovered, was where the infamous "Terrible Twos" got their name.

After a few major clashes, I sat down and analyzed the situation. I realized upon reflection that Megan wasn't so much rebelling against my authority as she was simply trying to become more independent. I decided to allow her to do everything for herself that she was capable of, as long as no danger was involved. I even allowed her occasionally to try things she wasn't capable of, such as tying her shoes, to help her learn her limitations.

I stood behind her to make sure she didn't fall while she climbed into her car seat, and I found that it worked well to offer her alternatives in potentially dangerous situations, such as the aforementioned crowded store: "Megan, you may ride in the cart if you like. Otherwise, either Mommy must hold you or you must hold Mommy's hand. Which do you want to do?"

I asked her to "be a big girl" and help me with small fetch-and-carry tasks, and encouraged her sincerely when she did. She was so eager to grow up that she willingly took on all the "big girl" tasks I would give her. She often surprised me with the number of things she was capable of, and our relationship improved dramatically. Megan's responsibilities have become more involved as she has grown older, but she still takes great enjoyment from her status as a productive member of the family.

For some reason, we mothers tend to think that the more we do for our family the better we are at our job, and we feel guilty when we begin to cut the apron strings. But the general attitude among our moms is that you do your child a big favor when you teach him to take on responsibility as soon as he is able.

I heard songwriter and author Gloria Gaither say once, speaking to a group of women, that a mother's primary goal should be to work herself out of a job. That's hard to accept, because it means gradually making yourself physically, although not emotionally, dispensable to your child. But it's the only way to raise capable, responsible, emotionally healthy children.

■ *Open Defiance.* Here is another nearly universal toddler phenomenon, and a natural result of the push for independence. Even so, it's hard to take. Probably the most crushing thing a toddler can do to his loving mother is answer her instructions with a rebellious "No!" And probably the most difficult thing for the toddler's mother to do is deal with her child's rebellion in love, without giving up on the command—which would give the toddler a sense of power and guarantee a repeat performance—or losing her temper and becoming authoritarian.

Remember, your child isn't really attacking you personally when he first tries this—although he soon will be if you show him that it pays off. He's testing his limits, and whether or not he becomes chronically rebellious depends on how you handle these first few experiments. "When my children said no to me," says Glenda, "I asked, 'What did you say?' If they repeated it, I explained to them, 'You don't tell Mother no,' and spanked them for it after that. If you let that sort of thing go, even at that very young age, your child will lose respect for you and your authority because he knows you'll just take whatever he dishes out." Dana adds, "It's strange how children have a certain age where you can start to see the rebellion. My sister used to not believe in original sin—the idea that we're born with sinful natures because of Adam's fall. Then she had kids of her own!"

At four years old, Donna's little girl came out with an even more disturbing statement than "No": "I hate you!" But hard as it was, Donna kept her cool. She knew that April was feeling threatened because her baby brother had just arrived, and she responded to April's anger with, "But I sure do love *you*."

Cheryl says, "At ages two, three, and four, my boys began to sometimes equate discipline with levels of affection. They'd say,'I like Daddy better than you, because he didn't spank me today.' Don't let that discourage you." Children begin early to test the effectiveness of words as weapons, and if you want to stop this type of behavior before it has a chance to grow it's vital not to let on even if something your child says does hurt. "But never let them say that and get away with it," says Glenda. Such times are good opportunities to deliver the well-known lecture, "Mommy disciplines you because she loves you and wants you to learn to behave." And you might want to point out that Daddy has a habit of disciplining too.

A word about tantrums: Many of our moms never had to deal with them, but whether your child tries them or not will most likely have more to do with his personality than with your child-rearing methods. But just because your child tries them probably doesn't mean you have to live with them. As with other unacceptable behavior, the way you deal with tantrums will usually determine whether or not they continue. It's important to note, however, that our advice on dealing with tantrums doesn't necessarily apply to children with special emotional or mental needs. For one of these children, consult your pediatrician or a child psychologist.

Our moms whose children tried them found that not all tantrums are alike, and thus they can't all be dealt with in the same way. My daughter Megan was blessed to inherit a strong personality from both sides of the family, and she tried her hand at two different kinds of tantrums before discovering that they didn't work. The first kind, a minor fit involving an exasperated yell and maybe a kick or two when her purposes were thwarted by Mommy, could usually be stopped by my telling her calmly, "No. If you throw a fit, Mommy will spank," and then following through if she disobeyed. But there were times when, either because she had become over-tired or for some other reason, she completely lost control of herself, and at those times spanking simply made the matter worse. I, along with many of our other mothers, found that a full-fledged tantrum is best left alone—in fact, Megan's tantrums halted abruptly when I began to put her into her bedroom and close the door, with me on the outside, as soon as one started.

None of our moms had to deal with self-destructive behavior during tantrums, but if your child is inclined to use head-banging or other such ways of venting his frustration check with a qualified family counselor for ways to deal with the behavior without allowing your child to injure himself. Our moms feel that *under no circumstances* should you give in to your child when he or she throws a tantrum—unless of course you like tantrums and want them to continue.

As with any other kind of discipline, spanking for rebellion and defiance must be preceded by an explanation and followed with a big hug and kiss, and then forgotten about. It's essential that you and your little one not harbor resentment toward each other. "As my children grew older," says Dana, "I've observed that what they convey after being punished for disobedience is often the exact opposite of their real desires.

"Bryan, for instance, will try to pull away from me. So I take him by the hand and make him come and sit down with me. Then I pull him onto my lap and hug him to me tightly. He resists for a matter of seconds as if that's the last thing in the world he wants, but then suddenly he clutches me with all his strength. Then we cry together and talk it out. He's so much more content when he knows he's been disciplined for wrong actions and then the slate is wiped clean. We may have to repeat the process over and over for the same type of disobedience, but it's important to always follow through."

Along with the hugs and talks, Patty W. recommends praying with your child after he has been disciplined. She says, "It teaches him what repentance and forgiveness mean, early on."

■ *Matching Wits.* The drawback to helping your child reach his full intellectual potential is that sooner or later he'll use that blossoming intellect to outwit you. "Children are smart," says Marilee. "The times when they pull things are the times when they know you don't want to deal with it—when you've worked hard all day and have just fallen into your chair exhausted, or when a phone call comes, or when you're kneading bread and your hands are covered with flour."

Our moms agree that a lot of poor discipline happens because Mommy just doesn't want to drop what she's doing and take care of the situation. "But then Mom ends up with the problems and the headaches," says Glenda. The parents who won't spend time, effort, prayer, and emotional energy making sure their children are reared with fair, loving discipline will pay for that mistake the rest of their child's life—and, tragically, so will the child.

Dana firmly believes that the way to handle any type of misbehavior is to nip it in the bud. She became a single mother after her children reached grade-school age, and she says, "I often think God knew what was going to happen in my family, and He knew I'd need to have a stiff backbone and be able to discipline my children. Sometimes my stubbornness comes in handy when I decide, in a loving way, that I'm just not going to let that child get the best of me."

■ *Bedtime Blues.* "Be firm about bedtime," says Patty W. "Nearly all children resist their naps." Enforcing bedtime isn't too hard with a young toddler. When he becomes tired and cranky it's a fairly simple matter just to rock him for a few minutes, tell him a story or do whatever bedtime ritual you've established, and then gently but firmly put him into his crib. Even if he protests, his only option is to grump himself to sleep. But as he grows older, sooner or later he's going to have a regular bed and you'll have to make sure he stays in it. And some of our moms' toddlers even learned to climb out of their cribs.

A local psychologist tells the story of his visit to the home of a young mother and her three-year-old son, whom we'll call Eric. After dinner was eaten and he played for an hour or so in the living room while the adults talked, Eric's mother told him it was time for bed. He protested, but she was firm. She put him into his pajamas, had him distribute good-night kisses all around, then tucked him into bed and told him to stay there. Five minutes later Eric toddled back into the living room. His mother took him by the hand, led him back into his room, spanked him, and put him back to bed while the psychologist listened with approval. She came back out, apologized for the interruption, and they continued their visit. After a few more minutes Eric again appeared and was again dealt with calmly and firmly.

Imagine the psychologist's surprise when this happened again not once but two times. He was beginning to wonder whether the poor child had masochistic tendencies when, the fifth time Eric toddled out, his mother rolled her eyes upward and said, exasperated, "Oh, all right, you can stay up a little longer. But you have to be quiet." This mother's show of discipline had been just that—a show—and Eric knew it.

Our moms weren't bedtime ogres. Most of them read their children stories. Chris bought Ashley some story-time tapes and let her listen to them while she fell asleep, and all our moms allowed their little ones to have their favorite animals, dolls, and blankets in bed with them. But, as in any other area of discipline, consistency at the start will prevent headaches later on.

■ *Stalling*. Rarer than the proverbial hen's tooth is the

toddler who has never tried to ignore Mommy when she told him to do something he wasn't in the mood to do. "When Ashley first started toddling," says Chris, "I went on a trip with my dad, who's a psychologist, and while we were riding I asked him how he thought I was doing as a mother. He said, 'Great, except for one thing. You don't make Ashley do what you say the first time you say it.'

"At the time I wasn't even sure she understood me when I told her to do something, but now I wish I had taken his advice because I'm having to repeat myself over and over. And it's not fair to her for me to tell her again and again to do something, then all of a sudden swat her. Believe me, you're better off to do the best you can to make sure your toddler understands, and then discipline if she doesn't obey."

No one likes to be rudely interrupted, and our moms agree with Dr. James Dobson's suggestion to give a child the courtesy of a few minutes' warning rather than telling him out of the blue, "Put your toys away. It's time to take a bath." Set the kitchen timer for five or ten minutes and say, "It's almost time to take a bath. When the bell rings, you must put your toys away." Then be prepared to see that your instructions are followed when the timer goes off. Marilee says, "If you wait to discipline your child until you've called several times and finally become upset, you're teaching him that he doesn't have to respond until you get upset."

■ *Misbehavior in Public.* If you've taught your child from infancy not to grab things off the store shelves or play with Grandpa's stereo knobs, chances are he won't turn into a little monster now. But he will probably challenge you, so following through is still vital.

Several moms stress the importance of, just before you enter a public place, telling your toddler exactly what behavior is expected and exactly what the results will be if your instructions are disobeyed: "Joshua, you must hold Mommy's hand in the store and not touch anything. If you run away or touch things, Mommy will spank." Sofia says, "I remember trips to the bathroom where pants were taken down and the children were spanked for repeatedly ignoring my warnings about their behavior. It's difficult to stop what you're doing and discipline, but it takes only a few times to let the child know you *will* follow through. It got to the point where I had only to say, 'Do you want to go to the bathroom with Mommy?'"

But don't stop only to take note of poor behavior. If your child is following your instructions, stop in the middle of the department store, give him a big kiss, and say, "Joshua, I'm so proud of you! You're doing exactly as Mommy told you—you haven't touched anything, and you're holding Mommy's hand."

Glenda says part of the problem with consistency in public, when both parents are there, is that the parents have never gotten together on strategy. "If one disciplines the other objects, and if the other disciplines the first one objects. So rather than have an argument in public they just sit there, which is disastrous!"

Another problem is interference from well-meaning friends and grandparents. If a child senses that Grandma will shield him from Mommy's discipline, he'll run to her without hesitation. Virginia says, "I've had my in-laws get mad at me because I wouldn't allow them to do that. They did it with the other grandkids, and they thought I was just awful!" Of course, Virginia's children are now the grandkids her in-laws brag about most for their good behavior.

■ *Not Completing Assigned Tasks.* "Train your child to put toys away as soon as he can walk and carry things," says Patty W. "Don't be his maid. It doesn't do you *or* him any favors." Donna agrees with chagrin: "April was an only child until she was four years old, and I always picked up after her, and now that we have another baby I'm picking up his toys *and* her toys. I've got problems! And it's hard on April as well as me, because I failed to teach her to pick up after herself when she was little. I can't blame her; I can only blame myself."

For many of our moms, it was no problem to get their children to pick up their toys or perform other little tasks, the reason being that they didn't make the mistake of expecting them to do it alone. To a toddler, working with Mommy or Daddy is fun; working alone is punishment. I began teaching Megan to put her toys away when she was about fourteen months old. I sat by the toybox and told her, "Bring Mommy the doll (or clown, or ball, or whatever)." She didn't always understand what toy I was asking for, but I gave her lots of encouragement and a big kiss as she brought me each one, and I told her its name as she handed it to me. She quickly learned the names of her toys and came to look on putting them away as a game. Telling her that the toys were going "Night-night" helped keep her from wanting to take them right back out.

Before long she was helping me put her toys into the box rather than just handing them to me, although it was months before she was ready to do the whole job by herself and even then it was necessary to give her encouragement and supervision. Chris says, "If you start when your baby is a year old, she might put only one toy in the toybox, and she might not even realize she's putting the toy *away*, but if you can just help her get the idea that she's helping Mommy you've accomplished a lot." "A patient mother is well worth her weight in gold when it comes to teaching her children to take on responsibility," says Adrienne. "You can always build from there. You've got a long time to work on it."

Using praise and hugs can work through the years, to the time when you're ready to let your little one help with such jobs as straightening her room, making her bed, helping to set the table, and putting her dirty clothes into the hamper. And even when your child graduates to the point where she's able to do these things alone she'll need lots of encouragement. Thank her sincerely and let her know how much you appreciate and depend on her help. Children aren't born able to do work just for the pleasure of a job well done—that ability has to be cultivated by you, the parent, helping your child feel good about herself for completing an assigned task.

■ *Sibling Jealousy.* A child's first four years are often the time when a little brother or sister comes along, and much has been said about the jealousy a toddler feels at having a little intruder usurp his throne. But several of our moms found that the above method of hugs, praise, and participation kept their toddlers from feeling any noticeable jealousy.

Terri took a set of individually wrapped matchbox cars to the hospital with her, and brought them home as a gift to Zachary from his new little sister. She says, "My little boy was never jealous of his baby sister. He thought she was the greatest thing ever. He said, 'Oh, boy, my new baby sister brought me a birthday party home from the hospital!'"

"It's all in how you handle it," says Glenda, "and how you let the toddler take part in the new baby's care. Our first two were only fourteen months apart, but we never experienced any jealousy with Greg because he thought of the baby as 'his' and was allowed to go and get diapers and help in other small ways. You have to promote the idea of the new baby coming, and then follow through afterward. A lot of times the mother is afraid to let the toddler be around the new baby, so she just shuts him off. That breeds resentment. You have to be very, very careful not to lose that toddler when the baby comes in." Cheryl adds, "Even if the baby's already here and the problem's already started, you can begin right where you are to involve the toddler. It may require a complete change of attitude, but it can be done."

Dana says, "When I brought Bridget home from the hospital, Bryan was the third person to hold her, after me and his daddy. I realized that a blue-eyed baby girl was going to get a lot of attention, so I made sure I gave Bryan *more* love and attention than I had before Bridget came. I honestly don't think that to this day it has ever crossed his mind that we might love her more than we do him."

In the midst of all the love and reassurance you're giving your toddler, make sure you don't let up on your discipline. In Glenda's family, everyone was so concerned that Greg would feel displaced by his new sister that they overdid it, and Greg decided that since he was receiving all this attention he might as well try getting away with a few things. "We had to put our foot down," says Glenda, "and that's difficult with grandparents around. They didn't like it when we disciplined him."

Even if your toddler adores his new little sister, put a childproof gate across the nursery door and make sure you never leave him alone with her. He doesn't yet know how to pick her up without dropping her, or what kind of hugs are okay. And there may be some jealousy there you haven't yet seen. Glenda says, "To protect the baby, we put her in an infant seat in the middle of a mesh playpen. She stayed occupied watching her big brother, but he couldn't reach her. I still had to watch them, though, because he dropped toys in when she cried, trying to get her to play."

As the new baby in the house approaches toddlerhood and learns to play with her big brother or sister, there's bound to be a clash of wills every now and then. But our moms dismiss as a cop-out the idea that sibling rivalry is just a natural part of growing up. It may be natural, but it's certainly not healthy, and it can cause deep emotional scars.

Most of our moms require their children to kiss and make up after exchanging harsh words. Dana goes even further and doesn't allow her children to fight at all. She says, "All their lives they've got to get along with people, and I decided that the best place to start is in the home. I've seen a lot of families who treat everyone else better than they treat each other, and I decided we weren't going to be that way—we were going to be examples. We were going to treat each other better than we treat our best friends."

How does she go about working this miracle? "I just don't allow them to argue. I tell them, 'You resolve it quietly; you don't fight.' If they're hateful to each other, they get disciplined, then they kiss and make up." In the event that each of them blames the other for starting it, Dana refuses to play referee: "I ask, 'Can you work it out calmly and lovingly with each other, or will Mommy have to discipline you both? Don't you think it would be much better to work it out yourselves, calmly and quietly, before I have to step in? Because if I step in, I'll discipline both of you.' That way they're motivated to compromise and give in to each other.

"Bridget and Bryan are very loving and close—Bridget wants to marry her 'Bubba'—because they've had no choice. They don't have the scars that come from fighting and ugly words because those things haven't been allowed." Dana concedes the necessity of staying within earshot of your children to learn whether one is consistently instigating the arguments or is being made always to give in, and the need to discipline separately a child who is a habitual bully. But she says that in her family Bridget, the youngest, is usually both the instigator *and* the first to yield.

▪ *Rudeness.* When Megan was about two years old she learned the magic words, "I want," and she said them loudly and often. After putting up with it for a while because of her extreme youth, I decided that any child capable of saying "I want" was also capable of saying "May I please." Sure enough, she was, and within a month or so she was amazing our friends with her politeness.

The way I went about her training in etiquette was by applying a healthy dose of what psychologist Kevin Leman calls Reality Discipline: Quite simply, when she said "I want" instead of "May I please," she didn't get what she asked for. I did a fair amount of motherly prompting ("How do we ask, dear?") and I usually allowed her to repent and ask again politely when she forgot. And I tried to reward her for asking politely by granting her request if it was reasonable and by giving her a good explanation and an alternative if it was not.

We made up funny little songs about the situation—real Grammy material, with lyrics like: "We don't say 'I want,' 'cause that's a yukky thing to say; we say 'May I please,' 'cause that's the polite thing to say."

Table manners are another major area where mothers run into etiquette problems with their children. You can't expect too much in the way of decorum at the dinner table from a two or three year old, but you can require that he eat with his fork or spoon—not his fingers.

Several of our moms found that the best way to deal with violations of this rule was, after one warning, to confiscate the child's dinner. That sounds harsh, but it shouldn't be necessary to do it more than once or twice before your child realizes you mean business. And with Megan I found that I needed to take her dinner away for only a couple of minutes in order for her to learn to obey.

A few warnings: Make sure your child understands and is capable of what you're asking. Give thorough explanations and demonstrations, and encourage him sincerely when you see him doing a good job. Also, if you choose to have your child skip the rest of a meal because of etiquette violations, don't give snacks later. If anything, serve your child the same meal again, reheated, and confiscate it again—with no reprieve this time—if he continues to break the rules. And don't confiscate a meal consisting entirely of foods your child hates. He'll think you're doing him a favor.

As your child grows older, he'll need to learn such niceties as putting his napkin on his lap before beginning to eat, not talking with his mouth full, keeping his left hand in his lap, and keeping his elbows off the table. Using games to teach these lessons, as psychologist James Dobson suggests, will create an awareness of good manners while at the same time making dinner a fun family time rather than an ordeal.

Have each of your family members watch the others for infractions, and establish a penalty such as having the violator march around the dinner table or hop up and down while chanting five times, "I will not talk with food in my mouth," or use Dr. Dobson's idea of counting loudly to ten from the back of the house. Your children will squeal with laughter if you let them catch you breaking the rules every now and then.

■ *Peer Influence.* The parental struggle against the negative effects of peer pressure starts early, mainly because children show just as much talent for imitating each other as they do for imitating adults. "Jason is four," says Cheryl, "and we never had trouble with rebellion until just recently. I know that our main problem is a couple of kids in the neighborhood, so I'm having to decide whether or not I'm going to let him play with them. It's hard to know where to draw the line—I want him to have friends."

Wanda says, "You can't pick your children's friends for them, but you can help them cultivate good friendships. Michelle is an only child and there aren't a lot of kids in the neighborhood for her to play with, but I can take an active part in her friendships by having the children I approve of over often. And it's good to point out the things you like about your child's behavior and the behavior of her friends."

Even though our moms know it's impossible to shield

a child from all negative friendships, most of them have chosen to at least partially screen their children's friends. But don't make certain friends off-limits without explaining why. Even a two or three year old can understand when you tell him, "No, I'm sorry, but Johnny can't come over because he runs in the house and doesn't obey Mommy."

Many of our moms are also cautious about the homes where they allow their children to play. "Get to know their friends' parents," says Wanda. "Just because your child met a friend at day care or Sunday school doesn't always protect him from wrong influences." Our moms are also adamantly against letting a young child spend the night in the home of a child whose parents are not trusted friends.

Even if his only public exposure *sans* Mommy and Daddy is Sunday school or a good Christian day-care center, your toddler will probably bring home a bad word or two and try it out on you to see your reaction. When he does, Debby says, "Try not to blow your top. He probably won't know what it means, so just explain very simply that it's not a nice word and he's not to use it again." The same goes for bad attitudes and behaviors that are transferred from day care to home. Explain that they're not allowed (and, if possible, why not), and be prepared to discipline if you're disobeyed.

"When the neighbor kids come over," says Marilee, "I make sure I can listen to their conversation with my children. Sometimes it takes me and my husband two weeks to finish explaining things the neighbor kids spent five minutes talking about!" "You have to explain those things, though," says Glenda, "because you can't shelter your children from what they're going to face outside, from the influence of other children. You have to teach them. Pretty soon you'll hear your little one telling the other kids, 'But my mommy says . . . '"

The best protection you can give your child against negative peer influence is to keep an open, honest, loving relationship with him, making yourself an example of good behavior and educating him as to why bad behavior is bad. And do try to help him cultivate friendships that will reinforce the values you're trying to teach. Marilee says, "I've told David, 'It's important for you to choose friends who act right, because the people you're around all the time are the people you're going to start acting like.' Even though he may not completely understand that right now, it's laying the groundwork for his friendships when he grows older."

■ *Lying.* Cheryl says, "It seems as if our culture teaches us that it's okay to lie if it gets you out of trouble, or it's okay to tell stories if it's not going to hurt anyone. As soon as Jason and Brian were old enough, we began teaching them Bible verses about not lying, and about loving one another and being kind to one another.

"We've had a problem, though, with Jason's being confused when he hears an adult say something untrue, then laugh and say, 'Oh, I'm just kidding.' I've tried to explain it to him, but for the life of me I can't come up with a good explanation of the difference between teasing and telling a lie. I told Rodger, my husband, 'We're really going to have to listen to what we say and what other people say, because right now Jason can't understand the difference.' I finally told him that sometimes even adults tell stories, but it's never the right thing to do." Glenda points out that children see morality in black and white, not shades of gray: "A child can't understand. All he sees is that you're allowed to tell stories because you're 'kidding,' but he's not."

When you're beginning to educate your child about honesty, it's important to realize from the outset that a very young child has no concept of the moral ramifications of lying. He doesn't even know what lying is, and he certainly doesn't realize that it's wrong.

Here are a few basic guidelines: First, avoid asking your child questions in a manner that will tempt him to lie. When you snap, "Josh, did you break this lamp?" little Josh will probably answer "No" out of pure self-preservation. He can tell from your tone of voice and the look in your eyes what the consequences will be if he confesses. Besides, breaking a lamp isn't a punishable offense unless it's the result of disobedience.

Second, patiently and calmly teach your child what it means to be truthful: "Josh, when I ask you to pick up your toys, don't tell me you already did it if you really didn't. That's called lying, and we don't do that." It also helps to find a storybook where the protagonist learns to tell the truth even if it gets him into trouble. There are a number of storybooks on the market dealing with kindness, honesty, unselfishness, and other virtues. Check your Christian bookstore for them. They can be invaluable teaching tools.

Third, be an example of honesty to your child. Don't ask him to lie for you on the telephone or at the front door. And if you slip and tell a lie, apologize to your child: "What I just said wasn't true, and I shouldn't have said it. Let's pray and ask the Lord to forgive me and help me be a good example for you."

Finally, don't include harmless childhood fantasies in the same category as lies. When Megan came up with tall tales such as, "Today I flew in a big balloon on 'Sesame Street,'" I generally answered, with a smile, "Oh, really? Was it fun?"

As their children grew older and began to understand why lying is wrong, several moms adopted the policy of disciplining their children twice if they misbehaved and then lied about it—once for the transgression, and once for the lie. Be sure you're right before you follow that course, though, because children have an acute sense of fairness, and an unjust punishment will stick in your child's mind for years to come. One of our moms says, "I remember that when I was little my dad wouldn't even let me tell my side of the story. If he accused me of something and I said, 'No, I didn't,' I got spanked for backtalking. I want to keep my relationship with my kids open so they'll feel free to confide in me. I want them to be able to look back and say, 'My parents were always fair when they disciplined me.'"

Dana adds, "This didn't happen with my children until they were older, but there have been times when I had to tell one of them, 'I'm not sure that what you've told me is the truth. But you know that sooner or later I'll probably find out. And even if I don't, God knows, and you know. If what you've told me isn't true, why don't you come clean and tell me the truth and ask Jesus to forgive you, and we'll go on from there.' It got to the point where I was able to tell. There was a certain indignation about them when they were lying that gave them away."

Finally, be quick to apologize if you discipline your child for lying, then discover later that he told the truth. Cheryl says, "All you can do is go to him and tell him you've asked Jesus to forgive you, and now you want his forgiveness too."

To Spank or Not to Spank

Our moms generally agree with James Dobson's recommendation that spanking be used only for direct disobedience and rebellion—the felonies of the juvenile world—and that more creative methods be employed to handle rambunctiousness, grumpiness, irresponsibility, and other misdemeanors. They've found that one of the best disciplinary methods for an active toddler is to make him sit still for a few minutes, especially in a boring place where there are no toys and books around. Marilee says, "If my kids are chasing each other around and starting to hit and can't seem to settle down, we'll sit one down on one end of the couch and the other on the other end and make them stay there for five minutes or so." "I think a lot of times having to sit still and be quiet is more punishment for a toddler than a spanking is," adds Cheryl. "When Jason is being too rough with his friends outside, it's a real punishment for me to bring him in and make him sit still while Brian is out there having fun. That's a much more effective way to discipline him than just giving him a quick spanking and then sending him back out to play."

A kitchen timer is an essential piece of equipment to have when your child enters toddlerhood. When you sit him down and explain to him that he's going to have to sit still for five minutes because he ran through the house, say, "Mommy is going to set this timer so that it will ring when five minutes are up. When the bell goes off, you may get down." Then set the timer and put it up out of reach. This will keep your toddler from asking constantly, "Can I get up now, Mommy?" Unfortunately, it *doesn't* keep him from asking, "How many more minutes?"

Chris and Michele both cured their little girls of the early-morning and midafternoon grumps by letting them discover that their whining got the exact opposite results from the ones desired. Instead of giving Ashley more attention when she started whining, Chris says, "I told her she was acting like she was still sleepy, so she'd have to go back to bed for five minutes—which was an eternity for her. It's amazing how well that worked." When Sarah became grumpy and unmanageable, Michele told her, "Go into your room until you can be sweet." At first Sarah stayed in her room and pouted for a while, but she quickly caught on and before long would run into her room, make a sharp U-turn, then race back out with a big smile, exclaiming, "I s'eet girl, Mommy!"

When her two boys fight over a favorite toy, Cheryl disciplines by confiscating it. She says, "There have been times when I've said, 'This toy is not worth fighting about. Let's put it up and play with something else.'"

Marilee makes use of the kitchen timer when both of her children want to play with a one-child toy. When it goes off after five minutes or so, it's the other child's turn.

As your child grows old enough to have regular responsibilities—and to "forget" to do them—you can add other methods of discipline to your repertoire, such as checklists, forfeiture of TV or other privileges when assigned work isn't done, or of a dime's worth of allowance for each pair of dirty underwear Mommy finds on the bedroom floor. Most of our moms are devoted Dobson readers and they heartily recommend James Dobson's books, *Dare to Discipline* and *The Strong-Willed Child*, for advice on ways to discipline as your child grows older as well as ways to handle special problems. Another excellent resource for the discipline of children over the age of four is Kevin Leman's *Making Children Mind Without Losing Yours*.

A Reassuring Word

Here's a final word of reassurance to the mother who is afraid of losing her child's affection through consistent discipline: You won't.

"You're not going to lose that child's affection if you do it wisely," says Glenda, "because you're not always going to say no. You'll give him hugs and kisses, and you'll compliment him when he does things right. It's not all no-no's, although some days it feels like it!" Children go through cycles of testing their limits and then resting within them, and our moms generally found that if they stuck to their guns during the times of testing, the times of resting became longer and longer.

Love is not weak and conciliating; it's strong and persevering. Parents who enforce loving discipline give their child a happy legacy that will stay with him all his life, and a legacy that is all too rare. People today are losing jobs and breaking laws because they never learned to yield cheerfully to authority, and marriages are crumbling because the partners never learned to give as well as take.

Wanda says, "Toddlers learn that Mommy and Daddy love them and discipline them because they've done something wrong and must learn to obey. And that's a lesson they have to learn, because people in the real world won't be as understanding as Mommy and Daddy. They won't discipline; they'll punish."

When you're tempted to let a transgression slide by to keep from making your child upset, remember the scriptural teaching that God disciplines us out of love, because we are His children. He's not afraid to let us get mad at Him, and we must show the same loving courage with our own children. "A nine-month-old baby can't understand that yet," says Cheryl, "but you need to know it for yourself. Know for yourself that you're doing the right thing, and that you're not going to lose your child's love. You're going to gain his respect."

9
...
Someone Special, That's Me!

O ur moms' children are fairly typical in that they're all different. Some of our toddlers demonstrated the happy ability to shed peer rebuffs with little effort, while others, more sensitive, seemed to be struggling with a deficit in the self-worth department from birth. But our moms agree that home should be a sanctuary from which a naturally confident child can sally forth to win the world, or where a naturally shy child can remain for a while to build up his courage, secure in the knowledge that he's loved and accepted just as he is.

It would be impossible in one chapter to give a step-by-step formula for producing a happy, confident child—and the formula wouldn't be valid anyway, given the differences among children. Nearly every chapter in this book makes some reference to building a child's self-esteem, and you'll need to finish reading it to get a true picture of how our moms are trying to encourage their children. This chapter will be dedicated to sharing some simple do's and don'ts that our moms have found to be true, and to reiterating some vital points that have already been mentioned.

■ *Do* give even a shy child the benefit of firm, consistent, loving discipline. Selfishness and self-esteem are not the same thing, and it does your child's sense of security no good when the limits you set for him collapse at the lightest touch.

■ *Do* tell your child *daily*, both verbally and physically, how much she's loved. She won't just know, she has to be told. One of our moms says, "Not until I was married did I hear my parents say 'I love you,' even though they always showed it by their actions. The first time I said it to them over the phone, there was total silence. They didn't know how to react. Now I'm struggling to go beyond just showing it and thinking it with my children. I want to *say* it."

Our moms believe it's impossible to overdo telling a child how special she is, how much you love her, and how very glad you are to have her. "Hugging is a big part of self-esteem, too," says Chris. Terri says, "We give a good-night kiss *and* a good-morning kiss in our house. It started as a joke when Zachary was tiny, but now it's really important to both our children. When things get really hectic, like on a Sunday when we're all running out the door for church, Zachary will stop and say, 'We can't go to Sunday school—we haven't had a good-morning kiss!'"

■ *Do* go by the Golden Rule as much as possible. Your role as parent will dictate that you enforce unpopular rules at times, but do give your child the courtesy due him as a unique person created by a loving God. Several moms have brought out the point that any treatment you'd hate will probably bother your child just as much.

■ *Do* give your child the freedom to pass milestones at her own pace—don't compare her to other babies. This is a biggie, because friends, grandparents, aunts, uncles, cousins, *ad infinitum*, begin comparing your child to various standards from the moment of birth: "How much did she weigh?" "What was her Apgar rating? Oh, only eight? My Janie got ten." After you come home from the hospital, it's a race to see whose child can crawl first, cut teeth first, say her first word first, walk first, toilet-train first.

The only way to shield your child from this ridiculous contest is to refuse to take part in it. It's good to know what the average four month old, or nine month old, or one year old is doing, so that you can tell if your child has a problem. "But you never have to express it to your child," says Cheryl. Carol says, "Don't let Satan put thoughts into your head, like, 'My child isn't as good as . . .' He'll do that if he can. And the child senses it."

"And usually children all catch up with each other anyway," adds Terri. "By the time they hit kindergarten they're pretty much even, so it's not as if one child is necessarily brighter than the other. It's just that some babies catch on sooner." "There are very few five year olds who aren't toilet-trained!" says Patti. Several of our mothers found that when they stopped overreacting to their child's toilet-training problems he was able to eventually relax and accomplish what Mommy had been trying to get him to do all along. The challenge left when the power struggle ended.

Cheryl points out the need, if you have more than one child, to avoid comparing your children to each other and also to discourage comparisons by well-meaning friends and relatives. She says, "It has been hard, with Jason and Brian only seventeen months apart. Jason is very quick-minded, whereas Brian is more the playful, energetic type. When people say things like, 'Boy, Jason's the brain and Brian's the brawn in this family,' we just laugh it off and change the subject and try to compliment both of the boys on their strong points. Any comparison, even if you don't mean it to be bad, comes out sounding like a left-handed compliment." Ask day care workers and, later, teachers, not to openly compare your children to each other.

As they grew older, some of our moms' children tried taking part in this destructive game themselves. "We started very early telling each of our children that God has a plan for them, and because they're different, they shouldn't compare," says Carol. Virginia adds, "When one of my girls says, 'Ricky can do so-and-so, and I can't,' I answer, 'Yes, he's strong in that area, but you're strong in *this* area.' "

■ *Don't* force your child to go to someone she's afraid of. "It's cruel," says Adrienne, "and it doesn't work." Many babies go through phases when they cling to Mommy, and it's important to keep offering social opportunities without pushing them. If a person behaves in a friendly manner while keeping his distance, your baby will probably decide to trust him eventually after repeated non-threatening exposure. But your child needs to know that you'll never betray her by handing her over to someone she fears.

This situation can be embarrassing, especially if the feared person is a family member. Megan was terrified of my father's deep voice when she was about four months old. Every time he came near her, she began to cry. So Granddaddy stayed in the background for a while, smiling at her and playing with her—when she allowed it—as my mother or I held her. It didn't take long at all for him to win her over and become one of her favorite people.

▪ *Don't* take your child places where his behavior is important when he's tired. "If you do, you'll get negative feedback from everyone you see," says Carol. You'll also end up feeling exasperated and impatient yourself, which can hardly help but affect your behavior toward your child.

▪ *Don't* have hysterics every time your baby falls down. Pick him up and comfort him if he cries, and of course check to see whether he has hurt himself, but do try to pass it off as lightly as possible. If you regard every bump and bruise as a catastrophe, it won't take long for your baby to pick up that attitude. I found that most of the time when Megan fell down there was an interval of a second or two between the accident and her reaction. If I quickly smiled and said "Boom!" or made another funny noise, her crying was usually averted.

▪ *Do* watch your nonverbal communication. "I could always tell my mother was upset with me just by how she breathed," says Terri. "Now sometimes I'll hear myself doing that. Zachary will ask, 'What's wrong?' and I'll say, 'Nothing' but I'll know he could tell I was upset because I breathed just like my mother. I've learned to say, 'Mommy's upset right now, but she'll be okay in a minute,' because a lot of times we tear our children down by our attitudes. They get the idea, 'Boy, she wishes I weren't here.'" Kathy agrees: "My four year old knows I'm upset just by the way I'm doing dishes. He'll come up and ask, 'Mama, are you happy?'"

A little sigh of disgust or a roll of the eyes can speak volumes to a young child—or a spouse, for that matter. Ask the Lord to make you hypersensitive to your own negative attitudes and actions, and deliberately try to cultivate the attitude that it is not by tearing your children down and proving your own superiority that you are built up, but rather by seeing them encouraged and blossoming under your care. As your child becomes more confident and secure, your ministry as a mother is validated.

▪ *Do* treat your child like a welcome addition to the family. Chris says, "I think it's important to take your child with you, even to restaurants if you can. I never want Ashley to have the feeling that she's more of a pain than a blessing." Wanda adds, "Be sure your child can be up high enough to see in stores and in crowds."

▪ *Do* try to make sure your child has playmates of his own age and developmental level. Aside from his relationship with his parents, peer and sibling relationships are usually the main source of a child's self-esteem or lack of it. It's devastating for a young child to be always dominated by older playmates, or to be told constantly, "You can't play with us. You're too little."

The potential for hurt feelings is even greater for a small child with older siblings. Cheryl says, "There are times when Jason has a birthday party to go to and Brian isn't invited. And there are some other things he's doing, like playing softball, that Brian's just not ready for. I've tried to arrange for Rodger or me to do something special with him when he can't participate in one of his big brother's activities. We just explain to Brian, 'Jason is going to a four-year-old party, and when you're four you'll go to some four-year-old parties too. But tonight, when Mommy takes Jason, Daddy's going to take you for some ice cream.'" Our moms agree that it's best, whenever you can, to encourage your children to play games in which older and younger alike can participate. Several of them found it beneficial to encourage their elder children to take the younger ones under their wing, not to discipline or correct them—that's your job—but to defend them from the slings and arrows of older play-mates.

But, again, do figure out some way to give a younger child playmates his own age, even if that means organizing a play group or cultivating some new friends of your own who have children his age and who can be invited over, with their children, for the afternoon.

For the shy or slowly developing child, it may be good to provide playmates on the younger side. Rita's second son, Brian, had a hearing difficulty at birth that slowed his speech development. She says, "He's more sensitive than Billy, and was a little clingier when he was small. He played with younger children. They looked up to him, and that gave him the leadership role. It helped a lot to bring him out." Patti adds, "I noticed a big change in my second child when my oldest, Keva, went to school. He got to be the leader for the first time, and he really blossomed."

■ *Don't* play favorites. Most of our moms say they had no trouble with this, but if you do have a favorite you must try to cure yourself of it for both of your children's sakes. "Ask God to help you see what He wants to develop in your children, and what's special from Him in each child," says Patti.

Children are sensitive to favoritism, and there are times when an unsuspecting mother will find herself accused of it when it wasn't even in her thoughts. Cheryl says, "If Jason knows he would be disciplined for doing something, then I had better discipline Brian for the same thing. Otherwise, it looks as if I'm playing favorites—and he'll tell me it does, too." Rita found it helpful to tell her older son, when she disciplined him, that she wasn't just picking on him because he was older: "When I reprimanded Billy for the way he was treating Brian, I assured him that I wouldn't allow Brian to do that to him, either. I felt that idea was really from the Lord, because I saw his whole attitude change."

■ *Don't* discuss your child's problems while he's in the room. "Remember that children are people," says Rosemary. "Don't converse with another adult in front of your child as if he were an inanimate object or deaf. Children have the same emotions adults do." New parents fall into this nasty habit while their child is a baby. They figure, "He can't understand what I'm saying, so I'm not hurting him." The problem is, they never bother to get out of the habit when their child learns to talk. "And I believe even a young baby can recognize his name and tell by your tone that you're complaining about him," says Terri.

Many of these unintentional insults are self-fulfilling. Not long ago, on a visit to a friend's house, my friend and I began to discuss her two-year-old daughter, who was playing in the same room. "Boy, Shelley's strong-willed," said my friend. "She tests me every time I turn around." I glanced over at her little daughter, who was listening, and I could practically see on her face the thought, "Boy, I'm strong-willed. I test Mommy every time she turns around."

How much better it would have been for my friend to say, "Shelley has a very strong will, and I know it's hard for her to obey Mommy sometimes, so I'm very proud of her when she does!" I would have understood exactly what she meant, but her words would have reinforced obedience rather than disobedience. At the same time, Cheryl warns against making a problem area sound as if it's okay; it's easy to end up praising your child for being difficult when that wasn't what you meant to do at all.

All of this may sound as if we're quibbling about semantics—and we are—but if you're under the impression that your words aren't important I urge you to take a look in your Bible at the book of James, chapter 3. Many of the points in this chapter have to do with controlling your words, which can be done only through prayer, commitment, and self-discipline. But it can be done. More than that—it *must* be done. Instead of complaining, express hope about difficult areas: "Maybe she'll come to you next time."

Most importantly, our moms say you should never criticize your child, either to her face or behind her back, for something over which she has no control, such as the arrangement of her facial features, her hair color or texture, her build, or—worse yet—her sex. Chris says, "What worse thing could you say in front of a child than that she should have been something she can't do anything about?"

■ *Don't* expect your child to work for your approval. He shouldn't have to, and besides, he won't. Chris says, "If you're constantly negative, your child won't be accustomed to having any sense of your approval anyway, so he won't work to gain it." Don't be afraid to show strong disapproval of unacceptable behavior, but a parent's resting attitude toward his or her child should be love and strong, often expressed approval, rather than neutrality or indifference while waiting for good or bad behavior to tip the scales. Instead of expecting your child to work for your approval, give so much approval that he'll work not to lose it. And don't ever fall into the fantasy that approval can take the place of discipline. It can't.

■ *Don't* resort to insults and harsh words to modify your child's behavior. Unlike the sting from a spanking, the sting of harsh words never goes away. Included in the insult category are self-fulfilling labels such as "bad boy," "bad girl," and age-labeling: "the terrible twos."

"There are so many times when it would be easy to say, 'That was a stupid thing to do,'" says Terri. "And that does get the message across, but it also gets across another message : 'You're stupid.' And a lot of times we take it for granted that they know they shouldn't have done something when they don't."

Many of our moms have mentioned the importance of apologizing if you lose your temper and say something to hurt your child. That goes for the little digs as well as the big ones. Cheryl says, "There are times when I'm tired or have a headache, and those are the times when I usually ask the boys to come and pray for me. I say, 'Mommy's very tired, and I don't want to get upset or yell tonight, but my head hurts. Would you please pray for Mommy?' Not only is their faith working as they pray for me, but they're also made aware that I'm not feeling well and they try to be more quiet, or if I say something I regret I can apologize and tell them, 'Remember that Mommy told you she was very tired? I didn't mean what I just said, and I'm sorry.'"

■ *Do* praise or criticize the action, not the child. It's good to tell your baby how adorable she is, but it's even better, as she grows older, to devote your most enthusiastic praise to your child's good actions rather than to things she can take no credit for, such as having a pretty face. Praising your child's inherited looks can lead to problems, especially if you have two children, one of whom is a natural beauty while the other isn't. Cheryl says, "We compliment our boys on how they look if they've made an extra effort to dress nicely—'Hey, you're a sharp dresser!'"

Give credit where credit is due. For healthy bodies, bright minds, and cute faces, the credit belongs to the Lord. Credit goes to your child for being kind to her friends, for working to master tasks with her healthy body and bright mind, and for doing a good job of brushing the hair surrounding that cute face.

Give specific praise or criticism. Rather than saying, "You sure were a good girl today," tell your child, "I'm so proud of you! You helped Mommy put away the clothes, and you obeyed when Mommy told you to come inside." When your child knows exactly what she did that was right, she's more liable to repeat it. Chris is a great believer in "I" messages: "I like the way you...." And Kathy recommends telling your child when he is being disciplined for a transgression, "It was wrong to do thus-and-so." "Not, 'You were bad,'" she says, "but the action itself was wrong."

■ *Do* give your child a sense of purpose in life. Chris says, "Since Ashley was six months old I've been telling her, 'You are a child of destiny. You're somebody special. God has a plan for you.' She'll look up at me in wonder and say, 'He does?' It's so important, even when they're tiny, for them to get the idea, 'I'm special to God, and to Mommy and Daddy. I have a special place on this earth.'" As the Gaither song says, a child is a promise. And your child is much more likely to keep that promise if he knows you believe he can.

■ *Do* recognize that different children have different abilities, even within the same family. Carol, who has four children, believes every child has strong points that need to be brought out. But she says, "It's important for the parent to recognize them early. God has given us gifts, and we need to know what they are."

Knowing where her strengths lie can give your child a sense of identity and confidence, so look for her strong points and reinforce them. If she loves to help, praise her for being helpful and give her as much opportunity as possible to do it. If she's bright and loves to read, praise her for mastering new books, and expand her library. If she's active and good at games, praise her for working hard at them. If she's gentle with other children and shares her toys, praise her for being kind. Of course, you'll need to help your child develop a balanced lifestyle that includes all of these areas. It's also important to make sure that your own wishful thinking doesn't assign your child a strong point different from the ones she really has.

■ *Don't* allow your child to be given degrading nicknames, and don't allow degrading terms or sarcastic humor to be used in your home. "Ever since Ryan was born," says Kathy, "we called him Weasel, because he was so funny looking when he was a baby—his ears stuck out. But when he was about two years old he told Hugh, 'Daddy, I'm not a weasel.' He had started feeling hurt about it, so we dropped it."

"Rodger and I don't allow sarcastic, cutting teasing between us," says Cheryl, "because not only is it bad for us, but also the children will pick it up and use it against each other."

■ *Do* focus on your child's strengths rather than his weaknesses. Virginia says, "If you don't feel well or are in a bad mood, it's easy to see everything your child does wrong that day instead of seeing the good and thanking God for it."

■ *Do* praise honest effort wherever you find it. Try to see your child's world from his point of view, and don't expect him to accomplish tasks as well or as quickly as you would. "We expect too much of our toddlers," says Cheryl. "We want them to do things as quickly as we would, and when they don't tie their shoes quickly enough we jump in and do it for them even though they should be learning to do it for themselves. We expect them to walk as quickly as we do, or pick up their rooms as quickly and well as we would. We push and nag when we should be saying, 'You're really doing well!'"

Adopt a child's-eye view of the things your toddler does for you. Wear the nasty-smelling perfume he gave you for Christmas at least a few times, maybe on days when you don't have to leave the house. Accept gifts of dubious artwork with joy. Instead of asking, "What on earth is it?" say, "How beautiful! Tell me about it," and find a way to display his pictures for at least a few days. Rather than constantly correcting your toddler's speech, make yourself an example of good language and praise your child when he does use a new word in the right way. "Praise him for his accomplishments!" says Karen H. "Clap and cheer! He'll love it, and it will encourage him to do things right."

■ *Do* give commands and instructions in a positive tone. Terri says, "With my little boy, I can say, 'Zachary, pick up the toy right now and take it into your room,' and he'll do it. But my little girl became very stubborn when I tried that with her, even at eighteen months old. I discovered that it worked much better when I said, 'Ashley, show Mommy what a big girl you can be and take the toy into your room.' Now, with that approach, she cleans circles around her older brother. She wants to please me."

■ *Do* give your child some space of his own. Humans are territorial creatures—and before you deny that, try sitting in your husband's seat at dinner tonight or taking your best friend's spot at aerobics class. If you have two toddlers who must share a room, make the dividing line clear. "Every child needs a special place where he can hide his treasures," says Patti. And beyond that, give your child a special corner of the family room, a special chair, anything that says, "I belong here. I'm an important part of this family." The mother who keeps her house perfect and never allows her toddler to encroach on her decor sends him a clear message: "I'm important. You're not." Of course, several of our moms laughed when I brought up this subject and said, "The whole house belongs to my kids. I'm the one who needs some space!"

Marilee suggests also allowing your child to have a few toys that are inviolable and need not be shared with others—especially toys that have to do with his sense of security, such as a special stuffed animal, pillow, or blanket. "A child needs freedom from the feeling that anything he has is fair game for any kid who comes into the house and wants it," she says.

■ *Do* remember that childish hands and feet are awkward and that spilled milk and broken vases are bound to happen occasionally. Don't discipline your child for them unless they're the result of direct disobedience. And that means don't yell.

■ *Do* spend time talking with and listening to your child. Cheryl says, "So often, when children reach the toddler stage where they're talking all the time, we tend to tune them out. And it's bad to ignore them or just come back with an automatic 'No!' I've had to pray for help to think before I speak and to give my boys the courtesy of listening to what they're saying, even if I've heard it a hundred times and they're taking ten times too long to say it." "Something that has helped me is to keep in mind the need to show respect for the members of my family," says Virginia. "It's so easy to respect other people, then we come home and relax and treat our children as if they aren't as important as the people 'out there.' And they start feeling as if they really aren't. I've had to ask the Lord to help me respect each one of them as an individual."

Connie says, "When your child shares things with you, listen. Give him eye-to-eye contact. My parents were never too busy to listen, and to this day I love to share things with them. They make me feel as if they really care." ◗

Of course, as in all other areas, you need to maintain balance. Your child shouldn't be allowed to monopolize the conversation in a group of adults simply because you're afraid of stifling his personality; on the other hand, his narratives shouldn't be fair game for interruption because they're not "important."

■ *Do* teach your child to love her enemies. Children can be cruel at times, and when your child is the victim it's important that you not react by encouraging her to strike back out of hate or spite. "That's hard," says Patti, "because you want to go beat 'em up!"

Observe your child during playtime to see if she's making social mistakes you can help her correct, such as being bossy or not joining in. I found that role-playing with Megan helped her learn appropriate play behavior.

When one of Michelle's friends treats her cruelly, Wanda shares with her: "Usually, when someone is mean, it's because she's hurting inside and is trying to make herself feel better by hurting you—it's not because you've done anything wrong. Let's pray for her." This helps the child see that the meanness of her peers isn't her problem; it's their problem. "It also teaches her to reach out and meet their needs," says Patti.

And, by the way: *Do* allow your child to defend herself if she's physically attacked by her peers. The concept of turning the other cheek is hard enough for us as adults to adhere to; besides, a small child who can't defend herself is a sitting duck for any bully who happens along.

■ *Don't* bring up past transgressions when you discipline your child. "After you've disciplined, drop it and don't bring it up again," says Rita. "I had a tendency to think of past things every time my boys made a mistake, and I had to stop it. My husband Marvin set a good example for me. He showed me how to just drop it and go on."

■ *Do* encourage your child to make decisions and think independently. Even a two or three year old can decide between eating a banana or an apple, or whether he wants a story about David and Goliath or Zacchaeus up in the tree. Allowing your child to make decisions whenever possible teaches him to make right choices, as well as giving him confidence in his decision-making ability. "Teach him to live with his decisions, too," says Cheryl. "If you ask, 'Would you like a toasted cheese sandwich, or peanut butter and jelly?' and he says peanut butter and then changes his mind when you're halfway through making it, he learns that every decision has a consequence—even at two years old."

■ *Don't* leave your child at the mercy of the media. As soon as he's old enough to understand, teach him that not everything aired on TV or put into print is gospel truth. If you're watching a program and something contradicting your values is portrayed as good, don't let it pass. Say, "What that man just did isn't right. Can you tell Mommy why?" It's best to screen questionable shows, but if you inadvertently allow your toddler to watch one you can always use it as a bad example.

■ *Do* give your child responsibility as he becomes able to handle it, and praise him for jobs well done. "Two weeks ago," says Cheryl, "Jason's Sunday school lesson was all about taking responsibility for helping around the house. He brought the storybook home and showed it to me and told what he'd learned. After dinner, while Rodger and I were watching a football game on TV, Jason went into his room and picked up his clothes, picked up *Brian's* toys, and then came out and told me he'd done just what his Sunday school teacher had said. He was so proud. Brian is just two, but I try to give him responsibility even now for little things like putting his shoes into the closet and his dirty clothes into the hamper.

That teaches self-discipline, but it also builds self-esteem as I praise him for it."

▪ "*Do* show interest in your child's activities by physical attendance," says Ruth. "It will mean more than he'll ever say." Those little nursery school pageants and four-year-old T-ball games are more important than they seem. "My mom was always into other things when I was small," says one of our moms, "and she didn't come to a lot of the things I thought were so important. I think it would have made a big difference in my self-image if she had."

▪ *Do* continue seeking to build your child's self-esteem as the years go by. This isn't hard to do, because when you seek from the time of birth to encourage your child you develop good habits that are natural to continue. I read a lovely anonymous quote recently: "A parent's job is to keep her child's cup of self-esteem so full that the rest of the world can't poke enough holes in it to drain it dry."

▪ *Do* give your child a strong spiritual foundation, and encourage him to accept Jesus as Savior as soon as he's able to understand what that decision means. Nothing reinforces a person's self-esteem so much as knowing that Jesus died for him and that the Creator of the universe loves him enough to listen to his prayers. "That, to me, is the most important thing you can do for a child," says Terri.

▪ *Don't* take your child for granted. "Enjoy him, and treasure every minute," says Karen H. "We've almost lost Josh twice, and we know that God may call him home before we're ready. Children are a gift, but they're only ours to nurture for a while. They belong to God."

10
The Working Mommy

Don't skip this chapter if you have been blessed with the freedom to stay home with your baby. As Debby points out, the title "The Working Mommy" is really a misnomer. All mothers work, and anyone who thinks they don't has never been one. Besides, you may need to help supplement the family income someday, and before we talk about mothers who toil in the outside world we'll show we'll how some of our moms have earned money while remaining at home with their children.

And do stay with us through the first section if you work outside the home. Our purpose in putting it at the beginning of the chapter is not to make you feel guilty for something you can't avoid. It's to show you some options you may not have thought of.

Working at Home

We'll have to content ourselves with giving you some ideas and general pointers in this section, since it would be a book in itself if we tried to include everything you need to know about starting a home business. For specifics, consult libraries, bookstores, and newsstands—the bigger the better. You'd be surprised at the wide range of specialty books and trade magazines available for the home entrepreneur.

And now, before we start giving ideas, a few warnings are in order:

Warning 1. It's not uncommon to hear of a full-fledged family business that started as a way to keep Mommy at home. But a home business usually takes a while to get off the ground, so plan on having little or no income from it for at least the first month or so. You may even have to spend a little money in advertising and free samples to get started. And even once you've become established, your home business will most likely be a supplement to your husband's income rather than the family's sole source of support unless you invest an unusual amount of time and effort in it.

Warning 2. Home businesses tend to have on and off seasons. For example, the months right before Christmas are an on season for a craftsperson, whereas spring and summer, with their weddings, are on seasons for a dressmaker or home caterer. Summer break is an off season for private music teachers, babysitters, and home typists specializing in college term papers. These on and off seasons don't have to be a drawback if you budget and plan for them. You can even offset them by diversifying and becoming a Jacque of several trades.

Warning 3. Don't charge too much for your services, but don't charge too little, either. Do some market research to find out what your competition charges, and offer a comparable value. "A lot of times we tend to sell ourselves short," says Patti.

Warning 4. If you're going to do something professionally (i.e., get paid), go about it in a professional manner. Wear businesslike clothes and leave your baby with a sitter when you visit local merchants to advertise your product or service, and have inexpensive business cards printed if you can afford it. Draw up a simple written agreement, to be signed by both you and your client with copies to each, detailing what goods or services will be provided and what payment is to be given when. If you're custom making goods for a client, get a deposit in advance. Your potential customers will take you only as seriously as you take yourself.

Warning 5. Make sure your product or service is needed. A cobbler in Florida would have a hard time making a living from fur-lined boots no matter how well they were made. Again, this is the place to do a little market research.

Warning 6. Keep your priorities straight. If you provide a needed, high-quality product or service at a reasonable price, you'll soon have as much business as you can handle, and probably more. Accept only as much business as you can do well and still give top priority to your baby—after all, that's why you want to stay home, isn't it? Make sure you give yourself and your baby time in the fresh air and away from home. A lot can be done in the morning before your child wakes—if he's not an early riser—during naps, and after he goes to bed. I should know. That's when I wrote this book.

Warning 7. The life of the home entrepreneur is not for the shrinking violet. Running a home business takes the ability to promote your business with confidence and to say "thank you" with a smile to the potential client who tells you he doesn't need your services—which happens to all of us. It requires that you be a self-starter who can make yourself get up each morning and work whether you feel like it or not. But there's no law that says a shrinking violet—and a lazy one at that—can't turn into a top home businesswoman. It all depends on how committed you are to it.

Warning 8. Remember Uncle Sam. Save receipts, and keep strict records of all income and expenditures for income tax and social security purposes. If you have a special corner of your home reserved for your business, save your home utility stubs and tell your tax person about it. It's also a good idea to save a percentage of your profits against April 15th. And do check with your local government to see whether you need a permit for your type of home business.

Now that you know what you're getting yourself into, let's go down a list of home businesses our moms found profitable.

Home Typing Services. This kind of business is ideal for the mom with secretarial experience. But even if your typing up until now has been strictly amateur you can run a successful typing service as long as you turn out a professional product. It'll just take you longer, and you'll have to do a little studying to learn the proper formats for business letters, term papers, and resumes.

Probably the most lucrative place to run a home typing service is a college town, but the college doesn't have to be big. Remember, community colleges and business schools assign term papers too. There are three small colleges in our city, and several of our moms have found that they get just about all the business they want by putting up notices on the school bulletin boards. List your price per page, your name, your phone number, and by all means include any extras you can offer such as minor spelling and grammatical corrections.

Cheryl recommends visiting the front office as well: "Most of the work from students comes around midterm and at the end of the term, but it helps to get your name known in the office. Now, when an extra project comes up, the receptionist refers people to me." Dana charges a higher fee for midterm and end-of-term papers—inspired by hotels' seasonal rates, I guess—and Patti points out that even the professors at colleges often need typing and proofreading done, so take your business card around to them as well.

Small businesses are another potential marketplace for the home typist. Go in, ask to speak to the office manager, give her your card, and say, "I have a professional in-home typing business, and I'd like to offer you my services if extra projects come up."

Music Lessons. Patti is a state-certified music teacher, and she advertises her availability to teach private lessons by sending notices detailing her qualifications to local school band and choral directors. "Let church music departments know, too," says Dana, who works in one. "We receive an average of two calls a week from people who want their children to take lessons." Put up notices also at day-care centers that work with grade-school-age children, and don't forget the classified section of your newspaper.

Patti has one warning for the potential private music teacher: "I had trouble for a while with students who cancelled at the last minute, so I started charging by the month, in advance. Now if they cancel, they still pay."

Dressmaking and Alterations. This business is a natural for the woman who likes to make her own clothes. Put your business cards up on church, day-care center, and business bulletin boards, and leave them at floral shops catering to brides. If you do alterations, leave your card at local dry cleaners and laundromats and ask the proprietors to send business your way. You can also get your working friends in on the act by making them a dress for the cost of the fabric and notions, stipulating that they give their office co-workers your card when they start receiving compliments—which of course they will.

You can charge for this service either of two ways: by the hour, plus cost of fabric and notions, or at a flat rate determined by the article of clothing being sewn, plus cost. Whichever you choose to do, give your customer a reliable estimate and let her know if you're going to run over.

Crafts. The idea that craftspeople have to be naturally artistic is a common misconception. Speaking as a person who has done everything from crochet to decoupage to macrame to flower arranging to counted cross-stitch to handtwined wreaths to furniture refinishing to basketry, let me inform you that crafts take NO TALENT. What they take is the willingness to follow instructions and stick with a project until it's done right. Talent comes in when you take the instructions and modify them to make something uniquely your own—and even that can be developed with time.

Visit craft shops and stores specializing in handmade gifts to find ideas for things you can make quickly and well, and with as little expense as possible. Then take samples of your wares to local gift shops and see which ones will sell them on consignment. Or camp out on the weekends at local flea markets, or look for information in trade publications on participating in craft fairs. Or give samples to your working friends for their desks, again with the stipulation that they recommend you to their co-workers. A couple of moms even held parties in their friends' homes, *a la* Tupperware, at which they displayed their handmade products and took orders.

Home Babysitting Services. Once you're accustomed to taking care of your own little one, you may be ready to take on a couple of your working friends' children. Wanda says, "When Michelle was eighteen months old and Dennis was out of college I was able to quit work, but we still needed a supplement, so I babysat during the day. I did register with the health department, which made the parents feel a little safer."

Wanda's advertising was mostly by word of mouth among her friends: "The parents were comfortable leaving their children with someone they knew," she says. "And I didn't make any bones about the fact that I read Christian stories to the kids and that we sang Christian songs, and that if they fell down and hurt themselves I prayed with them. If anything, that helped my business increase, because I always had more calls than I could take." To simplify her bookkeeping, Wanda charged the same per-day price whether a child stayed for a full day or only a few hours.

One thing you'll need to do that a fully staffed day-care facility would not is make the parents aware of the need to have an alternate arrangement should you or your baby become sick. Also, obtain copies of local day-care center policies and use them to help you formulate your own policies, in writing, to give to each set of parents. And be sure to check with your county health department to see how many children you can babysit without becoming a licensed day-care facility. Right now, where I live, the limit is four children in addition to your own (eight children total is maximum), but the laws are changing and vary from county to county and state to state.

If you choose to babysit in your home, be prepared to give your charges all the love and attention you'd want your own child to receive in someone else's care. You'll need to have a fenced-in yard where the children can run and play, or at the very least a large, open room and lots of creative toys and books. And you'll without doubt have to adopt a relaxed attitude toward your house, since handprints on the walls and accidents on the carpet are inevitable. And finally, it's a good idea to get training in infant CPR, but that's really something all mothers should do anyway.

Paper Routes. If your baby does well in the car, you may want to look into this. Lois had an afternoon paper route when her children were toddlers, and she says they still remember the discussions they had as they drove along. "My daughter has told me, 'Mom, we sure got a good spiritual foundation on that paper route!'"

Home Catering. Rita's sister Janet bakes cakes for special occasions. "She worked in supermarkets and learned cake decorating a long time ago," says Rita. "She even makes wedding cakes." Even if you've never worked in a bakery or supermarket, many community colleges offer courses in cake decorating. Advertise your wares in the same places where you'd advertise dressmaking: day-care centers, floral shops, bridal shops, businesses, and churches. If the proprietors are reluctant to recommend you, offer them a free sample of your goods.

Patti made dinner for a working friend one night a week. She says, "I just doubled my recipe for whatever my family was eating that night, and she paid me for it." This type of home catering business can grow quickly by word of mouth. Require your customers to pick up their food at your house on their way home from work, and charge a price comparable to what they'd pay in a family-style restaurant.

Be sure to call your county health department before you embark on this kind of enterprise. In many areas, including mine, home catering as such is illegal. A caterer must do her cooking in a facility separate from her home kitchen, that facility must be inspected, and she must be licensed.

Miscellaneous. Examine the skills you've gained from school, volunteer work, or previous employment for ways they can be used in a home business. If you're quitting a clerical or secretarial job, ask your employer to consider you for extra projects that can be done at home. And don't neglect the contacts you've made while in school or the working world. Pene earns a good-sized salary proofreading at home for a news service, a job that came about as a result of a contact she made before her son Aaron was born.

If you spend a little time thinking about it, you can come up with all sorts of ideas for home businesses. All it takes to put them into action is a sizable dose of perseverance and nerve, both of which you'll develop if you remain a mother for very long.

A Word About Part-Time Jobs

For our moms who tried it, working at a part-time job was like buying a five-pound turkey. By the time they got rid of the skin and bones—i.e., the hidden expense—there was very little meat left.

A part-time job involves most of the hidden expense a full-time job does, with less pay to show for it. And that's especially true because most of the part-time jobs our moms found were in the sales and clerical fields and paid little, if any, more than minimum wage. High-paying part-time jobs are rare, but if you must work and can find one, it may be worth your while to grab it.

Cheryl says, "When I worked part-time at our church, I was doing it more for myself—to spend time with my husband, who also worked there, and with other people I liked, and to have some adult conversation. But I didn't get much money out of the deal, even though I paid only half-price for day care because I was a church employee."

Day care is probably the biggest hidden expense for the mom who works outside the home. But according to our working moms there are quite a few others that need to be taken into consideration when you're figuring how much spendable income you would earn at an outside job. You may find that you could earn a comparable amount with a home business.

Here's our moms' basic hidden expense list: Day care; withholding taxes; transportation (extra fuel and/or extra car, upkeep, insurance); working wardrobe ("Panty hose!" says Patti); baby formula and disposable diapers for your baby's time at the sitter's; more clothing for your baby, especially in cool weather ("Yes, your baby has to have a working wardrobe!" laughs Adrienne); higher doctor bills if your babysitter watches more than one child at a time (and our working moms agree that their doctor bills really did go up). Add to this basic list money spent on household help, convenience foods, and lunches out. "That depends on your working schedule," says Wanda. "A lot of times in our family it's dinners out too—not just lunches." Most of our working moms say they now spend much more on meals out than they did when they stayed home. "Going out one night a week used to be a real treat," says Cheryl. "Now it's, 'Not again! Can't we eat at home tonight?' It gets old very fast."

Working Full-time

Life is not easy for the working mother of a new baby or young toddler, and it's no use pretending that it is or that it can somehow be made that way. Aside from the sheer physical hard work of carrying on what should be the tasks of two women, all our working moms experienced at least some guilt at leaving their babies—even when they had no choice. "Working before my children came was a breeze," says Debby. "Working with a child was a different story. Sometimes there was so much stress that I felt I was being pulled in at least three pieces. My job pulled one way, my husband pulled another, and my child pulled still another. Each demanded first priority."

With all this talk about hidden expenses and how hard the life is both emotionally and physically, I realize that this chapter runs the risk of sounding like a diatribe against working full-time. The simple fact is, the overwhelming majority of our *working* moms believe that a full-time job outside the home should be the last resort for a new mother. But if you must use that last resort, as several of them did, be comforted by the knowledge that the Lord is able to give you strength and wisdom, just as He has done and continues to do for our working moms. Their children are happy, healthy, well-adjusted tributes to the fact that He is able to help a mother compensate for a situation she can't avoid.

For our working moms, two factors determined whether combining baby with job was merely difficult or nearly impossible. The first factor was whether or not they were able to have confidence that their babies were in competent, loving hands while they were gone; the second was the amount of help and support they received from their husbands.

"I found a fantastic lady who babysat in her home," says Wanda. "She had raised five of her own kids, and loved Michelle as if she were one of them. It made it easier for me in that I wasn't afraid to leave her, but it didn't help me want to leave her any more. I guess I probably cried for the first three days." Our moms agree that if you possibly can it's best to have a young baby cared for by a competent individual rather than a day-care center. Debby says, "I just wanted my child to have someone's personal attention. As soon as I found out I was pregnant I started praying about who would take care of my baby."

Wanda recommends checking with your friends who are good mothers and who may want to earn some extra money while staying at home with their own little ones. "Talk with people who have the same values and way of life you do," she says. "That way, at least they'll display the same general attitudes around your child that you would." Don't be afraid to spell out exactly what kind of care you're looking for.

If you're approaching an experienced in-home baby-sitter, ask to see her stock of toys and storybooks, and check to see where the dreaded TV set figures in her decor. Is it where your child will be spending most of her play time? Carol B.'s experience with TV and her toddler came from a day-care center, but it applies to home child care as well: "Kristie was thirteen months old when I had to go to work," she says. "I found a day-care center that was clean, they served good food, and they sat my child in front of a television set for eight hours a day.

"At the time I didn't know what damage that could do, but wow! is all I can say. She had a very limited attention span and it took her four years to learn to read, and I've just found out in the past couple of years that TV was the cause of it."

After a child is three years old, our moms feel better about putting him into a good day-care center rather than a home. Patti says, "By then they're more ready for the social atmosphere and the higher pupil/teacher ratio."

In any day-care situation, ask for the names of other mothers who have children there, and call to ask whether their children seem to be happy and doing well. Make drop-in visits to see what the children do at different times of the day, and ask what activities are provided for older babies and toddlers. Have a frank talk with the sitter or the proprietor of the day-care center and let her know that you're checking her out not because you don't trust her, but because you want to be sure you're doing the very best for your baby. If she resents that, she's not the right person for you anyway.

More and more churches today are sponsoring Christian schools and, along with them, day-care centers. Regarding them, Cheryl says, "A church day-care center may be just fine as far as having good, moral, Christian women watching the kids, but if they're just babysitting and you've got a toddler who is ready to hear stories and have some educational stimulation, that's not necessarily the way to go. When I was looking for a day-care center for my boys, I spent two days calling around, and then visiting and asking questions. I ended up putting them in a secular day-care franchise because I was so impressed with it."

Be careful that you don't put your child into a Christian day-care center with the thought that they'll do all his spiritual training for you. Your child's caretakers should support your beliefs and values—or at least not contradict them—but the responsibility for his spiritual upbringing belongs to you and your husband.

Cheryl says it's also important to have a day-care center that takes an individual interest in your child: "I really appreciated it when Miss Barbara told me last year, 'Brian's not ready for the two-year-old class yet. His attention span isn't long enough for him to sit down and listen, so let's keep him in toddlers for half a year.' She knew him well enough to know what was best for him, and she took the time to talk to me about it."

Most important in your choice of a day-care center is whether you have peace of mind after having prayed and hunted and called and asked questions and visited and then prayed some more. Trust the Lord's guidance and your own instincts if you feel it isn't the place for you, even if all the other factors seem right. And once you find the right caregiver, keep alert for changes in your child's behavior that could be danger signals, and, as soon as your toddler can talk, encourage him to tell you all the details of his day. Cheryl says, "It's my and Rodger's responsibility as our children's spiritual leaders to keep up with what's going on. The minute there's a problem or something hits me wrong, it's time to reevaluate and possibly make a change."

She adds, "Your attitude, your peace about the situation, affects your child too. Our boys attend a Christian day-care center now, and each day we pray in the car on the way there that the Lord will protect them and help them learn about Jesus. It gives them a sense of anticipation about the day."

And finally, here's a tip on acquainting your baby with his new caregivers: When you're preparing to leave him on a regular basis, begin by doing it for a short length of time—say, an hour. Build up to longer periods as he becomes accustomed to the people and surroundings.

How important is it for a working mom to have a husband who helps out at home? Our moms' reaction to this question is strong and one-sided. "It's the only way," says Carol B. Wanda adds, "I couldn't do it without Dennis. A helpful husband is worth his weight in gold."

Most of our working moms say that their husbands are very helpful—but they also say they didn't come prepackaged that way. For the most part, helpful husbands are made, not born. Debby says, "Husbands have to be made to realize that it's much harder on the mother to work at a job outside the home than it is on the father. Responsibilities of a mother seem to be just taken for granted, and many times the father simply doesn't realize the pressures on her. It's a mistake for a new mother to think that surely her husband must know how hard she has to work, and that he'll just pitch in and help. My husband didn't even know what needed to be done around the house, much less do anything. The only way to get help is to ask for it—communicate. Make that new daddy understand and acknowledge that you are helping him with *his* responsibility to provide for the family by working at a job, and he must help you with yours. Otherwise, no matter how hard you try, resentments creep in and serious marital problems can crop up."

With a little practice, much of the housework and babywork normally done by you can be done by your husband: cooking, washing dishes, laundry, dusting, vacuuming, straightening, changing diapers, bathing and feeding the baby. But you'll need to adopt an understanding attitude if he didn't, like you, have the benefit of years of motherly training in household responsibility. And for organization's sake make up a basic chore list that spells out when each job should be done and by whom. It's probably best to have as many distinct "Mommy jobs" and "Daddy jobs" as possible, but do rotate the more distasteful ones—like scrubbing the toilet.

You'll also need to face the fact that, no matter how helpful your husband is, the bottom-line responsibility for your baby's welfare is yours. As with our moms, you will probably be the one to say when it's feeding time or a diaper needs changing, or to detect when your little one feels feverish. But if your husband learns to enjoy time spent playing with the baby, or to get up in the middle of the night and rock her back to sleep when she wakes up crying, both he and your child will be the richer for it.

There are more benefits to having a husband who is involved at home than just the immediate ones to you. As your child grows, you and your husband are giving him or her an object lesson in what marriage is like. Rita's husband Marvin is a paragon of helpfulness, and she believes he is giving her two sons, who are now in junior high and high school, a priceless lesson that will benefit their own wives someday: "I'm so thankful! Children watch you so intently, and they pick up everything you do. Brian and Billy have really caught his spirit for helping."

A Day in the Life . . .

Our typical working mom's day begins at around six a.m., when she rises, grabs a quick breakfast, and dresses before the children are up. "My priority before they wake up is me," says Dana. "After they wake up, it's them."

When the children are awake, she feeds them, dresses them, and makes sure they have everything they need to take to the babysitter's. It seems that early mornings are the one time when our moms' helpful husbands aren't much help. About the most they do is make sure they get themselves dressed. This unfair arrangement makes me feel fervent gratitude for my mother-in-law, a wise lady who taught her sons to help around the house long before that became popular. I don't work outside the home, but for times when Jon, Megan, and I all have to be somewhere at once we've worked out a more equitable system based on who has the most to do in the morning. I rise early and eat breakfast, and, when Megan wakes, feed her. After Jon takes his shower I hand her over to him, and after he dresses himself and her they play together or read a story while I fix my face and hair. We're usually ready to walk out the door at about the same time.

To the question of who stays home when the baby is sick, the nearly unanimous answer is, of course, Mommy. But one of our moms says, "My husband and I alternate if our daughter is sick for more than a day or so, or if I have something particularly important to do that week. My husband's employer asked him why he stayed home when that was the mother's job, and my husband answered that he feels it's as much his responsibility as it is mine, and that there are times when what I have to do at work is more urgent than what he has to do that day." Whether you can do this depends on your and your husband's respective employers, and should probably be discussed with them beforehand.

According to Cheryl, lunch break is the working mom's big chance to catch some time alone. But she recommends that you don't do it at home. "If I go home," she says, "I feel as if I have to clean the house—and maybe I do that once or twice a week. But for the working mom, lunch hour is the ideal time to have devotions, or go down to a lake or a park and eat lunch and read, or take a walk. I know there are always things I could and should be doing—I *should* go to the store, and I *should* clean the house—but that's when I try to have some time to myself."

After work, it's time to pick up your child and head for home. "You'll find that on coming home your toddler will want your immediate attention," says Dana. "He may show it in different ways, such as disobedience, showing off, or even just coming up and saying, 'What are ya doin'?' as you're cooking dinner. What he really wants is for you to sit down and give him your undivided attention. It may not take long at all to satisfy him, but when you do he'll be assured of your love." With Kristie, Carol B. has adopted the habit of having a milk-and-cookie time immediately after arriving home to give her daughter a chance to share her day with Mom and Dad; this practice also helps tide their growling stomachs over until dinner is ready.

Speaking of dinner—who cooks? "At our house," says Wanda, "it's whoever's the least tired. We trade off." Patti says, "I'd rather have my husband take the kids outside to play while I cook dinner." Cheryl agrees: "I've always felt that's a good time for Rodger to spend some time with the boys anyway. Usually I give them a snack or a piece of fruit, since they're always hungry when they get home, then Rodger uses that time to play with them and unwind a little himself."

To make your dinner situation easier, try cooking two or three big entrees on the weekends, then freezing the leftovers in meal-sized portions and eating them during the week, with maybe a variation on the accompanying salad or vegetable. Once you get a leftover bank built up, you can have quite a variety of meals to choose from during the week. This method has worked well for me. By using recipes that serve 8–10 people, I'm able to put three meals into the freezer each time I cook. Currently my family is eating a homemade meal nearly every night even though I actually cook only two or three times a week. Setting aside the portions to be frozen before dinner will help keep your family from going back for seconds or thirds. Also, I have found it essential to label and date my containers and to keep a current list of my freezer's contents.

Getting back to our typical working mom: her typical toddler goes to bed at around seven-thirty (although a younger baby may stay up much later), so after dinner there is just enough time for a bath, a brief story-prayer-and-cuddle time, and then bed. But even though the baby's day is over, Mommy's and Daddy's is still going strong. There are still the dinner dishes, laundry, and miscellaneous housework to do.

"My mom worked while I was growing up," says Patti, "and all my childhood I thought the dish fairy came every night and washed the dishes, since she never did them until after we were in bed. I fully expected to have a dish fairy when I grew up—what a disappointment!" Of course, as your toddler grows older doing dishes together can be a good chance to spend time with her or him.

After the housework is finished, there's still the next day to prepare for. "I try to do as much as possible the night before," says Cheryl, "—lay out the clothes, pack the lunches, put together the diaper bag." Dana has gone as far as pouring the breakfast cereal, covering the bowls, and putting them on the table.

Oh Where, Oh Where Has Our Family Time Gone?

As you can see from the last section, the family in which both parents work full-time has few opportunities to sit around and enjoy being together. While the stay-at-home mother has to find ways to get out of the house, the working mother's struggle is to find ways to stay home—or at least spend as much as possible of what has become known as "quality time" with her family.

The most obvious family times are dinnertime, right before bedtime, and weekends, but our working moms feel you can't build a healthy family life on those few hours a week—especially when you consider that a good portion of your at-home time will be taken up by housework. They've had to develop the ability to say no to worthy activities, such as church choir or shopping with friends, in order to be with their families, and they've learned to steal time with their children from moments that would ordinarily have been wasted.

Debby says, "Having the baby in her carrier near the ironing board or in the kitchen as I prepared dinner provided time for me to talk to her and notice all the changes she went through from day to day. And even though her 'daytime grandmother' had her clean and nice when I picked her up after work, I always took the time to bathe my baby before bedtime. We had so much fun splashing and talking and sometimes crying with each other. It was a real release emotionally for me to hold and bathe and dress that child who was a part of me. It made all the extra work worthwhile. To have a sweet-smelling, beautiful baby ready for bed, and see her settle down to sleep, was my reward for the day—and I believe all mothers need some type of reward, even though it may be different for each mother."

Cheryl adds, "Some of the best time Jason and Brian and I have is driving in the car to and from day care, to and from the store, to and from the laundromat; and that's some of the best time they have with their dad, too. Even if Rodger is home and could watch the kids while I go shopping, I try to take one of them with me and leave the other with him. That way we both get a chance to talk with them. When they reach the age when they're talking as much as Jason and Brian are, at two and four years old, being in the car is really one of the best times to let them tell crazy stories, or have theological discussions, like, 'Where does God live?' You'd be surprised at how much time you spend in the car."

Lois agrees: "We have a wonderful Christian radio station in our area, but I don't play the radio when I'm in the car with my kids, because if I do we'll listen and not talk. I developed that habit when I had a paper route. I'd flip the radio off and say, 'Okay, let's talk.' They'd sit there for a few minutes and not say anything, but after that, boy, the in-depth questions started to come!"

Wanda adds, "We enjoy our family time together, but it's also good for Michelle to have time alone with me, just the two of us. And it's very good for Dennis and Michelle to have time just for them—and that's good for me, too!" Perhaps Saturday morning could be a time for your husband to take your toddler to the park or out to breakfast, giving you a couple of hours to escape the double responsibility of being a working mother. Help your child's father to understand that the bulk of responsibility for your little one's welfare rests on your shoulders, no matter how helpful he is, and that there are times when you simply need to get away—mentally, at least.

The working mother really doesn't have less time alone with her husband than the stay-at-home mother; in fact, she may have more if they work together or if she can sometimes meet him for lunch. But her priorities are often so divided that it's easy for her husband to slide to the bottom of the list. "Time with our husbands needs to be a priority too," says Cheryl.

"Have date nights out; plan on babysitters every now and then. Find times other than ten-thirty at night to be alone, whether it's meeting for lunch—Rodger and I try to do that at least once a week—or when the baby is taking a nap on the weekends. If you don't make your husband a priority there's going to be trouble, and he may even come to resent the child. Nurturing your marriage is as important as nurturing your baby." Actually, nurturing your marriage provides a secure family for your baby, thus nurturing him as well. "It's something you have to plan for," says Virginia. "It doesn't just happen."

As was typical of our working moms, Dawn hesitated to leave Melody for a night out with her husband, since she also leaves her during the day while she's at work. "Until Melody was six months old, we never went out without her," she says. "Brian never complained, but it finally got to the point where it was ridiculous. I had to realize that my marriage was important and that we really needed time alone together." Jon and I found it easier to go out on dates as Megan grew older and began going to bed at seven and seven-thirty. We asked the babysitter to arrive just before bedtime, and started our evening together then.

Rita recommends letting your husband know he's in your thoughts by giving him little cards and notes, and by doing special little things that really don't take extra time: "Marvin grew up on lima beans and rice," she says, "and the boys hate any kind of beans. So when I cook them we make a big deal of the fact that they're Daddy's favorites. He feels that's something special I did just for him. That sort of thing goes a long way."

Finding Help

To gain more free time with their families, several moms found a cleaning person to come in once every week or two to help with the heavy housework. Cheryl found her housecleaner by checking the bulletin board at church and asking other working moms if they knew of someone who would do a good job at a reasonable price.

But your housecleaner doesn't have to be a professional. Pat has used college students, and Pene's sister used a high school student with good results. A responsible teenager is less apt than a professional to have set ways of doing housework and is less likely to be offended when you spell out exactly what you want done—which is something you *will* need to do. And it wouldn't hurt to walk her through it at first.

If you don't already have a responsible student in mind, try asking among parents with teenage children or putting up notices on school bulletin boards, specifying the wage you can pay (minimum wage is fair) as well as the hours you want help. Cheryl says, "Don't make it sound like a permanent job the first time. Just say, 'I need some help getting my house clean. Could you come over for a couple of hours?' If it works out well, ask her to come every week. If it doesn't, at least you haven't committed yourself.

"Even if you can't afford or find a housecleaner," she adds, "there are many laundromats that wash, dry, and fold. That may seem like a little thing, but a load of clothes a day can begin to look like a mountain. You'd be amazed at what a difference it can make just to have someone else do your laundry."

11
...
Making Memories

Think back. What's your most treasured childhood memory? Your most precious keepsake? The reason these things are spotlighted in our minds and hearts is that they speak to our sense of self-esteem. They say, "I love you. You're important to me. I care enough to talk with you, listen to you, read to you, cuddle you, work with you, play with you, make this for you, save this for you, write this down for you." They give us a sense of belonging in a world where that feeling is rare.

We have to work hard for our special memories nowadays, and that's not surprising. Special memories are active and personal in an increasingly passive, public society that spends its days shuttling its children to and from day-care centers and its nights releasing the stresses of the day before the TV set.

You probably won't have too much trouble providing special memories for your children if your own parents provided them for you, since you'll just continue the existing traditions and think of others as you go along. But it can be hard to get started if your own family belonged to the sit-around, don't-talk-to-each-other, let-the-TV-do-the-babysitting school of thought. We'll give you a push by letting you borrow our memories. Eventually, you'll be able to use them to think of family traditions of your own.

Fleeting Moments that Last Forever

Of the two kinds of special memories, tangible and intangible, the intangible ones are by far the most important. They're the ones you can't put into an album or up in your closet. They're fleeting—they happen and then are preserved only in your mind. They're the most durable kind of special memory, since they can't be taken away from you or destroyed by fire, flood, or time.

They're also extremely unpredictable. In families accustomed to spending real time together, they tend to sneak up as you go about your daily life alongside the people you love. They tap you on the shoulder days or months or years later and say, "Remember me?"

"I remember one time my father let me draw a picture on his back," says Terri. "I must have been about four years old. I was down on the floor, and I had a pen and I was writing, and I think I got a mark on him by mistake. We started goofing around, and I told him, 'I'm gonna draw a whole picture on you.' He lay perfectly still and I just scribbled away on his back, which was something

I was of course never allowed to do. I'll never forget it."

Adrienne remembers the time when she was small, listening to the radio with her father, when suddenly he asked her to dance. They waltzed around the room together for a few minutes that are now preserved for a lifetime in her heart.

"I still remember my mother praying for us every morning," says Virginia, "and another thing I remember is making homemade doughnuts together, and the aroma in the kitchen as they cooked. She let us help punch out the holes and eat the dough. Those were such special times."

Kathy says, "Something I'll always remember is the contentment of going to sleep hearing my parents talking in the living room. And as they went to bed too they'd lie there and talk. I couldn't understand what they were saying, but I could hear the mumble of their voices—no arguments or anything. I always went to sleep that way. Just knowing that they were there, and that they were still awake, was very important to me."

The Daily Specials

We've talked for a few moments about our moms' childhood memories; now we'll switch gears and show how they're making memories for *their* children.

Special memories are people-oriented; they happen while you're doing things together. And, as the moms quoted above have shown, often the memories that stand above the crowd are ones that somehow break the daily routine. Cheryl says, "My boys started liking picnics from the first day we went on one when they were just one and two years old. Even when we don't have a car available, they like to just take their lunches outside and spread a blanket or sit on lounge chairs with a sandwich and a cup of juice. And on rainy days sometimes we spread a blanket on the floor and have a picnic in the house."

Another way to give your child special memories and a sense of belonging, says Connie, is to create family gestures and passwords. "Our favorite number is five," she says, "since there are five in our family. When we're at the beach and Stephanie sees five pelicans in a group, she says, 'There's our family!' or when we're visiting the mountains and April sees five fish in a stream, she says, 'There's our family!' And we have what we call a five-way kiss. We get in a circle and all turn and kiss the cheek of the one on our right, and then do the same with the one on our left." Jon and I do something similar with Megan. Since she's an only child right now, we make a "Megan sandwich"—we stand on either side of her and kiss the dickens out of her cheeks. She loves it!

Vacations, when you make a special effort to spend time together, can also yield special memories. Connie says, "When we go to the beach, we collect shells together. In my mind I can still hear the girls saying, 'Look at this one—it's purple!' and see everyone crowding around to see it. We brought the shells back and let each girl keep the ones she found in a pretty jar on her dresser."

Our moms who have several children find it useful to make sure their little ones get time alone with Mommy by allotting each child some special time during the day. Carol says, "Right after lunch is Andrew's time—he's three. We sit down, and he picks out the books and we read. Then, after school, the older children have their time." When Glenda's children were little, her husband

Joe started the habit of taking them for a walk around the block as soon as he came home from work. That became their special time with Daddy, and it gave Glenda a chance to relax.

Several of our moms and their husbands plan a weekly family night where the TV is not watched unless there's something very special on, and no commitments are made unless they can be done as a family. "Friday night was always our family night," says Virginia. "Sometimes we'd go out to eat and then play miniature golf afterwards, or if there was something special on TV we'd watch it and pop popcorn." Family night doesn't have to be fancy—talk, read stories, go for a drive, cook a special meal, play simple games, work on crafts or Christmas gifts. As Virginia says, "Whatever you do, being together is fun." Carol's family has a group family night: "We've opened our home for a family Bible study on Thursday nights. It's really been special. We keep it short because of the children, but the kids really love having other children there."

Special Times, Special Seasons

As might be expected, many of our moms' most treasured memories are of holidays, particularly Christmas—and that's also the time of year when they work hardest to make special memories for their own children. They feel a strong obligation to keep the focus of Christmas on Jesus without taking the fun away, and they've developed quite a few new traditions to do it.

Having a birthday party for Jesus, complete with cake, is a favorite, and several families even incorporate their Christmas gift-giving into the celebration. Karin says, "It was our little boy, Matthew, who brought up the idea of a birthday party. We had been trying to emphasize to him that Christmas is Jesus' birthday, and about a week before Christmas he came to me and said, 'But, Mommy, Jesus doesn't have a birthday cake.' He was really torn up about it. So I made Jesus a birthday cake."

Kathy and her family take Jesus' birthday cake with them when they go to Grandma's house to celebrate: "In one day," she says, "we'll have our Christmas in the morning, then go to one grandparent's house, and then this year we'll be going to another one later on. Our relatives don't always keep the focus on Jesus the way we'd like it to be there for our children, so this is just our little way of carrying Jesus' birthday into the other homes too." Marilee has older toddlers, and she includes Santa in their celebration of Jesus' birthday by telling her children the story of Saint Nicholas and how, many years ago, he began the tradition of giving Christmas gifts.

Another way our moms accomplish their dual purpose of keeping the holiday season both Christ-centered and fun is to tell lots of Christmas stories. Carol says, "During the month of December, I have a big basket by the rocking chair filled with books of Christmas stories. When my children want a story, we just reach into the basket and get one." "The more wonder you put into the Christmas stories you tell your children, the better," adds Cheryl. "Tell about the star leading the wise men across a whole country, and how they brought valuable gifts, and how the shepherds and even the animals came to see the baby Jesus. Make it so full of wonder that a couple of little elves and a fat man in a red suit pale in comparison. My two boys are more excited about Jesus' birthday than the other kids in the neighborhood are about Santa Claus."

Adrienne made her children an advent calendar in the shape of a green burlap Christmas tree on a brown background. She says, "There are twenty-four ornaments made of stiff fabric that hang around the edges until we need them. Starting December 1st, we read a little piece of Scripture every day and then put an ornament on the tree." The first six days are the six days of Creation; the seventh is Isaiah 11:1, the trunk; then the next two weeks' verses deal with Jesus' forebears—Adam and Eve, Noah, Abraham, Isaac, Jacob, et al., ending with Mary. The last three days are the Christmas story from the books of Matthew and Luke, with the last decoration being the baby Jesus lying in the manger. As each day's verses are read, Adrienne tells her children a simple story about the circumstances surrounding them. "The kids love it!" she says. "It's their favorite Christmas tradition—they wouldn't miss their Advent calendar for anything."

To a child, a nativity set is a bunch of dolls in a straw house—and dolls are to be played with. Carol keeps two nativity sets: a high-quality plastic one for the older children, and a safe, wooden one on a low table for the toddlers. Kathy also keeps an inexpensive nativity set and allows her little ones to act out the Christmas story with it. "It helps them visualize the story," she says. "You can put your nice, handmade nativity set up out of reach."

Another aim our moms have at Christmastime is to teach their little ones the joy of giving rather than reinforcing the "gimme-gimme" attitude that usually mars the spirit of the season. Terri encourages Zachary and Ashley to give birthday presents to Jesus each year by helping them clean out their toy boxes and give toys that are still in good shape to charitable organizations, citing the verse from Matthew, "I tell you the truth, whatever you did for the least of these brothers of mine, you did for me" (NIV).

She says, "The first year, I tried and tried to explain it to Zachary, but he was so little. Finally he came to me and gave me a book and said, 'Here.' I asked, 'Is that all you're going to give?' He said, 'Yeah, it's the only thing I've got two of.' But he looks forward to it now, because I've tried to teach him that there are some kids whose mommies and daddies can't buy them toys, or who maybe don't even have mommies and daddies. We take the toys down to the church and unload them, and that's big-time to him. He can't wait. It also helps both Zachary and Ashley to see, when they open their own gifts a week or two later, that many times when you give you also receive." Terri says this tradition is also a great way to clear some space for the new toys your child will receive during the holidays.

If you adopt this tradition, let your child choose the toys he wants to give, and don't rebuke him if he doesn't give as much as you'd like. But don't be surprised if he, like Michele's four-year-old daughter Sarah, chooses to give the very best. "Sarah's nursery school class was told to bring toys for underprivileged children," says Michele. "She went into her room that afternoon and came out carrying her tape recorder and the bear she sleeps with. She told me, 'Mommy, these are my very favorite toys, so I know those poor little boys and girls will like them.'"

"Something we've done since our kids were little," says Glenda, "and it's one of the things they remember most, is making all kinds of goodies together. Then on Christmas Eve or Christmas Day we pack them into little bundles to send to all our neighbors and friends, and the kids get to go with their daddy to deliver them." "That's the fun part!" adds Carol.

Carol and her children make simple "gingerbread houses" from graham cracker squares glued together with icing from a squirt can. She says, "They're very small and simple, but we put them on cardboard bases and decorate them with icing and gumdrops and candy, and the kids give them as presents to our neighbors. My three year old loves it."

Several of our moms downplay what has, in our society, become the primary focus of Christmas: the family gift giving itself. Karin chooses to give little gifts throughout the year rather than swamp her children with toys and clothes at Christmas. She says, "We do give Matthew and Meagin presents at Christmas, but some parents just go nuts. We want to emphasize to our children that the whole thing isn't 'What do I get? How many more presents? What else is there?' It's Jesus' birthday.

"I used to feel guilty about it, because my parents gave me tons of presents when I was a kid. I thought, 'We need to get them something more.' But then I heard the Lord's still, small voice say, 'Karin, that isn't what Christmas is about.'" "Besides," adds Glenda, "later down the road, they don't remember the big Christmases where you think you went all out and gave them everything. It's the things you did, not what you gave them, that they remember."

Another few words on toys: "Kids would rather have a jar of bubble soap and you out in the yard blowing bubbles with them than a big expensive toy," says Karin. "It means a lot more to them"—that is, of course, unless they've been brainwashed by Saturday morning TV. Your child may think she wants the latest doll for Christmas. Maybe she really does, and that's okay. But in fifteen or twenty years the doll will most likely be forgotten and it'll be the handmade Christmas ornaments and the memory of long evenings spent reading Christmas stories together that count. The toys our moms remember are the ones they spent special times with, not the ones that were the most expensive.

When it comes to the presents your toddler gives the people he loves, try not to resort to buying them for him. If you possibly can, find the time to help him make simple gifts. The hours you spend working on them together will create special memories, and he'll have a warm sense of accomplishment at being able to give something he made himself. At the very least, go shopping with him and let him pick out inexpensive gifts with a little guidance from Mommy. And do always make sure your toddler has *something* to give on holidays or family birthdays and anniversaries, even if it's just a handmade card. Children are devastated when, like the little drummer boy, they're the only one with no gift to bring.

Even if you have both sets of grandparents and hordes of uncles, aunts, and cousins all within shouting distance, Glenda feels it's important to take some time for a private family Christmas celebration—perhaps making Christmas Eve your family time and devoting Christmas Day to relatives and friends. She says, "For many years we lived far away from our families and were never home at Christmas, and for the first couple of years Joe and I felt kind of lost since we're both from large families. But, you know, as the years went by it became more and more precious to have just our immediate family there, and now our kids really cherish the time we spend together as a family at Christmas. We're back now close enough to be with all the relatives, but the times the children remember most are the quiet times with just us, sharing and reading the Bible before we open our presents, thanking the Lord for His goodness, and talking and listening to Christmas music afterward."

Aside from Christmas, Halloween is probably the most-publicized children's holiday—which is too bad, when you consider what the All Hallow's Eve celebration is about. In our area, though, Halloween is no longer a big problem for Christian families. Even non-Christian parents are refusing to allow their children to trick-or-treat because of the scares, more and more frequent in recent years, with poisoned candy and boobytrapped apples.

Glenda says, "Halloween was dangerous years ago in Los Angeles when my kids were little, so they weren't allowed to go trick-or-treating. We got together with our friends in the neighborhood and planned games and fixed food, and every time the kids played a game they all got candy for their bags—not just the kid who won, although he got something special. I guess we went to about a half-dozen of our homes, and did something special at each house—bobbing for apples or whatever. They loved it!"

Terri's neighborhood is one that has a safe Halloween party for the kids: "My children have never known trick-or-treating the way I did," she says. "When the reports of candy-poisoning started coming in, I said, 'Forget it. We'll do something else.' And that's just what we did. It started with just a couple of families, but now a lot of them are involved. And it's a good way to get to know neighbors. When we notice a new child in the neighborhood, we go down and invite him and his parents. Kids love to dress up, and we still let them, but it's a lot safer than trick-or-treating. It's in a fenced-in yard, the parents are all there, and they know right where their children are. We don't have any unattended kids." Joyce says, "Our church has a Fall Festival for the children on Halloween, and we let the kids dress up in fun things—no ghosts or demons."

For Christian parents, Easter ranks right up there with Christmas as a special holiday—and, as with Christmas, the focus in the secular world has somehow shifted completely away from Jesus. Our moms found that using simple Bible storybooks helped their little ones understand the meaning behind the holiday much earlier than might be expected for such a complex subject as death and resurrection. Karin says, "Matthew was two at Easter this year, and he went around telling people, 'He's alive again! He's alive again!' And he would turn the cross on my necklace over and ask, 'Is Jesus dead on there?' When I answered, 'No, He's alive again!' he'd give a big smile and repeat, 'He's alive again!' He ministered to a lot of people just by knowing the story."

Virginia started a family tradition reminiscent of the Jewish Passover celebration by asking her children as soon as they awoke Easter Sunday morning, "Why is today special? What does Easter Sunday mean?" She says, "Although I had already explained it to them, I wanted to make sure they remembered. And I also wanted to start them thinking about it at the beginning of the day. They told me what they thought it meant, and I explained a little more if I needed to. We just had a little story time first thing in the morning. When you do that each year, it becomes instilled in them." Glenda's husband Joe is much in demand as a singer, and she believes the musicals and cantatas her children attended to hear Daddy sing helped them understand early the real meaning of Easter. Kathy adds, "The Easter Bunny and colored eggs become minor when you make Jesus major."

Speaking of the Easter Bunny and colored eggs: Our moms are aware that these traditions are thought to be based on ancient pagan festivals, but most have chosen to turn the symbolism around and connect it to new life in Jesus. After all, if you're going to be a real stickler about having only holiday symbols with their origins in the New Testament you're going to have to give up your Christmas tree. The traditional new spring clothes, too, can be worn in honor of Christ's resurrection.

Several moms still hide Easter baskets filled with candy for their children to find, a tradition which is one of my most vivid childhood memories. (Another is the two live chicks my Sunday school teacher gave me and my sister one Easter. I'm sure my mom blessed her for that.) "We put the emphasis of Easter on Jesus," says Virginia, "but we have the little fun times too."

Carol chooses to forego the Easter eggs, but she says, "We didn't want our kids to miss out on the fun, so this year I wrapped peanuts in bright foil, and after we came home from church I hid those in the yard for them—the foil catches the sunlight and makes them easier to find. Then I scooped out a watermelon and filled it with punch. I poked holes in the top, put straws through, each with a child's name on it, and put it in a red wagon in the middle of the back yard. So all the kids hunted for peanuts, then ate them and sipped punch out of the watermelon."

Other holidays, as well as private family celebrations, can also provide special memories for your children if you use them to start family traditions—and a family tradition doesn't have to be fancy. It's just something fun and meaningful that you do at special times.

Whenever there's a holiday, whether it's a birthday, anniversary, or Father's Day, Carol has her children help her decorate the honored person's breakfast chair with balloons and crepe paper. "Any time I can blow up a balloon and have a celebration, I do it!" she says.

She adds, "The anticipation of birthdays is sometimes hard on children. Even if you don't overemphasize the presents they still have the anxiety of knowing they're getting something special that day. So instead of waiting until evening for all the presents, we give them one present or something special at breakfast along with all the balloons and decorations. That starts the day out right." By the way, don't ever "forget" someone's birthday, child or adult, in anticipation of a surprise party at the end of the day. The joy of the surprise doesn't come near to making up for the misery of going all day thinking everyone has forgotten you.

Kathy allows each of her toddlers to plan the menu for the evening meal on his or her birthday. Terri says, "We take ours out and let 'em pick the restaurant."

On the subject of the traditional birthday cake, Karin says, "Birthday cakes are more special when they're made by you. I'm not a cook, and there have been times when I've gone out and bought a cake for my children's birthdays. But last year for Matthew's second birthday I made him a clown cake that took me three days to finish. He still takes the pictures out and says, 'Look, my mommy made me a clown cake!' It touched his little heart that I spent three days making him a cake. Now Meagin's birthday is coming up, and he's telling me, 'Mommy, Meagin needs a clown cake too.' It's important to them. And it doesn't have to be a clown cake, it can be anything as long as they know you took the time to do it rather than just going to the store and buying it."

Tangible Memories

As we've already said, intangible memories are without doubt the most important kind. The tangible ones are really just extras, and if you meet your child's emotional need for intangible memories she'll probably forgive you if you don't shower her with sentimental doodads.

Now that we've gotten duty out of the way by making that statement, let us add that tangible memories are very nice extras, and that our moms cherish theirs as concrete mementos of those fleeting, intangible moments. Again, these are just ideas to help you get started. Once you begin you'll find ideas for tangible memories coming out of the woodwork, and your biggest problem will be figuring out where to store them all.

"How Can I Say 'Cheese!' When I Can't Talk Yet?"

Photographs are probably the easiest and most common tangibles to collect, but our moms have come up with some creative ways to use them.

■ Connie says, "I held April's foot in my hand and had Shelby take a picture of it, and also of her hand in mine. It showed how tiny they were."

■ When Kathy bought Brandon his first little pair of sneakers, she took a picture of them side by side with his daddy's shoes. She says, "It's especially cute when they have identical sneakers, except one pair's big and the other is tiny."

■ Our moms recommend investing in a good 35mm camera if you can afford it. And take lots of candid shots. "You get some of your cutest pictures that way," says Terri. Several moms follow Sofie's example: "Every now and then I take the negatives of my favorite snapshots in and have them enlarged into 5 × 7s or 8 × 10s and put them into frames. I enjoy them just as much as formal pictures—sometimes more." These enlargements are quite inexpensive and, when framed, make wonderful presents for grandparents. Each year Kathy takes her favorite family snapshot to the photography department of a local drugstore and has it made into Christmas cards.

Beware of photographers who call you at home after learning that you've had a baby. Check them out before accepting any offers.

■ "Take lots of pictures," says Wanda. "It's so much fun to look back at them and tell stories about the circumstances surrounding the special occasions. Kids love to hear about things they did and said when they were 'little.' They also love to hear stories of when you were small." "One mistake we made," says Debby, "was that we took a whole bunch of pictures of Lisa, fewer of Angie, and even fewer of Marsha. Now my two younger kids are asking why I didn't take as many pictures of them as I did of Lisa."

Connie learned another lesson by hard experience: "My mother advised me to write my child's age on the back of each picture, but I ignored her, thinking, 'How could I possibly forget such important memories?' But a few years and two more babies later I did forget. I'm so glad that on some of the pictures I did jot down the names and ages, but on many of them I didn't, and I regret it."

■ Glenda keeps duplicate copies of her children's pictures behind the originals in the family photo album. Now that her kids are older, she says, "I've started an album for each child, so that when they get married they'll have some baby pictures, and some of themselves while they were growing up." Terri says, "When I got married, my mother-in-law gave me a little book of my husband's baby pictures. It was really special." It will be special to your grandchildren, too, to see the pictures you've saved of Mommy and Daddy when they were small.

■ Terri used her children's pictures to make Christmas ornaments: She cut a slice off one side of a styrofoam ball, which left a flat place to mount a picture that had been trimmed to fit. She then covered the rest of the ball with velvet and gold braid (although glued-on sequins and beads would do just as well), glued the picture to the ball, and trimmed it around the edges with the remaining gold braid. Carol's preschooler made her a simpler ornament by gluing a trimmed picture onto a round piece of cardboard, covering the edges with gold braid, and hanging it by a ribbon. Carol says, "It really is darling, and the kids love to see their ornaments hanging on the tree year after year."

■ Zachary, Terri's little boy, was badly burned when he pulled a pot of hot grease over onto himself at six months old. Terri says, "To this day I don't know why I allowed my husband to take a camera into the hospital, but once Zachary reached the point where we knew he would live we took all kinds of pictures. It was as if the scars didn't matter and we wanted to get pictures of this part of our baby's life. He didn't have to have skin grafts, which was a miracle, and he was released from the hospital three days after the doctors told us he would have to stay there for at least another month.

"Right after he got out of the hospital I looked through those pictures and panicked—I wanted to rip them up— but my neighbor said, 'Don't you dare! They're a record of what God has done, and unless you keep them no one will believe that your baby was ever that badly burned.' Now Zachary looks at the scrapbook and says, 'Did I look like that?' and he looks down at his side and his leg, and he sees what God did for him."

The Baby Book and Other Great Literary Efforts

The second most common memento of babyhood is the infamous baby book, which most mothers start and few finish. Our moms had the usual amount of trouble with writing milestones down before they were forgotten, and their advice to you on this subject is, "Do as I say, not as I did."

■ The mothers who had the most success keeping their books up-to-date were the ones who made a habit of jotting events down as they occurred. Patty W. says, "To keep track of new things Jennifer did, such as crawling, walking, and new words, I kept a calendar on the wall and quickly wrote it down when something happened. Then, later on, I transferred it from the calendar to my baby book."

Kathy kept a special baby calendar and began recording events even before Brandon was born: "I wrote down the first time I felt him move, and things like, 'You kept me up all night last night. I can't wait for you to be born!'" As Zachary and Ashley make their way through toddlerhood Terri has continued her practice of jotting down milestones on her calendar for later transfer to their baby books. She says, "It's fun to look back and see your child's progress, and to read and reread all the cute things she's said. Ashley's almost two, and she's doing and saying things almost daily that need to be written down." Connie kept a separate spiral notebook of her girls' funny childhood sayings. "We laugh and laugh when we go back and read them," she says. "Be sure to put your child's name and age by each quote."

■ If your baby book doesn't have keepsake pockets, Terri recommends keeping a separate scrapbook for such firsts as first checkup receipts, first shoe receipts, and a lock of hair from your baby's first haircut. Adrienne's mother saved her dried-up umbilical stump!

■ A friend of Chris's keeps a birthday diary for her little girl. Each year on her child's birthday she takes a few minutes to record her current height and weight, things she learned to do that year, new words, special friends, and favorite dolls and toys. I'm doing something similar, except that I write in my book two or three times a year and, since I plan to give it to Megan someday, I'm addressing it to her and spreading it with a thick frosting of you're-so-special's and we're-so-blessed-to-have-you's. I hope it will be a precious keep-sake for her someday.

Terri has adopted yet another variation on this tradition: Each year on her children's birthdays she writes them a long letter on a blank greeting card. She says, "I already write to Ashley. Even though she doesn't understand right now, the letters will be there for her when she does."

■ To protect your written mementos from time and leaky roofs, always write on good paper with a ball-point pen, not a pencil or water-soluble felt-tip pen.

■ Along with your baby's personal milestones, Kathy recommends keeping track of family history and current events in your child's diary. She says, "Kids like to know, 'Who was president when I was born? Where did we live? What kind of car did we have?'" A couple of our moms saved the front page of the newspaper from their children's birthdays. Adrienne says, "My mother saved the newspaper from the day I was born in 1951. It shows the styles—it's incredible what they wore back then—and tells all about the things that happened. If your baby has already been born you can buy front pages from the newspaper companies." Carol adds, "That's a neat gift, too. My neighbor saved the front page of the newspaper while I was in the hospital and brought it over after I came home."

■ Adrienne is the most ambitious of our moms in that she keeps a daily diary—but it's not just for keepsake reasons. She says, "It comes in handy for keeping track of immunizations, and also for when one of my children isn't feeling well. It prevents me from being stuck for an answer when the doctor asks, 'How long has she been sick?' Otherwise I might answer, 'Let's see . . . two or three days,' when it's really been seven."

With six children, Adrienne has learned to write in her diary during the only real time she has to sit down: in the bathroom. Connie says, "I know you probably don't feel you have time to keep a journal, but I'm so very sorry I didn't. I keep one now, but all those daily memories I could have kept . . . gone . . ."

■ Adrienne adds that written records are helpful, whether they're kept daily, weekly, monthly, or yearly, because children love to hear about the things they used to do even while they're still young. "That's important to kids," she says. "They love it—they'll listen for hours. Sometimes at night my children and I get started talking. They'll ask, 'What did I do when I was two?' and I'll tell them everything I remember."

Kathy says, "I tell Ryan how he was in the breech position up until three days before he was born, and how the doctor told me that if he didn't turn around I'd have to have an operation so he could come out, and how the Lord woke me up one night and I went out and found a Scripture meant just for me and him, and at my next appointment the doctor told me, 'He turned over!' He weighed nine pounds three ounces, and I hadn't even felt it! I tell him how special he is, and how even back then the Lord was with him. They love to hear that sort of thing." Dialogues like this also form a good foundation for the sex education you'll be providing for your child.

Everyone, no matter what his age, enjoys being told he's special and loved. Getting into the habit of writing to your children can produce lifelong memories. Virginia still writes to her son even though he's away at college. "Now that Rick's gone," she says, "I can think of so many things to tell him. So I write and tell him how precious he was when he was little, and how much he's grown and how proud I am. He likes it even now."

Other Doodads

■ Chris's husband David is a music director, so it's not surprising that they took the first possible opportunity to put their baby's voice on tape: "We began when Ashley first started making little cooing noises," says Chris. "We just stated her age and then recorded her for maybe three minutes. We did it every three or four months, so now we have a tape of how she's sounded all along."

■ When Megan was two and a half, we began helping her make keepsake tapes as gifts for her grandparents' birthdays. She sang "Happy Birthday to You" and other little songs, said "I love you" and told a little story or two. Her grandparents were thrilled.

■ Once you baby is old enough to stand, Carol cautions of the need to buy a height chart rather than making notches on the closet door. "That way you can take it with you if you move," she says. "We moved and had to leave ours behind. It's been painted over by now." Virginia adds that children love being able to ask, "How big am I now, Mommy?" and to see how much they've grown since the last time you measured them.

■ "I keep a baby girl named Monica," says Rosemary, "and her mother has used a stamp pad since her birth to sign cards with prints of her hands and feet for Father's Day, grandparents' birthdays, and other special occasions." If you do this, you might want to stamp two or three months' worth of cards at a time to keep down the number of days your baby spends with black hands and feet. And do be sure to use a nontoxic ink.

▪ "I traced Lisa's tiny feet and hands on pillowcases for Grandma and Grandpa," says Connie. "Then I wrote 'Good night, Grandma' on one pillowcase and 'Good night, Grandpa' on the other, and went over it all with liquid embroidery fluid. It was a hit!"

▪ Terri has traced her children's hands every year, starting from the very beginning. She says, "I want to make a quilt someday from all of them when Zachary and Ashley are older, but for the time being I use the patterns to make gifts and Christmas ornaments. On Zachary's first Christmas, I traced his hand and cut it out of calico fabric, then got a plain brown hotpad and zigzagged the handprint onto it. I embroidered underneath, 'Me-mom's Helping Hands,' and gave it to my mother from Zachary. She has it hanging on her stove and she uses it all the time, even though it was simple to make and cost almost nothing."

Here's how Terri makes Christmas ornaments from her children's handprints: "I just cut two of each hand out of red and green felt, sew the two layers of felt together, maybe stuff them a little bit, and hang them on the tree." She says Zachary and Ashley love to take their ornaments off the tree and stretch their hands over them to see how much they've grown.

▪ Adrienne suggests making a Christmas tree door decoration—perhaps even an advent calendar—from your child's handprints. Make a pattern by tracing your little one's hands on brown paper, then cut eight pair of hands from green felt and one pair from brown. Glue the hands, upside down and in the shape of a Christmas tree, onto a big piece of red felt backing—one hand at the top, three on the second row, five on the third, seven on the bottom, and the brown pair right side up for the trunk. For a bigger tree, add more green rows. Decorate with gold braid, colored sequins, and beads. This is the sort of thing a toddler would love to help with. And if you make your hands fairly easy to remove you can replace one pair with an up-to-date pair each year. Write the year on each pair of hands in small gold-glitter numbers.

■ I made a Christmas ornament from Megan's first pair of soft white dress shoes by stitching them together near the heel and hanging them by red and green ribbons.

■ Carol B.'s little girl Kristie had a beautiful wooden crib mobile that Carol couldn't bear to part with, so when the time came to take it down she cut the figures off and hung them on the Christmas tree as ornaments.

■ When her children receive Christmas ornaments as gifts from grandparents and friends, Carol marks the year and the giver's name on the back. "That way," she says, "they can go back through their own little box of ornaments and remember who gave which to them."

■ "I Like to do counted cross-stitch," says Terri, "so each year I make an ornament for each of my children that reflects their special interests—a train, a teddy bear, a doll—and embroider the year on it. I plan to give the completed set to them when they marry, so they'll have at least twenty or so ornaments for their first Christmas tree."

■ Virginia says a child old enough to help Mommy bake Christmas cookies is old enough to help make cookie-type ornaments from salt-and-flour dough, and Terri has yet another Christmas tradition that mixes the tangible with the intangible. She says, "I never thought I could make a gingerbread house, but on Zachary's second Christmas he saw one and got excited when I told him it was all made out of a cookie. He said, 'Make me one!' So I bought a book of instructions for an ornate gingerbread house decorated with candy, and I've made one every year now. They're really easy to make, and the kids love to help. You can let them dry out and save them—my mother has my first one, and my mother-in-law has my second one. Some people shellac them, but my mother didn't do anything to hers and it's holding up just fine. She has a country-style house out in the woods, and she keeps it out on display year-round on an old-fashioned porcelain-topped table." This would also make an adorable decoration for a child's room. Just put it up on a shelf where your little one can't get to it without your help.

■ When your child becomes old enough to start coloring pictures "just for you," our moms recommend saving the special ones that are of manageable size in a notebook to keep them from wear and tear. Write your child's name and age on the back first. There are notebooks on the market that are ideal for this purpose, since they bind the pages together between two clamps rather than forcing you to poke holes in them. Other pictures can be matted on construction paper and used to decorate your little one's bedroom, your bathroom, your kitchen—wherever they work best. When the time comes to throw pictures away, Virginia suggests that you don't let your child see you tossing her masterpiece into the waste-basket. No artist enjoys seeing her work thrown out, especially by someone she loves.

■ An often unexplored source of potential keepsakes is your child's toybox. Our moms don't save toys indiscriminately, but the better-made ones can be kept to serve several generations. "My grandmother still has some fifty-year-old Fisher-Price toys from back when they were made of wood," says Kathy. "She saved them from her own children, and has given them now to her great-grandchildren."

Handmade wooden toys are making a comeback, although they tend to be expensive. My sister gave Megan a beautiful hand-carved wooden duck pull-toy, complete with mahogany egg, and you may be sure that when Megan has outgrown it, that duck will waddle on up to my mantel to wait for my grandchildren to make their appearance. When her children receive wooden toys as gifts, Carol writes her child's name, the giver, and the date on the bottom with a woodburning kit.

"We took Kristie's first tricycle apart and boxed it up and put it in the attic," says Carol B. "When she gets married and has children, we'll give it to her again." Kathy is saving her children's cradle and bassinet, and Glenda says, "I've got six boxes of all my children's special dolls and stuffed toys, and a baby carriage that looks brand-new, that I'm saving for my grandkids. It means a lot when your children can give their children toys that were theirs when they were little. When I got married I had a little stuffed teddy bear that I was given when I was four years old, and my kids played with it until it wore out. They liked it better than anything else."

These second-hand toys will have even more meaning for your child and grandchild if you have pictures of your own little one playing with them. Just make sure that all handmade toys have nontoxic finishes and meet the safety requirements we talked about in Chapter 5.

■ Well-made clothes and baby outfits in classic styles can also be kept for future generations. Carol says, "A friend of mine has a beautiful quilt on her family-room wall that her grandmother made, and she can point to the different squares and tell which of her baby clothes they came from." Terri has saved scraps from Ashley's clothes and plans also to make a quilt someday. It's even possible to applique a special dress—such as a christening gown—on top of a finished quilt for a real showpiece heirloom.

12
Daddy to Daddy

It would hardly be fair to end this book without giving some fathers a chance to have their say. Parenting is no longer primarily a one-person proposition, with Daddy expected only to provide the daily bread and, on occasion, corporal punishment. Ironically, the same society that now sees more and more one-parent families is also seeing fathers awaken to the joys of active participation in their children's lives. Perhaps this trend is a result of necessity, since so many new mothers are now forced to work outside the home and must have help from their husbands in order to survive.

But in the group of fathers interviewed for this chapter, I found that even those whose wives are able to remain at home are trying to take an active part in such nurturing tasks as feeding, diapering, cuddling, bathing, playing—even getting up in the night! They do it not only to help their wives, but to become acquainted with their children as well. More than one of them expressed the thought, "If I weren't involved in my child's life, I believe I'd be missing out on more than she would."

A note to the new fathers reading this chapter: If you really want to be an involved parent, read the rest of this book. Its advice is not for mothers only, and much of it deals with issues on which you and your wife will need to present a united front to your child. You may want to skip some of the nuts-and-bolts tips in the early chapters, but do be sure to read Chapter 1, since it will explain many of the changes you'll see in your wife as she adapts to new motherhood, and Chapter 6, which will give you some good playtime ideas. Our dads say that playing with your new baby is one of the best ways to get to know him or her.

Most of the dads in this chapter are husbands of the women whose advice appears in the rest of the book. To learn a little more about them and their families, look them up in our "Meet the Mommies" section under their wife's name.

Involvement—Right From the Start

Nine of the fifteen fathers interviewed for this chapter participated in natural childbirth classes with their wives and were present when their babies were delivered. The number would have been almost unanimous but for the fact that five of them have older children who were born before natural childbirth became popular, and Karin, Wayne's wife, developed toxemia and had to have an emergency Caesarean section. Only one of our dads says, half facetiously, that if he could do it over again he would still prefer to wait in the "daddy room" rather than sweating it out with his wife.

Childbirth was hardly what our dads expected it to be. "It sure took away a lot of modesty!" says Hugh, laughing. "But seeing my kids born, and being there with Kathy, I felt like I was part of it. It made me feel a lot closer to my children." Dick and his wife Adrienne have six children, and Dick participated in natural childbirth classes for the first time with their youngest, Stephanie, who is now a year old. He says, "I regret that I wasn't there for all of them. It's an awareness thing, and it begins with all the classes you take with your wife, right up to the delivery. Certainly, I'd recommend it to anybody. We even took the whole family to one of the follow-up classes after Stephanie was born—all eight of us."

In one of our mommy meetings, Adrienne mentioned that Dick treated her much differently after their last baby was born. With their other children he had expected her to jump right back into her regular schedule, but after seeing what childbirth is actually like he was much more willing to let her convalesce.

David says, "We were very lucky in that Chris had a short labor—from the time we got to the hospital until Ashley was delivered was about four hours. Being there just made me that much more a part of what we were doing. The thing that amused me after it was all over was how different the techniques we practiced in the childbirth classes—the puffing and blowing and he-he's—were from what actually happened in the delivery room. The intensity level is greatly increased when it's the real thing!"

"My going through natural childbirth with Stella made us feel like a team," says Tim. "It made her able to say to herself, 'We're going through this together. I'm not doing it alone.' Also, it was really special to have the opportunity to be in the delivery room and witness a miracle happening right before my eyes. Someone can explain it to you, but until you witness the birth of your child you have no idea what it's like."

A brand-new father of my acquaintance says that his main feeling now after seeing his baby born is one of helplessness. "I don't know what to do with this baby!" he says. "I don't know how to hold her, or feed her, or change her diaper. I've been buttonholing the nurses in the halls and asking, 'Show me how to change my baby's diaper.'"

Truth to tell, most new mothers feel as inept as new fathers do when presented with their babies for the first time. It's just that they have no choice. Somebody's got to change the diapers and give the baths, and they're the most likely candidates. And our dads say that the way to overcome your feelings of awkwardness with your baby is to do what new mothers do: jump right in. Read the little how-to pamphlets your wife brings home from the obstetrician, and collar the nurses and ask if there are any training films for new fathers offered at the hospital. The more knowledge and experience you gain, the more confident and competent you'll feel with your child. Watch the way your wife and the nurses hold and diaper the baby. And David recommends asking your wife for instructions, or at least being tolerant when she inevitably starts to kibitz. "I couldn't figure out why my diapers never looked as neat as Connie's," says Shelby. "And what really bothered me was when she laughed at them!"

"Karin had a rough time with her Caesarean," says Wayne, "so I was forced to more or less jump in and help. I was pretty awkward at first, never having done it before. What bothered me most was that Matthew was just so tiny! I was afraid to do much with him because I thought I might hurt him. I was really careful." Tom adds, "I was unsure exactly how to hold Aaron. It wasn't so much that I felt scared as it was that I wanted to make sure I did it right." A hyper-awareness of their babies' frailty, manifesting itself in reluctance to touch them for fear they'd break, was common among our dads. But relax. You do have to be careful when handling your baby, but he's not as fragile as he seems—and he won't stay little for long. Tom says, "Our boys went through that stage so fast—Pene and I hardly remember it."

Jon took a week's vacation when our daughter Megan was born. Not only was he able to help me as I convalesced, but all the little things he did—changing Megan, holding her, playing with her—helped him feel comfortable with her much more quickly than he would have if he'd had only an hour or so with her after he came home from work each day.

Ralph, a Christian school principal with two children, strongly recommends having someone come and help your wife for the first week or two, after you stay home for a few days yourself. "Billie had a difficult delivery," he says, "and there was no one who could come and stay with her after the baby was born, and I was teaching and couldn't take time off from work. That was a hard time for her, and she has never forgotten it. I'd give anything to go back and change it."

Most of our dads got up at least occasionally during the night to help with the baby while their wives were convalescing. David says he also took over with Ashley when he came home from work in the evening. His main purpose was to give Chris a break, but he had other reasons as well: "I just felt that I had such little time to spend with Ashley that I wanted to use those hours to let her get to know me. That was our time to get acquainted and become comfortable with each other."

He continues, "The first four months were an extremely difficult time for us. It wasn't uncommon for Ashley to wake up ten or twelve times a night, or for her to cry for forty-five minutes and then sleep for forty-five minutes all night long." Ashley suffered from colic, an ailment that is discussed more thoroughly in Chapter 5. Fortunately, more babies don't have colic than do, but David's advice to new fathers with a colicky baby is to hang in there: "I tell everybody who approaches me with the same problem, 'This, too, shall pass.' And it did. She grew out of it. But there were times in the middle of the night when Chris just couldn't take any more, and I would have to step in and take over. The Lord really helped us get through those difficult times, and I felt it was very important as the head of the home to minister to Chris and keep building her up, especially since she tended to get depressed about it and think she had done something wrong to give Ashley colic."

"Wanda and I took turns getting up," says Dennis, whose daughter Michelle also suffered from colic. "The Lord always made sure one of us had just a little more energy or patience or understanding when the other one didn't. I was both working and going to school back then, and I missed out on a lot of sleep, but the Lord pulled me through."

Several of our dads also helped out around the house

during their baby's first few weeks, or at least adopted an understanding attitude about the housework. David says, "Don't expect the house to be spotless every time you walk in the door. Babies are a full-time job. Your wife will have more time as your baby gets older."

Marvin found that his helping Rita, far from making her take advantage of him, made her appreciate and treasure him even more. Wayne believes that his active role in fathering and husbanding has been good for his marriage: "Karin and I had to pull together as a team," he says. "Karin was under stress after Matthew was born for several reasons. She lost her mom right after he came, and that made things even rougher on her. We did a lot of extra praying and seeking God, and the Lord brought us through some hard times. It really brought us closer."

Our moms who had helpful husbands valued them tremendously, and those whose husbands didn't help found themselves fighting resentment. In an earlier meeting, one of our moms said, "Life will never be the same for a woman after she has a baby, and her husband needs to understand that it's not going to be the same for him either." A husband who comes home from work, takes a look around and says, "What on earth have you been doing all day?" contributes greatly to a new mother's falling sense of self-esteem.

"I think a lot of new fathers don't realize just how time-consuming a child is," says Jon. "You know it's going to take some time, but you don't realize that some days it's going to take 24 hours a day to take care of that child. I remember my wife had some tough adjustments toward the beginning when Megan was waking up a lot, and again the first time Megan got sick and wouldn't go to sleep. There were a lot of times when I had to pitch in and help when I really didn't want to. There are still times like that, come to think of it."

One of the best definitions of maturity is the ability to make oneself do something that isn't on one's current Top 10 list of favorite things, simply because it needs to be done. A husband who is trying to fulfill the scriptural command to love his wife as Christ loved the church will avoid leaving her in the lurch during perhaps her most vulnerable time in their married life. Most of our dads came through this stage with flying colors, but a couple of them did retreat behind the masculine excuse, "I'm providing the money, so I'm doing my job"—a mindset they now regret. We'll talk about that next, in our section on relationships.

Jon has another bit of advice to which Dick gives a hearty amen: "As soon as possible, I suggest that a new dad get Grandma or someone to come over to babysit and just take his wife away for a couple of hours. Megan was almost six weeks old when we left her to go out to dinner, and it was like a shot in the arm for both of us to be able to think just about each other for that short amount of time." Of course, Jon was too polite to mention the number of times during those two or three hours that he had to say, "Darling, would you *please* quit talking about Megan?"

Changing Relationships

When I asked our dads whether their relationship with their wife changed when their first child arrived, most of them burst out laughing. "That's an understatement!" says Dick.

Joe found himself struggling with the natural reaction

of feeling jealous of the new baby. "Debby and I had been married for three and a half years before Lisa was born," he says, "and after several months as a new father I suddenly realized that the time I was getting from Debby had been, at its very best, cut in half. Talk about an adjustment! For more than three years we'd done everything together—back-packed, camped, bowled. Then when the baby came it stopped short. I'm not sure I can say how I adjusted, other than sulking. My first reaction was to stay away. I felt really unsure of myself with Lisa, and I thought that if I could just continue providing for them I'd be fulfilling my responsibility. I had no hands-on experience with Lisa."

Joe has become an involved father since those days thirteen years ago, and he deeply regrets his lack of involvement back then. Given the chance to go back and change things, he says, "Oh, I'd love to be involved—everything from natural childbirth to sharing the nurturing of the children." His wife Debby says it wasn't until years later that Joe shared his feelings with her, probably because jealousy is not an attractive trait in a new father. But Joe says now, "Communication is the best route to healing. If you and your wife can just talk about why you're no longer getting all her attention, you'll work through it all right."

Our other dads claim that jealousy—or at least ambivalence—toward the new baby is normal. But it's interesting that the fathers who had little or no trouble with feeling displaced are the ones who jumped into daddyhood both feet first and became actively involved in their children's caretaking. "When Wanda was pregnant, there were times when she couldn't share with me how she was feeling," says Dennis. "And we didn't go through natural childbirth ten years ago, but once Michelle was born she became a focal point for our family. She became just one more thing Wanda and I had in common—something else to share. We became much closer and had more to talk about, especially since Michelle was so close to our hearts. I think we planned more and dreamed more."

If you find yourself feeling envious of your new child, try becoming involved with him or her instead of focusing on your own hurt feelings. Of course, new mothers being what they are, you may have to pry your wife loose at times. Mothers can become so wrapped up in their babies that they tune everything else out, but your wife really needs frequent breaks even if she seems reluctant to take them. Your involvement can help relieve that obsession and restore some balance to her life and to your family.

Most of our dads' wives breastfed their babies, and our dads were all for it once they got used to the tendency of their wives' milk to let down at intimate moments. "Nursing sure is convenient!" says Chris. "Amen," adds Jon, "Especially when the baby wakes up at 2:30 in the morning!" By the way, just because your wife nurses doesn't mean you'll never get to feed the baby. A nursing baby should be given a small bottle of expressed milk or formula every other day to keep her accustomed to it so that you and your wife will be able to leave her with a sitter at times for an evening out. Ask your wife to make those feedings your domain. And if you want to earn her undying gratitude, volunteer occasionally to do your feedings at night while she sleeps.

"The only drawback to nursing is that it interferes with making plans for a weekend away, unless you want to take the baby with you," says Dick. "But we found that the advantages of breastfeeding, from every aspect, far outweighed the disadvantages." Jeff agrees: "I was never more appreciative of Marilee than when she breastfed our kids. There's a warmth that's transferred from mother to child that can be lost if she doesn't do it. We put aside the idea of going a lot of different places for a while so our kids could get a good start. We assigned so much importance to it that everything else took a distant second place."

Several of our dads say they found the sight of their wives breastfeeding their babies a pleasant one—not only emotionally, but sensually as well. Hugh says, "I thought it made Kathy sexier, and I think somehow it made her feel more womanly. It was a very beautiful thing, especially with our first child." Chris adds, "One of the most touching experiences I remember with our first baby was when we brought her home from the hospital. Carol was nursing, and I was sitting there beside her, just watching. I felt very much part of that." Quite a few of our dads say that seeing their wives blossom into good mothers raised them in their esteem. Suddenly they saw untapped potential in the woman with whom they had been sharing their life. If you find yourself feeling this way about your wife, *tell her*. Especially now, she needs to hear it.

David points out the need to encourage your wife and support her in her breastfeeding, letting her know she has your enthusiastic approval. It's also important that you gently encourage her if she becomes depressed during her adjustment period after the baby is born. The nursing moms in this book say that nursing their children was one of the most rewarding experiences of their lives, but whether this becomes true for your wife is something over which you, as her husband, have a great deal of control. Milk production is intimately tied in with a woman's emotions, and the mother who lacks emotional support from her husband may fail to produce enough milk to nurse, or may give up in despair during her adjustment period even if she has plenty of milk—especially if the baby seems to have trouble figuring out what Mom's nipple is for. (To learn more about the advantages, joys, and trials of breastfeeding, read Chapter 3.)

As you probably have already discovered, women in the latter stages of pregnancy and the first few weeks postpartum can be subject to unpredictable mood swings. "Sometimes Adrienne will be in a mood and not really know why," says Dick. "It just compounds the problem if I come at her aggressively and ask, 'What's the matter with you?' It works much better for her if I'm just helpful and wait until she's ready to communicate." It wouldn't hurt, though, to ask a few gentle questions, such as, "Honey, is something wrong? How can I help?" And be ready to run for the tissues when she starts crying.

Two themes kept recurring in our talks, and even our most involved dads are still working on them: communication, and the willingness to change as a result of the things learned through the communication. These are both essential to a healthy marriage at any time, but especially when a new baby enters the household. New parenthood is a time of rapid change for both of you, and unless you keep the lines of communication open your marriage is going to suffer, even if it has until now been skimming right along.

Shelby says, "Before Lisa was born, when I did something Connie didn't like or she did something I didn't like, we were ready to work things out right away. Wherever we were, whatever room we were in, she gave her opinion and I gave mine, and then it was all over and we understood each other. And it didn't matter if we got a little angry, because no one else was there. It was fast and easy that way.

"After the kids came, and especially when they got a little older, sometimes they were around and it wasn't convenient to talk. I'd be ready to hash it out, but she'd say, 'Shh—the kids. We'll talk about it later.' It put a cramp on when we could get together to work out our differences."

"Don't wait until you feel you aren't communicating to improve your communications skills," says Dennis. "Read at least one book a year that relates to your family's development. Begin with *Dare to Discipline* by James Dobson." *What Wives Wish Their Husbands Knew About Women* and *Hide or Seek*, both by James Dobson, are excellent too—in fact, I'd go as far as to recommend that you read everything by Dr. Dobson that you can get your hands on.

Included in the need for communication is a strategy meeting with your wife to decide whether or not she will breastfeed, what discipline methods you both will use, and other basic issues, so that she will know she has your support when she runs into well-meant but ill-conceived advice from family and friends. A woman's self-image is inseparable from her feelings of success as a mother, and it's hard to feel successful when everyone around you is trying to tell you how to do it differently. "Jan's biggest need right now is reassurance that she's doing the best things for our son," says Steve.

Another aspect of your relationship that will change when your child arrives, according to Dick, is your love life—and with six children he should know. "A lot of times babies interfere with husband-wife intimacy," he says, "and you have to adjust." But it's an adjustment that can be made fairly easily. Just learn to plan ahead, and be willing to reschedule if your plans don't work out. That's another sign of maturity: the ability to delay gratification.

With the birth of your child, your wife will no longer be able to just pick up and go along to special activities. David recommends, for the sake of your family, resisting the temptation to do as you please and leave her behind. "Put your family ahead of sports," he says. "You'll have a happier home if you try to keep a balance between the things you know you should do as a husband and father and the things you want to do for yourself. If you work at it, you'll have all the time you need for sports and exercise. And God will reward your efforts."

Finally, Steve says that his relationship with his wife wasn't the only relationship that changed when Jordan David was born. His friendships changed too: "Jan and I chose our friends carefully, because we believe friends are a mirror of ourselves and our personality. When we develop friendships with people we respect, we can talk with them about our fears and apprehensions about raising Jordan David, and many times they've already worked through that particular problem. Or sometimes they're experiencing something at the same time we are, and we can compare notes."

Recipe for an Involved Father

"With an infant," says Chris, "I think the first thing is observing. You learn a lot by watching what the baby does and seeing how your wife handles her, so that when you do it you won't feel as awkward." Feeding, changing, holding, talking to, singing to, and just sitting and watching are all ways to get to know your new baby.

Our dads' general feeling is that a father is eligible to help with any nurturing task within his power. There were certain jobs they avoided, not because they felt they were "Mommy work" but because they simply didn't have the stomach for them. "I never put alcohol on my kids' navels," says Chris. "I changed diapers, but I didn't mess with the navel." Joe adds, "It's not within my power to clean up after my kids when they throw up—Debby would have to come along and clean up after *me!*" Of course, if Debby weren't there Joe would undoubtedly muster the wherewithal to clean it up rather than look at it all day.

Several dads became acquainted with their little ones by lying on the floor with the baby on their stomach. A nursing mother gets plenty of cuddle time simply by feeding her baby, but a daddy must go out of the way to hug and hold his child—something that doesn't come naturally to many fathers. Tim says, "It's important to have that close contact, and it's something I neglected at first, expecting Stella to do it all. The children need it, but *I* need it too, not only to help Stella but to get to know my children. I'm still working on it." Of course, a newborn won't be able to react to you as much as she will when she grows older, but those early interactions are important. Don't say, "I'll get involved when she's old enough to play with me." It'll never happen.

Dennis says, "The thing that made me comfortable with Michelle more than anything else was the first time Wanda left her with me at about two weeks old. She'd always been there, and she could always comfort her better than I could and she did a better job changing diapers. But, the first time she left for a couple of hours, all of a sudden it all depended on Daddy. It's amazing what you can do when you have to, and the close relationship it builds."

David is a music director whose ministry frequently keeps him out at night. He says, "I work during the day and am home for maybe two or three hours in the afternoon, and I'm rarely there when Ashley goes to sleep at night. I've had to learn to make the time I do have with her of good quality. It's extremely important, when I walk in the door, to put everything else aside." To other new fathers intent on building their careers—but not at the expense of their families—he says, "Make the most of your time at home. If you come home tired, put yourself aside for a while and interact with your child. The floor is one of the best places. Don't make whatever you do half-hearted—make it valuable time, something that will fulfill your child's need for a father."

Chris discovered that playing with a little person who loved him unconditionally was a great way to relax after a hard morning at work: "Carol and I used to live in town," he says, "and I would come home for lunch every day. The kids would yell 'Daddy!' and it wasn't hard for me to throw off whatever was on my mind and play with them and hug them and pick them up. I was always able to have a close relationship with them when they were small, and that has carried over to today." All of our dads recommend that you *not* turn the TV on while you play with your baby. Your child needs and deserves your undivided attention. "Put the TV in the closet!" says Chris.

"When I'm at my best as a parent is when I work at it," says Joe. "Children don't always need you during one of your good times or when it's convenient. They need you when you're busy, tired, or after a hard day at the office. It's hard work sometimes to put down my book or get up from watching the TV to give them my attention. But when I put myself to the task, God's wisdom and strength help me give and give again."

It was interesting for me to see the change in Megan's attitude toward her daddy when Jon began taking time for active play with her when she was about a year old. He had always helped care for her and played with her before, but this was different—suddenly Daddy became more rowdy, and therefore more fun, than Mommy. He put his arms out like Frankenstein and chased her around the house, then turned around and let her chase him, and she loved it. Before long her first word when I went into her room each morning was "Papa?" and whenever there was a noise in the house during the day she would quickly turn and whisper, "Papa!"

Of course, it's important to be considerate of your child's feelings. Megan dearly loves to be startled when she knows it's coming, but, if your child doesn't, you can figure out some other way to have fun together. And do be careful—medical research has recently uncovered the fact that it's dangerous to shake or jiggle a young child too much.

Tom says, "I used to think 'quality time' meant sitting down and helping my kids learn the alphabet or studying the Bible together, which is all fine, but some of the most special times I've had with Aaron, who is three now, have been just doing yard work. He'll ask me how the lawn mower works, or why you change the oil on a car—

just ordinary, everyday things that you wouldn't think would be important to a child. He was fascinated by the way I repaired the lawn mower. He has a toy one, and now he never uses it without turning it over and checking to see if the blade is 'sharp.'"

"Never let a day go by without expressing your love to your family in both word and deed," says Dennis. "Find the time to spend doing the little things that count in a child's life. Time spent wrestling in the yard, giving piggyback rides, or playing games is a valuable investment in later years when peers and your child's own independent nature become significant forces in his life."

He goes on, "There have been times, very special to us, when I just cut some time out of my schedule to be at home with Michelle and allow Wanda to get away. Michelle looks forward to those times tremendously. For some reason they're more special to her than just an evening when everybody happens to be at home."

Shelby says, "Every now and then Connie or I will take out just one daughter, and that becomes her special day. She's all by herself with her mom or me, and she doesn't have to compete with anybody. But another thing we've done that has helped me grow closer to my kids is take a vacation together. My vacation is not for my personal use. We go off in a tent or in our camper and spend that time together."

Playing together and caretaking are not the only ways a father can grow close to his children, of course. As head of the household, it's vital that you participate in the more serious side of your child's life as well.

"A mistake I made, and have tried to correct," says Dick, "was letting Adrienne do the praying with the children at night instead of my sharing that responsibility with her. I think it's a common mistake of fathers to turn that responsibility over to their wives, but it's important for the father to do it too."

Joe says, "Debby and I wanted to make sure that I as a father participated in the correction of my children. It's too easy to let the wife do it all, especially if she's home all day. It may sound funny, but I got to know my kids largely through participating in their discipline. And that wasn't always spanking, although it was included. Our technique for spanking dictated that I spend some time with them, holding them while they cried, explaining things to them. I got to know the girls, and they got to know me, through that."

I asked our dads how they see their role: spiritual leader, provider, disciplinarian, caretaker, teacher, friend, playmate, encourager, role model? Their answer is that a father is all these things—but not necessarily what his child wants him to be at the moment.

Regardless of whether your wife's pregnancy was planned or accidental, good parenting isn't something that just happens. It's a commitment consciously made and consciously kept.

The final thought on this subject is for when your child is older, and it comes from Dennis: "Don't forget to let your child beat you at racquetball every so often," he says. "Someday you'll want him to return the favor."

Changing Times

The roles of men and women in our culture are undeniably changing—sometimes for better, often for worse. But the dads in this chapter are unanimous in their opinion that the current trend toward fatherly involvement is a healthy one. When I asked whether there were any nurturing tasks that are strictly "Mommy jobs" and not to be done by Daddy, the only reply was "Nurse the baby."

Our dads are not suggesting—and certainly I'm not either—that you try to become a surrogate mother. Children need both parents, and Daddy isn't just a stand-in for Mom. He's a completely different person with a different set of actions, reactions, and play styles.

By the way, take lessons from your wife in baby care, but be yourself; don't try to imitate her style. It's not necessary, and it won't work. There are times, especially with a nursing baby or when the baby is sick, when a mother simply cannot be filled in for. "There's an emotional quality that only a mother can give a child," says Dick, "especially from, say, newborn to one year. When I notice this is when Adrienne goes to choir rehearsal or somewhere and I'm home watching the children. Stephanie will become fussy, and I just can't quiet her down or meet her emotional needs the way Adrienne can. Of course, the more time I spend with her, the more relaxed she is with me." Joe adds, "But there are emotional needs we fathers can meet for our kids too, especially as they grow older, that Mom can't."

To our dads at least, keeping your role as a father clearly defined seems largely a matter of attitude. There is a quality about you as a daddy and about your wife as a mommy that transcends whatever job you happen to be doing at the moment. And there will be household tasks—although not necessarily ones directly associated with your child—that fall naturally into the daddy slot while others fall into the mommy one. The man who is confident in his own heart that he is the spiritual head and final authority in his household, and who is encouraged in that role by his wife, is strong enough to encourage his wife and help nurture his children without feeling threatened with emasculation.

All of this is a pretty big change from the way fathering was viewed in past generations, and our dads reflect that change. The majority don't seem as sure of themselves as fathers as the moms in this book are of themselves as mothers, and several feel caught between two different worlds. They're still trying to make the change from being the type of father they've been taught to be and the type they really want to be for their children.

"I felt that pressure," says Shelby. "When I was a kid, there was pressure for the man to be the provider, and when he'd done that, he'd done his duty. But Connie taught school for a year when our first baby was three, and so I did my church business in the morning, picked Lisa up from the nursery at noon, brought her home and put her to bed; then after she woke up from her nap I took care of her. I enjoyed it, and it was a challenge to get that little critter to go to sleep—that's a tough job! Sometimes I didn't know whether to spank her or lie down and take a nap with her, and I thought, 'Boy, if my dad or my granddad saw me doing this, they'd think I was henpecked.' I didn't want to feel that way, but I did feel some pressure. Now I'm glad I came through it okay."

Ralph says, "There was a big difference between the way I handled our first child and our second one. I knew how to take care of children because I had come from a large family, but when Heather was born I was working two jobs and didn't do much to help Billie. I remember thinking, as I was teaching school and then working at night, 'Well, she's home all day long, and I'm working these two jobs. She probably feels more like taking care of the baby than I do.' I didn't really put myself in her position and think about what she was going through. I felt I was fulfilling the traditional male role of provider, and I focused on that with the excuse that I didn't have time to meet other emotional needs that should have been met.

"I know I didn't have a valid excuse, though, because I did realize her needs at the time. What has helped us is just talking problems out. It has helped me understand her better, and I know it has helped her understand me better. And as we talk with the children we're able to better understand them too."

A common feeling among our dads with older children is that they'd like to go back and do it again, knowing what they know now. "I'm sure Connie wouldn't go along with this," says Shelby, "but I'd like to start all over again and raise another family!"

Like Father...

Inevitably, our dads are using their own fathers as examples—mostly negative, unfortunately. One says, "I had a father who was a very moral, hard-working, diligent person, but he came from a family that was not expressive of emotions. I never felt close to him while I was growing up, although I loved him and wanted him to spend time with me and talk to me and tell me he was proud of me. So, even when he died, it didn't affect me that much. I regret that now. I'd give anything to have my father back and be able to tell him how much I love him.

"But because of that lack of contact and expression of love, we do a lot of hugging in our house now—even with the boys. I think that's probably more important than anything else you can do in a family relationship." "So often we're afraid to share emotions," says Ralph. "Kids need to learn that sometimes Daddy cries too."

My husband Jon was a "Marine brat." His dad was a wonderful man, but he says, "Dad was hardly ever around. At the time, it was just a normal part of life—I only miss it in retrospect. But I realize now how much I missed out on, and when we had Megan I decided I was going to be there as much as possible."

Another dad says, "My father was gone a lot too, and I've also had some unpleasant memories of extremely harsh, cruel discipline that the Lord has had to heal me of. It's challenged me in some areas to be a better father than my father was. When my daughter looks back she may see some mistakes I've made too, but I'm going to give it my best shot."

Still another of our dads says, "My father was there, but I never had a close relationship with him when I was younger. I really envied people who had that. I looked at them almost with an astonishment, like, '*That's* the way a family's supposed to be?' It wasn't until after I left home—and even that was under bad circumstances—that I was finally able to have man-to-man talks with my dad. I don't know if I consciously geared myself to be his opposite, but I never want to feel I can't have personal talks with my kids. I have strong feelings about that."

Wayne's father set him a different example, and with it we will close this chapter and this book: "I lost my father when I was five," he says, "and Mom never remarried, so I was without a father for practically my whole life. My fondest memories are the days I did spend with my dad. I remember that he always had time for me, and anytime he went somewhere where he could take me, he would. So I've purposed in my heart that I'll always be there for my kids, and that I'll never be too busy for them."

APPENDIX

■■■

Meet the Mommies

*T*he *Mommy Book* was compiled primarily through a series of meetings in which groups of carefully chosen mothers were interviewed; it also includes the results of one-on-one interviews and written advice submitted by mothers who live outside our area. As my research went on, any stereotypical image I may have had of the average housewife was demolished. There's no such person—not in this bunch, anyway.

In this appendix I'll try to give you a glimpse into the lives of these very special women. You'll notice that some have common interests, and many have common family goals, but the Lord has combined and recombined those goals, interests, and thousands of other traits to make each of them a unique individual. I wish you could meet them in person.

If our moms' children seem older in this section than they do in the rest of the book, it's because they are. *The Mommy Book* was more than a year in the making, so the moms who began the project with infants ended it with toddlers. Rather than changing each child's age throughout the book as each month went by, I decided to leave the children at the age they were when each chapter was written.

And now, before I get down to the business of introducing our mothers, it needs to be acknowledged that this section includes only the women directly quoted in the book. There were a number of others who attended our meetings and confirmed, by a silent smile and nod of the head, the advice given by our more vocal mothers. I apologize that they are not publicly recognized here, and offer this word of thanks: The Lord knows who you are. Remember, they also serve who only sit and nod.

In Alphabetical Order

Adrienne—Adrienne bears the distinction of being the mother in this book with the most children: Jennifer, 12; Richard, 11; Jeffrey, 10; Georgia, 7; Mary, 4; and Stephanie, 1. When tuition at the accredited Christian school her older children attended grew beyond reach, she decided to continue their education at home. "In order to do it legally, I had to take out a charter and become a private school," she says. "We use an accelerated Christian education curriculum, and I let the older kids choose electives in addition to the basics to keep their interest high. We're having a lot of fun with it." Adrienne's hus-

band, Dick, is a branch manager of a life insurance firm
and is one of the fathers in Chapter 12.

Carol—Carol's children are Peter, 10; Lini, 8; Andrew,
3; and Mary, 16 months. "We're a very outdoorsy
family," she says. "We love to go camping and to the
beach." She goes on, "Our focus right now is the awe-
some job of raising these children and spending the
proper amount of time with them. Our primary ministry
is to our family—both our children and their grandparents." Carol's husband, Chris, is a lawyer with a business
practice. He also participated in our daddy chapter.

Carol B.—Carol's daughter is Kristin, 14. "Our relationship is very special," says Carol. "Kristin talks to me
about everything." Aside from being mommy to Kristin
and wife to her husband, Chuck, who works in sales,
Carol is office manager at WCIE in Lakeland, a Christian
radio station. Asked to describe her job, she laughs and
says, "I'm an organizer and a prodder!"

Cheryl—Cheryl works as office manager for a chemical
supplier and her husband, Rodger, runs an engineering
business. Their jobs keep them very busy, and Cheryl
says, "One of our main goals is to spend time together.
Another is to develop our individual disciplines: personal
devotions, and physical fitness. We've found that when
our individual lives suffer, our family life does too."

Their children are Jason, 4½, and Brian, 3. Both boys
are fascinated by electronic toys now—probably in imitation of Daddy—and they spend as much time as possible in the pool at their new house.

Chris—Chris is mother to Ashley, 3½, and newborn Amy. Mothering is taking most of her attention right now, although Chris says she still finds time to pursue her favorite hobbies: cooking, reading, and painting ceramics. "Ashley's very outdoorsy right now," she says. "She loves to play outside. And she loves to play school. We do that together every day." Ashley's artistic side is also blossoming—a trait she most likely received from her father, David, a music director—and she spends hours with creative toys such as watercolors, crayons, and playdough. David also participated in our "Daddy to Daddy" chapter.

Cindy—Cindy's little girl is Lindsey, 2. Her husband, LaRell, is a pastor, and Cindy finds herself busy with counseling and church activities. "I teach the college and career Sunday school class at our church," she says, "and I love it!" Cindy and LaRell are now planning to have their second child.

Connie—Connie and her husband, Shelby, are in charge of the children's ministry at their church—a big responsibility, since their congregation consists of over 500 impressionable children. Their three daughters, Lisa, 17, Stephanie, 13, and April, 10, all help with the children's church services. "They're all puppeteers," says Connie, "and they help in other areas as well. It's a neat chance for us to be together as a family, and it's also their ministry." Connie also writes children's stories for denominational magazines. Shelby participated in our daddy chapter.

Dana—Dana is the single mother of Bryan, 9, and Bridget, 6. She has her hands full rearing her children and working as music department secretary at her church. "Bryan loves reading right now," she says, "and he's very interested in school. Bridget, on the other hand, loves her Barbie dolls."

Dawn—Dawn and her husband, Brian, a landscape architect, adopted their daughter Melody after being told that the chances were small for Dawn to become pregnant. But the improbable happened, and 14-month-old Melody will have a little brother or sister by the time this book reaches print. Dawn is overjoyed. "I've been called to be a mommy," she says. She adds, "Melody is getting into everything now. She likes to try new sounds, and she loves playing outside."

Debby—Debby's three daughters are Lisa, 14, Angela, 12, and Marsha, 11, and she and her husband, Joe, recently adopted Michael, 7. Debby works as secretary to Joe, who is the minister of evangelism at a large church. She's also in charge of the deaf ministry at her church and, in her words, "I try to keep up with my kids' activities. Lisa, especially, has become active lately, and it's quite a job to get her from place to place." Joe is one of the dads in Chapter 12.

Donna—Donna's children are April, 5, and Aaron, 1. Her husband, Michael, is a youth pastor and also performs in a contemporary Christian music ministry.

Glenda—Glenda is mother to Greg, 20, Michele, 19, and Julie, 16. Her main goal right now? "Getting them all through college—that's a challenge!" she says. Glenda works as office manager for a local contractor.

Her husband, Joe, a chemical engineer and sales representative, travels quite a bit with his job. "He's done it ever since we've been married," says Glenda, "so we've adapted to the lifestyle. Everyone pitches in and takes up the slack. It keeps life interesting, because we never know when our plans are going to change."

Helen—Helen's children are Barbara, 37, and Brad, 30. Helen and her husband, Harold, are also the proud grandparents of two grandsons and one granddaughter. Helen regards her job as an executive church secretary to be her primary ministry now, not only because she undergirds the ministry of the pastoral staff, but also because she is often called upon to counsel parishioners who phone in with problems. Harold is the minister in charge of pastoral care at the church.

Jan—Jan is mother to Jordan David, a very active two year old, and is pregnant with her second child. In addition to working with her husband, Steve, in their home marketing business and helping with the young marrieds' Sunday school class at her church, Jan is a naturally empathic person who is often called upon to give encouragement and counsel to other mothers with young children. Steve is an associate pastor and Christian TV producer; he is also one of the fathers who participated in our "Daddy to Daddy" chapter.

Janet—Janet's children are Derek, 4, and Rachel, 2. She and her husband, Kenny, both work in the office of

a large grocery store chain, ...
likes to work on sewing and ...

Janice—Janice is mother to Bran... Her husband, Rob, is a pastor, so Ja... with a built-in volunteer career at the ch... pecially enjoys leading Bible studies and do... her spare time.

Joyce—Joyce's children are all grown now: Steve, 2.; Danny, 26; Karla, 24; and Dawn, 21. Her husband, Karl, is pastor of one of America's largest churches. Joyce keeps herself busier than most of our younger mothers in her roles as a pastor's wife, writer of magazine articles, hostess of an award-winning 15-minute radio program, and counselor. One of her very favorite roles is that of grandmother to Jordan David, Jan and Steve's little boy. "That's the most fun!" she says.

Julie—Julie has three sons: Sean, 4; Ian, 1½; and Brian, four months. Her husband, Larry, is a high school history teacher. She says, "Right now, the Lord is renewing my devotional life. There was a while there when things were pretty dry. And He's also teaching me and Larry to work together for the common good of the family, without complaining."

Karen H.—Karen is kept busy by two active sons: Joshua, 3½, and Jeremy, 9 months. When asked what Jeremy is into now, she says, "Everything! He's just learned to walk and open cabinets." Joshua is getting his first taste of education: "We have a preschool curriculum we go through every day," says Karen. "Lots of creative things

away from the TV." As the wife of Randy, an
pastor, Karen also is frequently called upon to
other young mothers in her church.

arin—Karin is mother to Matthew, 2½, and Meagin,
Her little family is very active: "We're involved in a
of outside activities, but they always include the chil-
ren," she says. "We're very family-oriented, even
though most of what we do is outside the home." Wayne,
Karin's husband, is a landscaper and is one of the fathers
who participated in our daddy chapter.

Kathy—Kathy's children are Brandon, 8, Ryan, 4, and
Jessica, 2. Her husband, Hugh, is the assistant business
manager in a large church and is also studying for his
master's degree in business administration. Kathy says,
"We're really trying to work on our priorities: Christ first,
then each other, then the children, then jobs, then outside
activities. For a while there our outside activities took
over. We were meeting each other coming and going."
Hugh also participated in our "Daddy to Daddy" chapter.

Kristy—Kristy's two daughters are Julie, 10, and Jennifer, 6. Her husband, Milton, is a pastor. "I'm a family-
oriented pastor's wife," she says. "I teach an adult Sunday
school class and I'm also writing a book for ministers'
wives." Kristy's girls are learning what it means to share
their faith: "They both love to tell their friends about the
Lord," she says.

LeEtta—LeEtta's little girl is Lindsie, age 2. Even
though LeEtta feels called to be an at-home mommy, she

was recently forced back into the job market. "I'm hoping it's just temporary," she says. "It has been a hard adjustment. My heart is at home, and my body is at work." LeEtta's husband, Mark, is a real estate investor.

Linda—Linda is mother to Philip, 2½, and Heather, 19 months. Aside from concentrating on her husband and children, Linda stays busy as a part-time bookkeeper as well as being a member of her church choir and piano player for her church youth choir. Linda's husband, Fred, is studying for the music ministry.

Her daughter Heather has been diagnosed as asthmatic and often has trouble breathing, especially at night. "I've gotten used to living on four or five hours of sleep a night," says Linda. "Going through this has really given me empathy for other mothers with chronically ill children." Philip is a bright, active little boy who is currently in the throes of toilet training.

Lois—Lois is mother to Michele, 16, Rindi, 13, Lori, 10, and Leslie, 7. The two youngest children are stepdaughters of whom Lois and her husband, Larry, have partial custody. Aside from her roles as wife and mother, Lois is a frequent soloist at her church and works in a home office as secretary and bookkeeper for husband Larry, who is an electrical and general contractor.

Lynda—Lynda is mother to Grant, 2½. "He's talking now," she says, "and he loves 'Sesame Street.' And he repeats words—we've already had a problem with that. I don't know where he picked it up."

Lynda is thrilled about her recently acquired part-time job. "I was an operating-room nurse for ten years before

Grant was born," she says, "and after he came I prayed for a part-time job so I could spend more time at home with him. Now I work three days a week as a medical consultant for an insurance firm." Lynda's husband, George, is a self-employed carpenter.

Lynne—Lynne's two sons are Jonathan, 3, and Michael, 18 months. Lynne works for the Freedom Council, and her husband, Bill, is studying to be a psychologist. Lynne says, "Our main focus is spending time with the children without getting too involved in outside activities—even worthwhile ones. Right now, our children are our ministry."

Marilee—Marilee's children are David, 5, and Althea, 3, both of whom are currently intent on copying Mommy and Daddy. "Althea doesn't go anywhere without a doll," says Marilee, "and David likes to play with construction equipment. He thinks he wants a backhoe." Marilee runs a home office for her husband, Jeff, who runs a surveying business, and she is investigating the possibility of home schooling for her children. Jeff also participated in our daddy chapter.

Mary Ann—Mary Ann's son is Joseph, 8. Another son, John, died at age 22 months. She and her husband, Joe, are itinerant missionaries currently assigned to China.

Michele—Michele is mother to Sarah, 3½, and Amanda, 7 months. Having worked at the telephone company until Amanda was born, Michele is enjoying the freedom to stay home with her little girls and is building her family's church involvement.

Her husband, Robb, a communications specialist, is an involved father, and Michele says he and Sarah have developed a special tradition: "Every Saturday morning they walk down to the restaurant on the corner and have breakfast together. It started out as a way to let me sleep late when I was working, but it's turned into a special sharing time for both of them."

Nancy—Nancy's four children are Christopher, 19, now a pre-med student; Greg, 18, about to enter college; Stephen, 15, entering high school; and Elizabeth, 12, in junior high. Her husband, Bob, is vice-president in an investment firm.

With the age difference between the two older children and the two younger ones, Nancy and Bob now find themselves going through a second set of adolescents. She says, "We're working to be as enthusiastic for the younger kids' interests as we were for the older ones. We need to attend their basketball and volleyball games and also let them entertain at home like we did with the older ones. Something else we're discovering is that there's no substitute for having a child spend time at home with the family. Sometimes it's too easy just to send them over to a friend's house or to a ball game."

Pat—Pat's daughter, Kimberly, is eight months old now, and Pat is leading a hectic life between her job, motherhood, and studying for a degree in business data processing. "If my husband hadn't encouraged me, I would never have tried to do this much," she says. "Kimberly's in an interesting stage now. She's more mobile, so she's getting into more things." Pat's husband, Thomas, is an electrician.

Patti—Patti is mother to Keva, 5½, Joel, 4, and Jonathan, 2½. She also has another baby due to arrive soon. She resigned a position as an elementary school music teacher when Keva was born, and her husband, Kent, is in sales. Patti says, "With four children, we're trying to put a real emphasis on family closeness, teaching our kids to support each other rather than tear each other down."

Patty M.—Patty's children are Scarlett, 4, and Ashley, 7 months. She and her husband, Steve, an advertising manager for a trade magazine, are lay ministers who do a lot of counseling and Bible study teaching.

Patty is also looking into the possibility of home schooling for her children. "I believe kids respond to their mothers much faster than they would to a teacher," she says.

Patty W.—Patty is mother to Jennifer Joy, a bright, playful 3½-year-old, and has recently discovered that she's expecting her second child. Her husband, Randy, is a computer programmer-consultant and serves as an elder for their local Christian fellowship. "Lately the Lord has been teaching me about dying to self," Patty says, "—the need to lay down my life for the Lord and my family. Randy's and my goal is to become more deeply committed both to the Lord and to our family."

Pene (pronounced *Penny*)—Pene is mother to two very active boys: 3½-year-old Aaron and six-month-old Ian. She works part-time as a public information assistant to the Phosphate Council, and her husband, Tom, is a radio announcer and producer of a dally hour-long Christian radio talk show.

"Our primary goal right now is raising our children the right way," she says. "But when I relax I like to do cross-stitch, and we ride bikes together. Tom and I have bike seats for the boys on the back of both our bikes." Tom is one of the daddies in Chapter 12.

Rita—Rita is mother to Billy, 17, and Brian, 14. She says, "Billy is thinking about college, so that's a big step for him. Also, both of the boys are very athletic, and we're trying hard to show up at games and support them." That's not easy because Rita is the public relations director at Christian radio station WCIE as well as being a popular radio personality herself, and she does quite a bit of public speaking. Luckily for her, her husband, Marvin, a maintenance mechanic, supports her ministry wholeheartedly. "He has been my best supporter from the very beginning," she says. "He feels called into this along with me." Marvin also participated in our daddy chapter.

Rosemary—Rosemary is a fervent believer in large families and has had the unique opportunity of raising two generations of children: Sherri, 22, and Laurie, 21, who are now both married; and Susan, 6, and Katie, 4.

She also has a granddaughter, Jannipher. "It's the most wonderful experience in the world!" she says. "I accepted Jesus after my two older children were eight and nine years old, and I wondered what it would be like to have two more children and raise them in the Lord from the beginning. Really, I always wanted five. I think being a mother is the most fulfilling profession there is."

Rosemary's husband, Doug, is a cost-accounting manager for a machinery corporation.

Ruth—Lately Ruth has been kept busy planning for the back-to-back weddings of daughter Jenny, 22, and son Russ, 20. She also is the executive secretary to her husband, Jim, who is the executive administrative assistant at their church and is in charge of the church's building program.

Sofie—Sofie presides over a large, closely knit family: Jimmy, 14; Debbie, 11; Joseph, 7; and David, 3. "In spite of their age differences," she says, "the children are very close and it's obvious that they really love each other. Their teachers at school seem surprised by it." Luckily for Sofie, her husband, Paul, is a pediatrician.

Sonja—Sonja's children are Tasha, 5, and Dustin, 2. Her husband, T. L., is in management, and she says, "Right now our main focus is building traditions and family values in our children. We want to show them that we spend not only mealtimes together, but other special times too, because we want to and because our time together is important." Sonja is also active in a local Christian women's club.

Stella—Stella's two daughters are Shauna, 9, and Dina, 4. Her husband, Tim, is assistant principal at a Christian school. Stella gave up an elementary school teaching position when she and Tim adopted Shauna. She says, "Right now Tim and I are working on having consistent family devotions. Even at their ages, the girls come away from their little friends with a 'gimme' attitude—discontent with the things they have, wanting to keep up with all the other kids. We've found that consistent spiritual emphasis really helps to get rid of that negative competitive spirit." Tim participated in our "Daddy to Daddy" chapter.

Sylvia—Sylvia has one daughter in college: Angela, 18; and two sons in high school: Phil, 16; and Scott, 15. "Our main goal right now is keeping the boys where they need to be spiritually," she says. "That's hard sometimes in public school. The main thing we're battling is peer pressure. Scott is dyslexic, and there are better programs for him in public school than in private ones." Sylvia's husband, Fred, is in real estate and insurance, and Sylvia works in the office with him.

Terri—Terri is mother to Zachary, 5, and Ashley, 2. "Zachary is just starting to learn to write," she says, "and he loves trains. Ashley's two favorite things are dishes and dolls." About her lifestyle, she says, "We're really family-oriented. We don't do much at all that doesn't involve the children." Terri's husband, Michael, has recently been licensed as a minister and hopes to have his own pastorate someday.

Trina—Trina's daughter, Audrey, is 14 months old, and Trina is thoroughly enjoying the freedom of staying home and watching her grow. "She's learning to pray at meals now," she says. "It's very special. She helps me see so many things spiritually." Trina's husband, Claude, is a paramedic.

Vicky—Vicky is mother to Lauren, 2½, and expects her next baby in three months. "Lauren is starting to be more independent now," she says, "Everything is 'mine' or 'I don't want any!'"

Her husband, Steve, works in the office of a large grocery store chain, and Vicky says, "Steve works nights, so our family time has to be in the morning. Our children are our main ministry right now. Steve and I feel *so* responsible to the Lord for them."

Virginia—Virginia's three children are nearly grown: Ricky, 20, is away at college; Tina, 18, will soon be attending a local Christian college; and Crystal, 15, is in high school and is doing some modeling for local dress shops. Aside from her children, Virginia feels her primary ministry is to other single parents, since she is one herself. "Going through a divorce and being single has given me real empathy for people who are hurting," she says. She has frequent opportunities to speak to church singles' groups. Virginia works as a church receptionist.

Wanda—Wanda's daughter, Michelle, is ten, and Wanda says, "I can see definite signs of preteen-ness!" Michelle is a bright, outgoing young lady who loves outdoor sports, school, and handcrafts—taking after her mommy in that area. She's in a program for gifted children at her school and hopes to start learning to use a computer soon.

Wanda works as assistant to her husband, Dennis, a Christian bookstore manager and audio engineer-director. She says, "Michelle, Dennis, and I have a good day-to-day family unity, and we're always trying to make it better." Dennis is one of the daddies in Chapter 12.

Karen Hull organizes and participates in "Mother's Forum," a monthly radio program on WCIE-FM in central Florida, and has been featured on "Focus on the Family," hosted by Dr. James Dobson. She and her husband, Jon, have two daughters, Megan and Anna.